PLANNING LAW
AND
PROCEDURE

PLANNING LAW AND PROCEDURE

A. E. TELLING, M.A.
of the Inner Temple and the Midland Circuit, Barrister
Principal Lecturer in Law, Trent Polytechnic

FIFTH EDITION

LONDON
BUTTERWORTHS
1977

England London	Butterworth & Co. (Publishers) Ltd. 88 Kingsway, WC2B 6AB
Australia Sydney	Butterworths Pty. Ltd. 586 Pacific Highway, Chatswood, NSW 2067 Also at Melbourne, Brisbane, Adelaide and Perth
Canada Toronto	Butterworth & Co. (Canada) Ltd. 2265 Midland Avenue, Scarborough M1P 4S1
New Zealand Wellington	Butterworths of New Zealand Ltd. 26/28 Waring Taylor Street 1
South Africa Durban	Butterworth & Co. (South Africa) (Pty) Ltd. 152/154 Gale Street
USA Boston	Butterworth & Co. (Publishers) Inc. 19 Cummings Park, Woburn, Mass. 01801

First edition	*September*	*1963*
Second edition	*October*	*1967*
Third edition	*February*	*1970*
Fourth edition	*June*	*1973*
First reprint	*July*	*1974*
Fifth edition	*April*	*1977*

ISBN—Casebound 0 406 66507 9
Limp 0 406 66508 7

PREFACE TO FIFTH EDITION

A new edition of this book is necessitated by the large amount of new legislation and by recent decisions of the courts.

The Land Compensation Act 1973, although mainly concerned with compensation for the acquisition and use of land for public purposes, has made important changes in the law regarding blight notices. The Town and Country Planning Amenities Act 1974 has enlarged the powers and duties of local planning authorities with regard to conservation areas, listed buildings and the protection of trees. I have therefore devoted a separate chapter to conservation areas.

Most important of all, the Community Land Act 1975 envisages a far more positive role for local authorities in town and country planning. Local authorities are now under a duty to consider the acquisition of land required for major development schemes; after a transitional period, major development will be permitted only on land which is either in or has passed through public ownership. The duty to acquire all land required for major development is to be introduced piecemeal by the making of "duty orders" applicable to particular areas; the process is to be completed by the naming of a "second appointed day". The marriage of planning powers with those of the landowner will affect not only the timing of development but the whole scope of development control.

The Community Land Act is supplemented by the Development Land Tax Act 1976 which, following the precedent of the short-lived Land Commission Act, imposes a special tax on the realised development accruing from the sale of land or the carrying out of major development projects.

I have endeavoured to deal with the salient features of these new measures in Part III which comprises four entirely new chapters.

The Minister has used the powers delegated to him to give greater freedom to local planning authorities to grant planning permission for substantial departures from the development plan; and he has also enlarged the powers of planning authorities to obtain planning permission on their own behalf without reference to himself. These measures will simplify administration; how far they are consistent with the new concepts of public participation is questionable.

The Minister commissioned Mr George Dobry, Q.C. to conduct a review of the development control system. Mr Dobry has made a number of significant and, in some respects, revolutionary suggestions. The Government has not yet accepted these suggestions which would in any event require legislation. It is in no spirit of disrespect to Mr Dobry that I have made only passing reference to his recommendations.

I have endeavoured to state the law as at 31st January, 1977. However, since the edition went to press, the House of Commons has given a second reading to a Town and Country Planning (Amendment) Bill. The main purpose of the Bill is to amend the law as respects stop notices by removing the anomaly that stop notices cannot be served in respect of unauthorised changes of use. The Bill was introduced by Mr. Dudley Smith, M.P. as a private member's Bill, but it has been welcomed by the Government and is likely to become law.

I am grateful to Mr T. G. Robson, B.A. (Legal Studies) of the City Secretary's Department, Nottingham for his valuable assistance in the preparation of this new edition.

Nottingham A.E.T.
February 1977

PREFACE TO FIRST EDITION

The comprehensive system of land use control introduced by the Town and Country Planning Act 1947 has now been in force for some fifteen years. The Act of 1947 and the subsequent amending Acts (now consolidated in the Act of 1962) together with the numerous orders and regulations have been the subject of a good many excellent works. Experience of lecturing and examining in planning law and procedure, however, has convinced me that there is scope for a more academic treatment of the subject, and this book is offered in the hope that it will be of value to students reading for degrees and professional qualifications requiring a knowledge of this subject.

I am indebted to Mr. V. W. Taylor, LL.M., Senior Lecturer in Law at the College of Estate Management for his helpful advice and criticisms; to Mr. Keith Davies, M.A., LL.B., Barrister-at-Law, Lecturer in Law at the College of Estate Management for undertaking the laborious task of revising Part I of the book to take account of the passing of the Act of 1962 and other changes, and for reading the proofs; to many anonymous students whose questions have sometimes opened up new channels of thought; to my publishers for their patience and helpfulness; and finally to my wife who typed much of the manuscript.

I have endeavoured to state the law as at 10th July 1963—the date on which the Town and Country Planning Act 1963 received the Royal Assent.

A.E.T.

16 Castle Gate
Nottingham.
July 1963.

CONTENTS

PART I.—PLANNING CONTROL

PAGE

PART II.—FINANCIAL PROVISIONS

PART III.—COMMUNITY LAND AND DEVELOPMENT LAND TAX

TABLE OF ABBREVIATIONS

Act of 1971	The Town and Country Planning Act 1971
Act of 1972	The Town and Country Planning (Amendment) Act 1972
Act of 1974	The Town and Country Planning Amenities Act 1974
Act of 1975	The Community Land Act 1975
Act of 1959	The Town and Country Planning Act 1959
Act of 1962	The Town and Country Planning Act 1962
Act of 1968	The Town and Country Planning Act 1968
DLT Act	The Development Land Tax Act 1976
Advertisements Regulations	Town and Country Planning (Control of Advertisements) Regulations 1969. S.I. 1969 No. 1532, amended by Town and Country Planning (Control of Advertisements) (Amendment) Regulations 1972, S.I. 1972 No. 489; 1974, S.I. 1974 No. 185; 1975, S.I. 1975 No. 898
Compensation Regulations	Town and Country Planning (Compensation and Certificates) Regulations 1974, S.I. 1974 No. 1242
Determination by Inspector's Rules	Town and Country Planning (Determination by Appointed Persons) (Inquiries Procedure) Rules 1974, S.I. 1974 No. 420
Development Plans Regulations	Town and Country Planning (Development Plans) Regulations, 1965, S.I. 1965, No. 1453.
General Development Order / *G.D.O.*	Town and Country Planning General Development Order 1973, S.I. 1973 No. 31, amended by Town and Country Planning (Amendment) Order 1973, S.I. 1973 No. 273; 1974, S.I. 1974, No. 48; 1976, S.I. 1976 No. 301.
General Regulations	Town and Country Planning (General) Regulations 1976, S.I. 1976 No. 1419
Inquiries Procedure Rules	Town and Country Planning (Inquiries Procedure) Rules 1974, S.I. 1974. No. 419
Listed Building Regulations	Town and Country Planning (Listed Buildings and Buildings in Conservation Areas) Regulations 1972, S.I. 1972 No. 1362, amended by Town and Country Planning (Listed Buildings and Buildings in Conservation Areas) (Amendment) Regulations 1974, S.I. 1974 No. 1336

Minerals Regulations	Town and Country Planning (Minerals) Regulations 1971, S.I. 1971 No. 756
Plans Regulations	Town and Country Planning (Structure and Local Plans) Regulations 1974, S.I. 1974 No. 1486
Tree Preservation Regulations	Town and Country Planning (Tree Preservation Order) Regulations 1969, S.I. 1969 No. 17
Use Classes Order	Town and Country Planning (Use Classes) Order 1972, S.I. 1972, No. 1385.
The Minister	The Secretary of State for the Environment or the Secretary of State for Wales
Franks Committee	The Committee on Administrative Tribunals and Inquiries, 1957, Cmnd. 218

TABLE OF STATUTES

References in this Table to "Statutes" are to Halsbury's Statutes of England (Third Edition) showing the volume and page at which the annotated text of the Act will be found.

TABLE OF CASES

In the following Table references are given to the English and Empire Digest where a digest of each case will be found.

PAGE

L

M

PART I

PLANNING CONTROL

SUMMARY

Chapter 1

HISTORICAL DEVELOPMENT OF PLANNING LAW

Introduction

The problems of town and country planning in Britain arise mainly from the profound revolution through which the country has passed in the last two hundred years. The most important feature of the revolution has been the enormous growth in the population, especially during the nineteenth century. In 1800 the population was about 10½ million; by 1850 it had increased to nearly 21 million and by 1900 it had nearly doubled again to 37 million. Since then the rate of increase has been considerably less but even so the population has grown to over 50 million. Such an increase could not fail to alter the physical appearance of the country and to bring in its train a whole host of problems.

It is doubtful whether the country could have sustained so large a growth in the population but for the industrial revolution which changed Britain from a predominantly agricultural nation to an industrial one. The early industrial revolution was centred on the coalfields and on the wool and cotton towns of the north, and was assisted by the building first of canals and later of railways. The result was to concentrate the population in certain parts of the country, chiefly the north of England, the Midlands and South Wales. The industrial towns grew in size more dramatically even than the general population and people left the countryside to find work in the new factories. During the first half of the nineteenth century the number of people in the countryside increased since the growth in population was greater than the migration to the towns; but with the decline in agriculture after 1850 the population of the countryside declined absolutely.

Conditions in the new industrial towns were often appalling. Factories and houses sprang up side by side without any attempt at zoning; although it must be remembered that until the coming of the railways, most people had to live within walking distance of their work. Still worse, there was no attempt even to control standards of building construction and sanitation. Although the housing conditions of the skilled artisan and the miners were often better than is now realised, conditions generally were very bad (*a*). The foul state of the houses encouraged the spread of disease and there were serious outbreaks of cholera and typhoid in the eighteen thirties and forties. Local boards of health had been set up after the cholera epidemic of 1831–1833 but were allowed to lapse. In 1838 the Poor Law Commissioners published a report showing evidence obtained when they employed a number of doctors to inquire into the causes of death and destitution in London. They then commissioned the energetic public health reformer Edwin Chadwick to carry out a similar investigation over the whole country. The publication of the results of this in 1842 led to the appointment of a Royal Commission on the Health of Towns, which published its first report in 1844 (to a considerable extent the work of Chadwick) and its second report in 1845. These reports were followed in 1848 by two Acts of Parliament which, although very limited in scope and effect, are significant as laying the foundations of permanent statutory restrictions on the freedom of landowners to build as they pleased. The Public Health Act, 1848, set up a General Board of Health with powers to create local boards on the petition of ten per cent of the inhabitants of a district and to enforce boards where the death rate was above 23 per 1000. The boards were given powers to ensure

(*a*) For a general account of conditions in the towns, see for instance—*The Town Labourer* and *The Bleak Age* by J. L. and Barbara Hammond; and *An Economic History of Modern Britain* by J. H. Clapham, Vol. I.

that both new and existing houses were provided with water and drainage: the building of new houses was not to be commenced until the board had been given notice of the position of privies and drains. The Nuisance Removal and Disease Prevention Act, 1848, applied throughout the country and made it an offence to build a new house to drain into an open ditch. This Act was replaced in 1855 by the Nuisances Removal Act, which enabled the local authority to complain to the justices where any premises were in such a state as to be a nuisance or injurious to health. The justices' order could require the provision of sufficient privy accommodation, means of drainage and ventilation to make the house safe and habitable: and, if the house were unfit for habitation, could prohibit its use for that purpose. The Act of 1855 was extended by the Sanitary Act, 1866, which *inter alia* enabled the local council or board of health to deal with houses lacking proper drainage by compelling their connection with a public sewer (if within 100 feet) or with a cesspool or some other place.

At the same time, the more enterprising municipalities were obtaining extended powers by petitioning Parliament for local Acts. These local Acts were of special significance in that they paved the way for the great Public Health Act, 1875. This consolidated the earlier public general Acts and gave national application to provisions previously found only in local Acts. Local authorities were given power not only to secure proper standards of drainage and closet accommodation, but also to make byelaws regulating the size of rooms, the space about houses and the width of the street in front of them; provision was also made for the making up and sewering of unadopted streets at the expense of the frontagers.

Builders were anxious to get as many houses as possible to the acre, and the byelaw minimum became accordingly the maximum and the minimum at once. The result was the sea of uniform rows of streets and houses which surrounds the centre of many of our industrial towns and whose dreary and unbroken regularity is too well known to require description. Nevertheless, byelaw control was an important step forward.

The powers of local government in the field of public health were supplemented by housing legislation beginning with the Artizans and Labourers Dwellings Act, 1868, which gave powers to deal with individual insanitary houses. This was followed in 1875 by powers to undertake slum clearance (*b*) and in 1890 by powers to build tenements and cottages for the housing of the working classes (*c*).

This activity in the fields of public health and housing was followed by a sweeping reform of local government. Outside the boroughs, local government was entrusted to a patchwork of authorities often of an *ad hoc* character such as the local boards of health. These were replaced by the establishment of county councils in 1888, and urban and rural district councils in 1894.

Thus, by the end of the century, there existed an effective system of local government with substantial powers in the fields of public health and housing. It soon became apparent, however, that something more was necessary. The possibility of more satisfactory conditions of living and working was being demonstrated by the building of such places as Bournville and Port Sunlight by enlightened industrialists. About the same time, Ebenezer Howard wrote the famous book *Garden Cities of Tomorrow*, which may be taken as the starting point of the new towns movement, as well as the immediate inspiration for the first "garden city" of Letchworth started in 1903.

THE DEVELOPMENT OF REGULATORY PLANNING

The Acts of 1909 to 1943

The first Planning Act was passed in 1909 (*d*). It authorised the preparation by local councils of planning schemes for any land "which is in course of development or appears likely to be

---

(*b*) Artizans and Labourers' Dwellings Improvement Acts, 1875 and 1879.

(*c*) Housing of the Working Classes Act, 1890.

(*d*) Housing, Town Planning, &c. Act, 1909.

used for building purposes", *i.e.* suburban land. Such schemes were to be prepared with the object of ensuring "that in future land in the vicinity of towns shall be developed in such a way as to secure proper sanitary conditions, amenity and convenience in connection with the laying out of the land itself and any neighbouring land".

Thus to the search for good sanitary conditions, which had characterised the nineteenth century reforms, there were added the claims of amenity and convenience. The planning scheme was far more ambitious and flexible than the byelaw. Not only could it regulate the number of buildings on a site and the space about them, but it could provide both for the control of their appearance and the way in which they might be used. The scheme might also define zones in which only certain specific types of building use would be permitted, and it could list types of development which could not be undertaken without specific application to the local authority.

The preparation and approval of a scheme was necessarily a lengthy process, and an Act of 1919 (*e*) introduced the concept of interim development control: that is during the period from the passing by the council of a resolution to prepare a scheme until the scheme became effective. Under interim control, a developer was not obliged to apply for permission but if his development conflicted with the scheme as ultimately approved he could not obtain compensation. On the other hand, if he obtained interim development consent, he was safeguarded.

The next major step forward was the Act of 1932 (*f*) which enabled local authorities to prepare planning schemes for any land in England and Wales and not merely for suburban land as hitherto. The Act of 1932 was purely permissive, but it was supplemented in 1935 by the Restriction of Ribbon Development Act which made new building within 220 feet of classified roads, or roads made the subject of a resolution under the Act, subject

(*e*) Housing, Town Planning, &c. Act, 1919.
(*f*) Town and Country Planning Act, 1932.

to control. And in 1943 (when 73 per cent of the land in England and 36 per cent of the land in Wales had become subject to interim control under the Act of 1932) it was provided that all land in England and Wales should be deemed to be subject to interim control whether or not the local authority had passed a resolution to prepare a scheme (*g*).

New Problems

The Acts of 1909 to 1943 had all been based on the concept of the planning scheme. Such schemes were undoubtedly useful in ensuring that new development conformed to certain standards of amenity and convenience and in controlling changes in the use of existing buildings. But new problems were coming into prominence and it soon became apparent that the planning scheme was unsuitable for dealing with these. The population continued to grow substantially although less dramatically than in the nineteenth century. The advent of road transport and a cheap supply of electric power was changing the face of the country. These influences resulted in a new growth in the size of towns and cities and of many places beyond their boundaries. Industry was no longer tied to the coalfields and railways, and between the two wars a major relocation of the nation's industrial power took place. Some of the older industrial areas went through a period of prolonged and at times severe depression which led to the appointment of Commissioners for Special Areas. The Commissioners, whilst emphasising that economic considerations must in the main determine the location of industry, drew attention to the dangers involved in the continued haphazard growth of the Metropolis and considered that much of the growth was not based on strictly economic factors (*h*). The result was the appointment of the Royal Commission on the Distribution of the Industrial Population (the Barlow Commission).

(*g*) Town and Country Planning (Interim Development) Act, 1943.

(*h*) Third Report of the Commissioners for Special Areas, 1936. Cmd. 5303.

The Barlow Report (*i*), after a lengthy examination of the advantages and disadvantages of the swollen state of the cities, came to the definite conclusion that (*k*)—

> "the disadvantages in many, if not in most of the great industrial concentrations, alike on the strategical, the social, and the economic side, do constitute serious handicaps and even in some respects dangers to the nation's life and development, and we are of opinion that definite action should be taken by the Government towards remedying them."

The Report also commented on the serious loss of agricultural land which they said (*l*)—

> " . . . since 1900 has been so rapid that it is stated to have covered with bricks and mortar an area equal in size to the counties of Buckingham and Bedford combined. Alike in urban extensions and in expropriation of land by Government Departments for military, Royal Air Force, or other national requirements, regard must be had to the agricultural needs of the country.
>
> Nor is it merely the agricultural needs of the country that should be borne in mind. Providence has endowed Great Britain not only with wide tracts of fertile soil, but with mineral wealth in the form of tin, lead, iron-ore, and, above all, coal; with abundant supplies of water, hard and soft, corresponding to the various needs of industry; with rivers and harbours apt for transport and for both foreign and internal trade; and last, but by no means least, with amenities and recreational opportunities, with hills and dales, with forests, moors and headlands—precious possessions for fostering and enriching the nation's well-being and vitality."

Publication of the Barlow Report was followed by the appointment of a Committee on Land Utilisation in Rural Areas under the chairmanship of the late Lord Justice SCOTT (*m*). Both the Barlow Report and the Scott Report urged that more effective action should be taken to control the siting of development and both

---

(*i*) Cmd. 6153.
(*k*) Cmd. 6153, para. 413.
(*l*) Cmd. 6153, paras. 36 and 37.
(*m*) Cmd. 6378.

pointed to the weaknesses of the Act of 1932. As the Barlow Report put it (*n*)—

> "While present statutory town planning tends towards producing a more pleasant, healthier and more convenient local environment, it is not adapted to check the spread of great towns or agglomerations, nor, so long as their growth continues, to arrest the tendency to increasing central density and traffic congestion. . . . Present town planning does not concern itself with the larger question of the general and national grouping of the population."

To remedy this situation both reports recommended the establishment of a central planning authority: the immediate extension of planning control to all parts of the country: and the formulation of a national plan for the location of industry and population.

The immediate results were the passing in 1943 of two Acts concerned with planning. The first provided for the appointment for the first time of a Minister "charged with the duty of securing consistency and continuity in the framing and execution of a national policy with respect to the use and development of land throughout England and Wales" (*o*). The other Act (*p*) extended, as already explained, interim control under the Act of 1932 to the whole country: legislation more suited to the control of land use generally, as distinct from local amenity and environment, did not come until the passing of the Act of 1947.

Problems of Redevelopment

The Act of 1944

In the meantime another problem had come into prominence: the redevelopment of older built-up areas. Existing planning legislation was concerned only with the preparation of schemes for regulating the activities of developers. These developers would normally be private individuals and companies, though there was a certain amount of development by local and other public

---

(*n*) Cmd. 6153, para. 219.
(*o*) Minister of Town and Country Planning Act, 1943, s.1.
(*p*) Town and Country Planning (Interim Development) Act, 1943.

authorities which was equally subject to the regulatory control of the planning scheme. Although the scheme would indicate what was desirable, it could not compel development to take place.

The limits of the approach became obvious during the Second World War when a good deal of thought was given to the physical reconstruction of older cities and towns. Although the immediate stimulus to this new thinking came from the opportunities created by the bombing, people were soon thinking of bolder schemes of reconstruction. For this purpose something more than regulatory planning was wanted, namely, publicly organised schemes of redevelopment. Although town improvement schemes had been authorised in part by local Acts, local authorities had no general powers to carry out redevelopment schemes until 1944.

The Town and Country Planning Act of that year (*q*) gave local authorities power to designate for general reconstruction areas which had been heavily bombed, or had been badly laid out and whose development was now obsolete. These were known as "declaratory areas" and the local authority could compulsorily purchase any land in a declaratory area and carry out their development either themselves or by disposing of their land to private developers for approved schemes.

(*q*) Town and Country Planning Act, 1944.

CHAPTER 2

BASIS AND OBJECTS OF MODERN PLANNING LAW

PLANNING LEGISLATION

The framework of the modern system of planning law was established with the passing of the Act of 1947. It repealed all previous legislation (with the exception of the Minister of Town and Country Planning Act, 1943) and made a completely new start with effect from 1st July, 1948.

In setting up the new system, Parliament was plainly guided to a large extent by the recommendations of the Barlow and Scott reports. For instance the Act of 1947 set up a powerful system of central administration. Although the Act did not create a "central planning authority" as recommended by the reports, the Minister was given very strong powers which, taken with his general duties under the Act of 1943, enabled him to act to all intents and purposes as a central planning authority. The recommendations of the Barlow report about the location of population and industry were given effect by providing that applications for planning permission to build all but the smallest factories should require the support of the Board of Trade. Certain powers were also given to the Minister of Transport.

The Act of 1947 also strengthened local administration. Under the previous Acts, non-country boroughs and district councils as well as county boroughs were entrusted with the preparation of planning schemes. The Act of 1947 provided that the local planning authority should normally be the county council or county borough council, the former providing a larger and more realistic area for the preparation of development plans.

Each local planning authority was required under the Act of 1947 to carry out a survey of the whole of its area and to prepare a development plan based on the results of the survey; the development plan was to be reviewed every five years from the date of approval in the light of a fresh survey of the area. By requiring that development plans should be based on the results of a physical, social and economic survey of the area, the Act moved away from planning primarily in terms of amenity and convenience to planning on the basis of securing proper control over the use of land. The plans embodied both concepts of planning as described in the previous chapter—regulatory and positive. In the sphere of positive planning, the Act provided for areas of comprehensive development similar to the declaratory areas of the Act of 1944, but including areas which required total re-planning for reasons other than extensive war damage.

With regard to regulatory planning, however, the development plan was materially different from the old planning scheme in that it did not confer any rights to develop. Henceforth, no development was to take place without planning permission; normally this would require an application to the local planning authority who would then decide whether to grant planning permission, with or without conditions, having regard to the provisions of the development plan and any other material considerations. There were additional powers of control in the case of buildings of architectural or historic interest, trees and outdoor advertisements.

The Act of 1947 also contained some complex provisions for dealing with the financial problems inherent in any comprehensive planning control. These will be discussed in more detail in a later chapter (*a*). It will suffice to say here that normally no compensation was payable under the Act of 1947 where permission was either refused or granted subject to conditions. However, where land had become incapable of reasonably beneficial use, certain persons falling within a somewhat artificial definition of "owner" might serve a purchase notice.

The following years were to see a number of amending Acts. The Acts of 1953 and 1954 radically altered the financial pro-

(*a*) See chapter 17, *post*.

visions of the Act of 1947. The Acts of 1959 and 1960 made some improvements in the system of planning control without disturbing the framework of physical planning established by the Act of 1947: the concept of the purchase notice was extended to cases of planning blight, provision was made for appeals to the courts on points of law, and the system of enforcement was strengthened.

The Act of 1947 and the subsequent amending legislation were repealed and consolidated in the Act of 1962. But it was not long before further changes were made. The Civic Amenities Act, 1967, introduced the conservation area and strengthened the earlier provisions regarding trees and buildings of special architectural or historic interest.

In the meantime, the Minister had appointed a Planning Advisory Group to review the system of town and country planning and to see what changes were required to meet the needs of the next twenty years and beyond. The Group reported in 1965 that the system of control was effective, but that control was based on plans which were out of date and technically inadequate. In 1948 it had been assumed that the population of Great Britain would become static round about 1953; this assumption had proved entirely false, and the more conservative estimates were suggesting an increase to over seventy million by the year 2000. Again, in 1948, no one forecast the enormous increase in the volume of motor traffic. In the light of these two trends, the Planning Advisory Group saw the need for a much more flexible type of development plan; they recommended that there should be broad structure plans which would require the approval of the Minister, and local plans which would not require ministerial approval. These, together with some other changes, were put into effect by the Act of 1968.

The Act of 1962 and the subsequent legislation have now been repealed and consolidated in the Act of 1971, which came into force on 1st April, 1972.

Outline of the Act of 1971

The Act of 1971 is now the principal Act dealing with town and country planning. It has been amended in some comparatively minor respects by the Acts of 1972 and 1974. The Local Government Act 1972 which took effect in April 1974, made some important changes in the local administration of town and country planning, and the Act of 1971 must now be read subject to certain amendments made by the Local Government Act.

The Act of 1971 continues the principle of a strong system of central administration. The former offices of Minister of Housing and Local Government and of Minister of Transport have now been combined in the new post of Secretary of State for the Environment (referred to in this book as "the Minister"). The Minister's powers and duties under the Act of 1971 enable him to control the policies of local planning authorities and indeed to initiate policies. The Minister has indeed a duty to secure consistency in planning policies (*b*). The extent to which he actually initiates policy will depend partly on the state of public opinion as to the desirability of forceful action by "Whitehall" (*c*) and partly on the personality of the particular Minister. Some aspects of planning policy—*e.g.* the moving of population and industry from London and the "green belts"—owe much to a strong lead by Ministers; though the London "green belt" was largely the result of the initiative of the London County Council shortly before the second World War.

The Secretary of State for Industry also has important powers under the Act of 1971. Applications for planning permission for new industrial development—whether by the building of new factories or by the conversion of non-industrial buildings to industrial use—require the support of the Department of Industry

(*b*) This derives from the Minister of Town and Country Planning Act 1943.

(*c*) See the Report of the Royal Commission on London Government, para. 352, for a comment on the desirability of *not* taking a strong lead in forming policy.

(*d*). In some parts of the country, office development is subject to a similar form of control (*e*).

Until 1974 the local planning authority was usually the county council or the county borough council. Under the new system of local government there are two tiers of local authorities concerned with town and country planning. Some planning functions—notably the preparation of the structure plans—are the responsibility of the county council as "county planning authority", but many matters are dealt with by the district council as "district planning authority" (*f*).

The new system of structure and local plans is being introduced into different parts of the country at different times. When, provision for the new system was first made by the Act of 1968, the Minister invited a number of authorities to prepare structure plans for certain specified areas. The first formal orders were made in 1972 to enable the authorities concerned to embark upon the statutory procedures for public participation and the submission of the plans to the Minister; some of these plans have now been approved by the Minister. The new system is now in force throughout the country in the sense that all the authorities concerned have started on the preparation of structure plans. However, this does not mean the 1947-type plans are no longer of any importance; these older plans remain in force until resolved by the Minister.

The structure plans will be in the nature of policy documents concerned with the main planning problems of the area and the best way of dealing with these problems. The detailed solutions, including land allocations, will be found in the local plans. An important feature of the new system is the emphasis laid on the positive aspects of planning. In preparing the new plans, the local planning authorities are specifically required to consider measures for the improvement of the environment and the

---

(*d*) See chapter 6, *post*.
(*e*) *Ibid.*
(*f*) See chapter 3, *post*.

management of traffic; and they will be expected to identify action areas, that is, areas requiring comprehensive treatment in the comparatively near future by way of development, redevelopment or improvement or by a combination of these methods.

The structure and local plans will also be of importance in regulatory planning; in considering an application for planning permission, for instance, the local planning authority will need to consider the policies laid down in the structure plan and the more detailed provisions of any local plans in force in the locality concerned (*g*).

The requirements as to planning permission are the king-pin of the whole system of regulatory planning. They depend on the definition of development in section 22 of the Act of 1971—namely, the carrying out of building, engineering, mining or other operations or the making of any material change in the use of buildings or other land. This definition is not as simple as might appear (*h*) and has given rise to a large number of High Court actions as well as numerous appeals to the Minister. Any person who is in doubt as to whether a proposed operation or change of use would constitute development may apply to the local planning authority for a determination and, if dissatisfied with that determination, may appeal to the Minister; there is also a further right of appeal to the High Court (*i*). There is now similar machinery for enabling interested persons to obtain a determination in some cases as to the established use rights of buildings or other land (*k*).

Where planning permission is required it is sometimes granted by the Minister by development order and there are a few cases in which planning permission is deemed to be granted. Otherwise application should be made to the local planning authority; if the applicant is aggrieved by their decision he may appeal to the

---

(*g*) For development plans see chapter 4, *post*.
(*h*) This definition is discussed fully in chapter 5, *post*.
(*i*) See chapter 5, *post*.
(*k*) See chapter 9, *post*.

Minister whose decision is final except for an appeal to the High Court on points of law (*l*).

Where planning permission is refused, persons entitled to a legal interest in the land may have a claim for compensation (*m*); and where the land has become incapable of reasonably beneficial use, or the chances of selling it are adversely affected by planning proposals, certain categories of owner may serve a purchase notice (*n*).

If development is carried out without planning permission or in breach of conditions attached to the permission, the local planning authority may serve an enforcement notice. There are certain rights of appeal to the Minister, but, once the notice takes effect, failure to comply with it is an offence punishable by fine; if the notice relates to the carrying out of building or other operations the planning authority have additional powers of enforcement (*o*).

A grant of planning permission may be revoked or modified before it is acted upon (*p*), and the local planning authority have certain powers to require the removal or alteration of existing buildings and uses (*q*).

The importance of conserving and where possible of enhancing the physical environment is recognised by giving local planning authorities certain additional powers of control which are not dependent upon the definition of development. These relate to the preservation of trees and woodlands, the preservation of buildings of special architectural and historic interest, the control of advertisements and the tidying up of waste land (*r*). The local planning authority may also designate conservation areas in

---

(*l*) See chapter 6, *post*.

(*m*) As to compensation for planning restrictions, see chapters 16, 17 and 18, *post*.

(*n*) See chapter 11, *post*.

(*o*) See chapter 9, *post*.

(*p*) See chapter 8, *post*.

(*q*) See chapter 10, *post*.

(*r*) See chapter 12, *post*.

which special attention will be paid to conservation and improvement (*s*).

The Community Land Act, 1975

The theme of positive planning has been developed further with the enactment of the Community Land Act 1975, which received the Royal Assent on 12th, November 1976. This Act is designed:

"(a) to enable the community to control the development of land in accordance with its needs and priorities; and

(b) to restore to the community the increase in value arising from its efforts" (*t*).

The Act of 1975 therefore makes provision for bringing land required for major development schemes into public ownership. The intention is that, after a transitional period of some years, "relevant development" (*u*) shall take place only on land which is either publicly owned or has passed through public ownership. Thus, having acquired land for "relevant development", the authority concerned will either develop it themselves or will dispose of it for private development,

The authorities concerned will thus have greater scope for deciding when and where development shall take place, and in disposing of development land will be able to impose conditions which would be *ultra vires* the Act of 1971. This marriage of planning control with the powers available to a monopoly landlord could in the long-term transform planning in this country. Whether this is necessary or desirable is, of course, a matter of argument.

Other Planning Legislation

The Act of 1971, as subsequently amended, provides the main statutory framework for town and country planning in England

---

(*s*) See chapter 13, *post*.
(*t*) White Paper "Land", Cmnd. 5730.
(*u*) See chapter 22, p. 335, *post*.

and Wales. There are in addition some other Acts dealing with special problems associated with planning, notably the New Towns Act 1965 (re-enacting the original New Towns Act 1946 and other legislation): the Town Development Act 1952; the National Parks and Access to the Countryside Act 1949; and the Countryside Act. 1968.

The New Towns Act 1965

The genesis of the new towns movement is to be found in Ebenezer Howard's *Garden Cities*, published in 1899. It led to the formation of the Garden Cities Association (*v*) and two voluntary experiments in the building of garden cities at Letchworth and Welwyn. The importance of garden cities was recognised by the Acts of 1925 and 1932 which gave the Minister power to acquire land required for garden city development by compulsory purchase, although these powers were in fact never used. Fresh impetus to the movement was given by the Barlow and Scott reports (*w*) which drew attention to the importance of securing the decentralisation of urban areas without at the same time creating fresh suburban sprawl. Finally, it was recognised that the redevelopment of older towns, on account of war damage or for other reasons, would inevitably create an overspill problem. In 1945 a government committee on new towns was appointed "to consider the general questions of the establishment, development, organisation and administration that will arise in the promotion of new towns in the furtherance of a policy of planned decentralisation from congested urban areas; and in accordance therewith to suggest guiding principles on which such towns should be established as balanced communities for work and living." In the first interim report (*a*) the committee came to the conclusion that the most effective agencies for the purpose would be state-appointed development corporations.

(*v*) Later known as the Town and Country Planning Association.
(*w*) See chapter 1, p. 9, *ante*.
(*a*) Cmd. 6759.

This recommendation was adopted and the Act of 1946 was passed "to provide for the creation of new towns by means of development corporations and for purposes connected therewith" (*b*).

The initiative in establishing a new town is taken by the Minister. If satisfied that it would be in the national interest that any area of land should be developed as a new town, he makes an order designating that area as the site of the proposed new town. Notice of the draft order must be published and an opportunity given for the hearing of objections (*c*). Although the Minister will be considering objections to his own scheme, it should not be assumed that it is futile to object; such objections have in fact resulted in a reduction of the designated area.

A development corporation will then be appointed (*d*), the Corporation will submit proposals to the Minister for the development of the new town (*e*) and subject to the approval of the Minister may compulsorily acquire any land in the designated area (*f*). Such land may either be developed by the corporation itself, or sold or leased for private development (*g*). The development of the new town will be financed partly by Government loans and partly by grants under the Act of 1965 (*h*) or under the Housing Acts (*i*).

When the development of the new town is complete, the development corporation will be wound up. The assets will be transferred to the Commission for New Towns set up "for the purpose of taking over, holding, managing and turning to account the property previously vested in the development corporation for a new town" (*k*).

(*b*) Act of 1946.
(*c*) Act of 1965, s. 1 and First Schedule.
(*d*) Act of 1965, s. 2.
(*e*) *Ibid.*, s. 6.
(*f*) *Ibid.*, s. 7.
(*g*) *Ibid.*, s. 18.
(*h*) *Ibid.*, s. 42, amended by Housing Finance Act 1972.
(*i*) Housing Rents and Subsidies Act 1975, ss. 2 (1), 3 (1).
(*k*) Act of 1965, s. 36.

The Town Development Act, 1952

This Act was passed "to encourage town development in county districts for the relief of congestion or overpopulation elsewhere" (*l*). It thus has the same fundamental purpose as the Acts of 1946 and 1965. But whereas the New Towns Act provides for the creation of new towns by state appointed corporations the Act of 1952 is directed rather to the extension of existing towns (*m*) by local authorities.

The scheme must be a substantial one and provide for the relief of congestion or overpopulation in an area outside the county in which the development is to be carried out (*n*).

The district in which the development is to be carried out is known as the receiving district (*o*). The council of the receiving district may compulsorily acquire land required for the development (*p*). The Minister will make substantial grants to the council to enable them to carry out the development (*q*) and he may also approve the making of grants by the "exporting authority" (*r*). It is usual in practice for the exporting authority and the council to work in close co-operation; for instance, the exporting authority may provide technical assistance for the development.

The National Parks and Access to the Countryside Act, 1949

The scope of this Act is considerably wider than its title might suggest. It covers the designation of extensive areas of the countryside as national parks: the designation of areas of outstanding national beauty: the establishment of nature reserves:

(*l*) Act of 1952.

(*m*) The Act of 1952 appears wide enough to permit the building of an entirely new town by local authorities, but this is not the primary purpose of the Act.

(*n*) Act of 1952, s. 2(1), as amended by the Local Government Act 1972, s. 185, Schs. 18 and 20.

(*o*) *Ibid.*, s. 1.

(*p*) *Ibid.*, s. 6.

(*q*) *Ibid.*, s. 2(2).

(*r*) *Ibid.*, s. 4.

the making of access orders and agreements: and the carrying out of a survey of public paths and the creation and diversion or closure of public paths.

The Act establishes a National Parks Commission with duties in connection with (*s*)—

(a) the preservation and enhancement of natural beauty in England and Wales particularly in areas designated as national parks;

(b) encouraging the provision or improvement of facilities for the enjoyment of national parks and for the enjoyment of opportunities of open-air recreation and study of nature afforded by them.

These functions have been extended by the Countryside Act, 1968, and the Commission is now known as the Countryside Commission (*t*).

National parks.—The object of designating a national park is to preserve and enhance the natural beauty of the area and to promote its enjoyment by the public. It must be an area which affords opportunities of open-air recreation (*u*) by reason of its character and its position in relation to centres of population (*a*).

The responsibility for seeing that these objects are carried out rests on the local planning authorities rather than the Commission (*b*). This will be done in three ways. First, there will be a strict control over development. A national park will not be exclusively devoted to enjoyment by the public. The life of the area is to go on and the various authorities are to have due regard to the needs of agriculture and forestry (*c*). Other land uses, such as mineral development, may be permitted in excep-

(*s*) Act of 1949, s. 1.

(*t*) Countryside Act, 1968, s. 1(1).

(*u*) "Open air recreation" does not include organised games: Act of 1949, s. 114(1).

(*a*) Act of 1949, s. 5.

(*b*) As to planning authorities in a national park, see chapter 3, pp. 46, 47, *post*.

(*c*) Act of 1949, s. 84.

tional circumstances (*d*). A national park will in fact be an area of special control in which amenity considerations will be predominant but not necessarily decisive.

Secondly, the local planning authority may provide various facilities for public enjoyment such as accommodation, meals and refreshment, camping sites and parking grounds; and they may compulsorily acquire land for these purposes (*e*). They may also improve waterways for sailing, bathing or fishing (*f*).

Thirdly, the Act provides for extended Government grants to encourage the local planning authorities to use their powers to preserve and enhance the natural beauty of the area. Thus an authority wishing to make an order under section 51 of the Act of 1971 for the removal of an authorised use (*g*) in a national park would get a special grant for the purpose.

Areas of outstanding natural beauty.—There will be many areas of outstanding natural beauty which are not suitable for designation as national parks either because they are too small or for some other reason. The Commission may designate such areas as areas of outstanding national beauty. In addition, some areas may be so designated pending designation as national parks. The local planning authority will be able to do all such things as appear expedient for preserving and enhancing the natural beauty of the area and special grants will be available for the purpose, but there is no power to provide facilities for public enjoyment as in a national park (*h*).

Nature reserves.—The local planning authority was given power in the Act of 1947 to define sites of nature reserves in the development plan (*i*) but it was left to the Act of 1949 to give any real

(*d*) See the Minister's statement on the Second Reading of the Bill: House of Commons Official Report, vol. 463, col. 1492.

(*e*) Act of 1949, s. 12.

(*f*) *Ibid*., s. 13.

(*g*) See chapter 10, *post*.

(*h*) Act of 1949, ss. 87 and 88.

(*i*) Town and Country Planning Act, 1971, Sch. 5.

meaning to the concept of a nature reserve. The phrase is defined in the latter Act as land managed for either of the following purposes (*j*)—

(a) "providing, under suitable conditions and control, special opportunities for the study of and research into, matters relating to the fauna and flora of Great Britain and the physical conditions in which they live, and for the study of geological and physiographical features of special interest in the area": or

(b) "preserving flora, fauna or geological or physiographical features of special interest in the area."

The establishment of a nature reserve will normally be undertaken by the Nature Conservancy Council (*k*) who may either enter into agreements with the landowners or compulsorily purchase the land.

Access to open country.—This is defined as any area consisting "wholly or predominantly of mountain, moor, heath, down, cliff or foreshore (including any bank, barrier, dune, beach, flat or other land adjacent to the foreshore)". Local planning authorities are enabled to secure public access for the purpose of open-air recreation by entering into an access agreement with the owner of land, or by making an access order, or by compulsorily purchasing the land (*l*).

Rights of Way (*m*)

The provisions as to rights of way apply to the whole of England and Wales and not merely to special areas such as national parks and open countryside. Local authorities are empowered to enter into agreements with landowners for the creation of new public paths (*n*) and in certain cases to make compulsory orders creating such paths (*o*). Local authorities may also make diver-

(*j*) Act of 1949, s. 15.
(*k*) Nature Conservancy Council Act 1973.
(*l*) Act of 1949, s. 59.
(*m*) These provisions are now contained in the Highways Act, 1959.
(*n*) Act of 1949, s. 39; now Highways Act, 1959, s. 27.
(*o*) *Ibid.*, s. 40; now Highways Act, 1959, s. 28.

sion orders or stop up an existing path and replace it by a new path (*p*). And, where the local authority consider that a public path is no longer needed, they may make an extinguishment order without having to provide an alternative path (*q*).

The Countryside Act 1968

This Act is an extension of the National Parks and Access to the Countryside Act, 1949, discussed earlier in this chapter. The former National Parks Commission is re-named the Countryside Commission and given new powers in relation to the countryside as a whole (*a*). The Act also provides amongst other things for "country parks" which will be the responsibility of local authorities (*b*).

The new functions of the Commission in relation to the countryside as a whole are general in character. The Commission has a duty to keep under review the provision of facilities for the enjoyment of the countryside, the conservation and enhancement of natural beauty, and the need for public access (*c*). The policy of the Commission is to stimulate other public authorities rather than take direct action, but it has power to provide technical assistance (*d*) and to carry out experimental projects (*e*); it also has power to make grants and loans to non-public bodies (including the National Trust) for approved schemes (*f*).

The country parks differ radically in concept from the national parks. A national park is a very large area which is not wholly devoted to public enjoyment; the ordinary life of the area goes on, and the authorities have a special duty to have regard to the needs of agriculture and forestry. A country park will be

---

(*p*) *Ibid.*, s. 42; now Highways Act, 1959, s. 111.
(*q*) *Ibid.*, s. 43; now Highways Act, 1959, s. 110.
(*a*) Countryside Act, 1968, s. 1(1).
(*b*) *Ibid.*, s. 6.
(*c*) *Ibid.*, s. 2(2).
(*d*) *Ibid.*, s. 2(5).
(*e*) *Ibid.*, s. 4.
(*f*) Countryside Act, 1968, s. 5.

a site to be laid out as a park or pleasure ground by the local authority (*g*). Having defined the site of a country park, the local authority have power to purchase land, lay out the site, provide buildings and such facilities as refreshments, lavatories, car parks, fishing and sailing on waterways (*h*).

There is also a general power (not restricted to country parks) for local authorities to provide camping sites for holiday and recreational purposes, to be used primarily for setting up tents; authorities may also provide picnic sites for motorists (*i*).

The Act also provides that, in the exercise of their functions relating to land under any enactment, every Minister, government department and public body shall have regard to the natural beauty and amenity of the countryside (*k*); the Act does not provide any machinery for enforcing this duty.

Current Planning Problems

What is the purpose of all this planning legislation? In Chapter 1 an outline was given of the development of our planning problems from the industrial revolution to the end of the second world war. Most of these problems still exist and indeed have been intensified by current trends. Some new problems have come into existence since the war.

The main planning problems of the nineteen seventies can be summarised as follows.

The National Economy

Throughout the post-war period the national economy has been under severe strain. In particular, there has been a tendency for imports to exceed exports which at fairly frequent intervals has caused major crises; in other words, the country has difficulty in paying its way. This problem has, of course, become particularly

(*g*) *Ibid.*, s. 7(1).
(*h*) *Ibid.*, ss. 8(1), 9(3).
(*i*) *Ibid.*, s. 10.
(*k*) *Ibid.*, s. 11.

acute in the middle seventies. The state of the economy affects town and country planning in two ways. First, it means that many desirable projects have to be deferred even though in the long run they would contribute to national well-being. Secondly, the requirements of the national economy have to be taken into account in deciding upon the right use of land.

The objects of town and country planning include general economic considerations, such as the need to boost exports, as well as such matters as the zoning of land for housing and industry or the preservation of the countryside. Sometimes these economic considerations come into conflict with other planning objectives.

> A company manufacturing steel castings sought permission to extend their factory to nearly twice the previous size. The local planning authority refused permission: the existing works constituted a serious injury to local amenities, and any extension would increase this injury; any reconstruction or extension should take place on the opposite side of the road on land which was likely to be zoned for industrial purposes.
>
> The Minister considered that the company's objections to the use of the alternative site well founded. The factory was wrongly sited but its complete re-siting could only be considered as a long-term project which might become practicable at some future date. In the meantime, there was immediate need for expansion of the existing works to enable the company to meet their commitments and satisfy important export demands. The proposed developments would also benefit amenity by improving the appearance of the works. The Minister accordingly allowed the company's appeal (*l*).

Distribution of Population and Employment

In 1940 the Barlow Report had commented on the over-concentration of population and industry in the large conurbations and on the tendency of industry to move from some of the older industrial areas to London and the South-East; the ten-

---

(*l*) Bulletin of Selected Appeal Decisions VIII/14.

dency of industry to move to certain favoured areas is just as strong today. There is also a heavy concentration of new office buildings in London and one or two large provincial cities. The result is serious congestion particularly in London. As a former Minister of Housing put it:

> "At the root of almost all London's planning problems is the evil of congestion and its effects upon living and working conditions. . . . It is the enormous number of offices and office workers which constitutes the greatest single cause of congestion" (*m*).

One of the major problems of planning therefore is to restrain these tendencies and to try to steer new factories and offices to less crowded areas. This is largely a problem of "regulatory planning"; the development plans will indicate where land is available for new factories and offices and planning authorities may also lay down density standards for new buildings; the Secretary of State for Industry has substantial powers of control over industrial development; and, if planning permission is granted for a new factory building, it may be subject to a condition that the building is occupied only by firms already established in the area (*n*). The Secretary of State for the Environment also has power to control the location of office development. There is also considerable scope for "positive planning" through the building of new towns and town expansion schemes.

The Boom in Development

During the nineteen sixties and early seventies there was a considerable boom in development schemes. Its most outstanding feature was the unprecedented demand for new homes; the total population continued to increase; the number of separate householders increased even more rapidly because couples were married at an earlier age; and, with a comparatively high level of prosperity, the effective demand for better homes was greater than ever before.

(*m*) Letter approving the County of London Development Plan, 1955.
(*n*) Circular 42/55.

Again more and more people were able to take holidays away from home with the result that there was a great demand for holiday facilities; much of this demand has been channelled into caravan sites, the location of which has produced special problems for planning authorities.

The economic recession of the middle seventies has restrained effective demand and reduced the number of new development schemes. However, as the country climbs out of recession, there may well be another boom in development.

The Outward Spread of Towns

With a high level of building activity, there is a natural tendency for many towns to spread outwards into the surrounding countryside. This outward spread has many disadvantages; those who live in the inner areas are further removed from the countryside; those who find homes further out have a long journey—often in crowded public transport—to their work; and in some cases towns may merge to form an almost continuous urban agglomeration. The Minister has urged planning authorities to establish green belts around expanding towns as a means of checking this outward growth (*a*) but this produces fresh problems—namely, a pressure for more intensive development within the existing built-up areas and a demand for building land beyond the green belts.

Urban Renewal and Reconstruction

The problems of urban renewal and reconstruction are difficult and urgent. At the centre and within the inner suburban ring of many large towns there are now large areas of obsolescent buildings and badly laid out development. Some of these are ripe for slum clearance under the Housing Acts, but there are also the "twilight areas". The rebuilding of these areas of obsolete development nearly always creates an overspill problem even when the new building is to a high density.

(*a*) See chapter 4, *post*.

Large scale redevelopment is also needed to cope with the problem of the motor vehicle. Professor Buchanan has described the traffic problem as one of the most extraordinary facing modern society.

> "It arises directly out of man's own ingenuity and growing affluence—his invention of a go-anywhere, self-powered machine for transport and personal locomotion, and his growing ability and inclination to invest in it. It is an extraordinary problem because nothing less is involved than a threat to the whole familiar physical form of towns" (*b*).

There is thus scope and need for a great deal of comprehensive redevelopment, but this presents formidable problems of finance, administration and land ownership. To quote the Buchanan Report again—

> "Local authorities can undertake it, provided they own the land, either themselves or by letting off the land on building leases. But this is almost certain to require compulsory acquisition on a big scale, with vast financial outlay bringing no returns in the early stages. Private developers can undertake it provided they can overcome the difficulties presented by multiplicity of ownership. These difficulties are acute. Moreover, as matters stand at present, private enterprise is, naturally enough, interested only in the profitable rebuilding of commercial and business centres and finds little inducement to tackle the enormous 'twilight areas' of obsolescent 'byelaw housing' of which there is so much in our towns."

When the Land Commission was set up in 1967 it was suggested that the Commission might finance the redevelopment of twilight areas by using the profit from the acquisition and disposal of virgin land to offset the loss on dealings in land in twilight areas (*c*). The Land Commission was dissolved in 1970 and no alternative provision has been made for financing the redevelopment of twilight areas.

(*b*) *Traffic in Towns*, published by H.M.S.O. 1963. An abbreviated edition was published by Penguin Books in 1964.

(*c*) Speech by Sir Henry Wells, Chairman of the Land Commission reported in *The Times*, March 7, 1967.

Dispersal of Population and Industry

One method of dealing with the problems created by the outward spread of towns and the overspill from the redevelopment of older urban areas is the planned dispersal of population and industry to new and expanded towns. Machinery for this purpose exists under the New Towns Act and the Town Development Act.

Agriculture and the Countryside

Both the Barlow and Scott reports laid considerable emphasis on the need to safeguard good agricultural land and to preserve the countryside as a source of amenities and recreational opportunities. These remain important objectives of town and country planning. Thus in a Development Control Policy Note, the Minister has stated that an efficient and prosperous farming industry is not only essential to the life of the countryside: it is a vital national interest (*d*).

Mineral Deposits

Although coal no longer has the importance that once it had as virtually the sole source of energy in this country, in recent years there has been increased interest in exploiting new coalfields. And other minerals—notably ironstone and sand and gravel—are of increasing importance. Since minerals must be worked where they are found, it must be one of the objects of town and country planning to see that valuable deposits are not sterilised by premature building or other forms of development. Mineral working (whether surface or underground) is a form of development for the purposes of the Act of 1971 and is thus subject to the ordinary processes of planning control: these are supplemented by special regulations made under the Act of 1971 and by the Mineral Workings Act, 1951 (*d*).

(*d*) Development Control Policy Note no. 4: Development in Rural Areas, para. 9.

(*e*) See (*e*) See chapter 13, *post*.

Traffic and Access Problems

In deciding upon the location of new development it is important to consider the effect on traffic and access to roads. Certain types of building—offices, hotels, and places of public entertainment—obviously attract traffic and create problems of parking and access. Or, to take a rather different example, the siting of a new housing development may depend upon the adequacy of public transport facilities.

Preservation and Enhancement of Amenity

One of the objects of planning control is to preserve and where possible to improve the pleasant appearance of streets and buildings and of the countryside. There are several aspects of this problem. First, to see that new buildings are of good design; thus planning permission may be refused for a building which is ugly or of poor design or which would be unsuitable in its surroundings (*f*). Or conditions may be imposed requiring the use of certain materials; for instance, requiring a new house in the Cotswolds to be built of stone. Secondly, permission may be refused for development which would be "unneighbourly", such as development which would give rise to noise, smoke, smell or dirt, or which would interfere with the daylighting of adjoining buildings, or which would obtrude upon the privacy of neighbouring residents. Noise, smoke, smell and other interference with the comfortable enjoyment of land may constitute a nuisance at common law or may be regulated under such legislation as the Public Health Acts, 1936 and 1961, or the Clean Air Act, 1956. Planning permission does not override common law rights or statutory restrictions and so in some cases it may be reasonable to permit development in the knowledge that neighbouring residents or landowners are adequately protected. But in other cases, the planning authority may consider that common law

---

(*f*) Selected Planning Appeals, Vol. III.

rights or other statutes do not afford sufficient protection and may accordingly refuse permission or impose conditions.

Thirdly, it may be necessary to give permission for development even though it involves some loss of amenity; mineral workings are an example. In such cases conditions may be imposed in order to minimise the interference with amenity.

Planning and Economic Competition

As mentioned earlier, planning has to take account of general economic needs, such as the promotion of exports or mineral supplies. It must also take account of local economic requirements, such as the need for shops or petrol stations. Where there is a conflict with other planning objectives—*e.g.* the preservation of amenity—the planning authority will have to decide whether the need outweighs the objections. If there is an appeal, the appellant may have to satisfy the Minister that the need exists.

Where there is no objection on other planning grounds, however, the question of need will not be relevant. For example, if a proposed petrol station would not be detrimental to amenity and the requirements of public safety, permission ought not to be refused on the ground that there is no need for another petrol station in the locality (*g*). Planning control, it is submitted, should not be used merely to restrict competition.

(*g*) Circular 25/58.

CHAPTER 3

CENTRAL AND LOCAL ADMINISTRATION

The administration of town and country planning in England and Wales is the responsibility mainly of the Minister and the local planning authorities. In England the Minister is now the Secretary of State for the Environment; he exercises the functions in respect of town and country planning which were previously the responsibility of the Minister of Housing and Local Government and the Minister of Public Buildings and Works (*a*). In Wales the Minister is the Secretary of State for Wales (*b*).

The Secretary of State for Industry (*c*) is also concerned with the administration of town and country planning in both England and Wales; he has important powers of control over the distribution of industry (*d*). There is also a Secretary of State for Transport; he is concerned with highway matters.

(*a*) The derivation of the Secretary of State's powers is as follows: The functions of the Minister of Town and Country Planning were transferred in January 1951 to a new Minister of Local Government and Planning; see the Transfer of Functions (Minister of Health and Minister of Local Government and Planning) (No. 1) Order 1951, S.I. 1951 No. 142. In November 1951 the style and title of this Minister was changed to Minister of Housing and Local Government: see the Minister of Local Government and Planning (Change of Style and Title) Order 1951, S.I. 1951 No. 1900. All the functions of the Minister of Housing and Local Government, the Minister of Public Buildings and Works, and the Minister of Transport were transferred to the Secretary of State in 1970: see the Secretary of State for the Environment Order 1970, S.I. 1970 No. 1681.

(*b*) In Wales and Monmouthshire most of the functions of the former Minister of Housing and Local Government were transferred to the Secretary of State for Wales in 1965—see the Secretary of State for Wales Order 1965, S.I. 1965 No. 319. See also Act of 1968, s. 104(1).

(*c*) The Act of 1971 refers simply to the Secretary of State. This is because in constitutional theory there is one *office* of Secretary of State although in practice there are always several Secretaries of State each in charge of a separate Department.

(*d*) See chapter 6, pp. 126 *et seq*.

The Minister

As the successor to the Minister of Town and Country Planning the Secretary of State for the Environment is charged by statute (*e*) with the duty of "securing consistency and continuity in the framing and execution of a national policy with respect to the use and development of land throughout England and Wales". It will be observed that the Minister's duty relates to the framing and execution of a national *policy:* he is not called upon to prepare a *plan* in the sense in which local planning authorities are required to do. Moreover, the Minister has over the years laid down *policies* rather than a single policy statement. Thus, he has laid down policies with regard to the dispersal of population and industry from London and other urban centres, green belts, the preservation of agricultural land and so on.

In fact, the real authority of the Minister derives from his specific powers and duties under the Town and Country Planning Acts and other planning legislation. The nature and extent of these duties may be illustrated by a few examples.

Duties of the Minister

(1) *Making of regulations.*—The law of town and country planning is to be found not only in various Acts of Parliament but also in orders and regulations made by the Minister in the form of statutory instruments relevant to planning. Their importance can hardly be exaggerated. The Use Classes Order (*f*) for instance excludes certain changes of use from the definition of development and thus removes them altogether from planning Control. By the General Development Order, the Minister has given a general planning permission for a wide variety of development with the result that it is not necessary in these cases to apply for permission to the local planning authority (*g*).

(2) *Approval.*—Some actions of the local planning authority

(*e*) Minister of Town and Country Planning Act, 1943, s. 1.
(*f*) See chapter 5, *post*.
(*g*) See chapter 6, *post*.

require the approval of the Minister. For example, the older type of development plan and the new structure plans do not become effective unless and until they are confirmed by the Minister (*h*). The same principle applies (with a few exceptions) to orders for the revocation or modification of planning permission (*i*), tree preservation orders (*l*), and orders establishing areas of special control for outdoor advertisements (*m*).

(3) *Appeals.*—Other actions of the local planning authority do not require the approval of the Minister, but persons affected may have a right of appeal to the Minister. The most important example is the right of appeal against a decision of the local planning authority refusing planning permission or granting it subject only to conditions. Although the Minister decides each case on its merits and does not move from precedent to precedent as does a judge in a court of law, his decisions nevertheless form something like a body of "case law" which is invaluable to local authorities and developers in that it shows what policy the Minister is likely to adopt in future cases.

(4) *Powers of direction.*—In some cases the Minister may give directions either of a general or a particular nature. Examples of general directions are the Housing Accommodation Direction, 1952 (*n*) which requires the local planning authority to consult the housing authority before giving a decision on an application to change the use of a dwellinghouse, and the Development Plans Direction, 1975 (*o*) which lays down the procedure to be followed where the planning authority wish to grant planning permission for development which does not accord with the development plan. The Minister may also issue a direction to a local planning authority with regard to a particular matter: he may for instance "call in" an application for planning permission so that he may

(*h*) See chapter 4, *post*.
(*i*) See chapter 8, *post*.
(*l*) See chapter 12, *post*.
(*m*) *Ibid*.
(*n*) This direction is included in circular 94/52.
(*o*) This direction is printed as an appendix to circular 96/75.

give a decision himself (*p*); this is often done where the proposed development would conflict with the development plan or where the development is of especial public interest such as the proposed development of the Monico café site in Piccadilly Circus.

(5) *Default powers.*—If the Minister considers that a local planning authority have failed to fulfil some function under the Act of 1971, he may himself take action. He may, for instance, prepare or alter a structure or local plan (*q*), serve an enforcement notice in respect of a breach of planning control (*r*), or make a tree preservation order (*s*).

(6) *Claims for compensation.*—Claims for compensation under Part VII of the Act of 1971 for refusal of planning permission or for conditions attached to a planning permission are dealt with by the Minister (*t*).

(7) *Judicial determinations.*—The whole machinery of planning control depends on the definition of "development" in the 1971 Act (*u*). Under section 53 of the Act of 1971 the Minister may, on appeal from the local planning authority or (if he so decides) at first instance, be called upon to give a determination as to whether a proposed operation or change of use would constitute development and, if so, whether an application for planning permission is required (*v*). Under section 95, he may be required to certify what is the established use of any land (*a*). And, on an appeal against an enforcement notice in respect of a breach of planning control, he may have to decide whether the matters complained of in the notice constituted development (*b*).

In addition to these statutory functions, the Minister is able to

---

(*p*) The power to do this is conferred by the Act of 1971, s. 35.
(*q*) Act of 1971, s. 17(1).
(*r*) *Ibid.*, s. 276(5).
(*s*) *Ibid.*, s. 276(2).
(*t*) See chapter 19, *post*.
(*u*) See chapter 5, *post*.
(*v*) See chapter 5, *post*.
(*a*) See chapter 9, *post*.
(*b*) Act of 1971, s. 88. See chapter 9, *post*.

shape planning policy through advice and information. Circulars are sent from time to time to local planning authorities on various aspects of planning control; these circulars are usually available to the public as well, so they are often of considerable assistance to landowners and their professional advisers in negotiations with the local planning authority and in conducting appeals to the Minister. Information and advice are also conveyed through handbooks and other publications on such matters as the density of residential areas and the redevelopment of central areas of towns.

Obviously the Minister cannot exercise all these functions personally. Most of the decisions are made on his behalf and given in his name by senior civil servants; and, in the case of some planning appeals, the decision may be given by the Inspector who conducted the inquiry. Nevertheless, the Minister is responsible for every decision, and (except perhaps for the judicial determinations mentioned above) answerable for it in Parliament.

Nature of the Minister's Decision

The Minister's decisions are of two kinds: policy decisions and judicial determinations.

Policy decisions.—The most important examples arise in connection with planning appeals and development plans. When considering an appeal against a refusal of planning permission or in deciding whether or not to confirm a development plan, the Minister's concern is to achieve or uphold good standards of planning and to ensure that land is not used in a manner detrimental to the public interest. In other words, he is concerned with questions of policy rather than law. He must act within a legal framework—that is, he must not exceed the powers given him by the Planning Acts and he must observe the relevant statutory procedures—and, if he fails in either of these respects, the decision may be challenged in the courts. But the courts will not go into the question whether the Minister's decision represents good planning policy. Subject to his responsibility to Parliament, the Minister is the final arbiter of what is good planning.

Before reaching the decision in any particular case, the Minister usually has to give the parties concerned the opportunity of being heard by a person appointed for the purpose, usually an Inspector from the Ministry. The hearing by the Inspector often takes the form of a public local inquiry at which the persons immediately affected—that is, the landowner (or developer) and the planning authority—will state their case and members of the public can make representations. The parties will often be represented by counsel or a solicitor, and will usually call witnesses on questions of fact or expert opinion. The hearing thus has some of the characteristics of a court of law. But the Inspector is not a judge. Although the Inspector may now give the decision in certain minor planning appeals (*c*), his duty is usually limited to making a report to the Minister presenting the facts (as they have emerged from the evidence at the inquiry or from his own inspection of the land in question) together with his own conclusions and recommendations. The Minister is not obliged to accept the report but will reach his own decision (*d*).

Public inquiries of this kind have for many years formed part of the procedure for slum clearance schemes made under the Housing Acts and for compulsory purchase under a number of statutes. Recently, however, there has been much controversy as to their nature and purpose. In some quarters they have been regarded simply as part of the machinery by which the Minister collects information and opinion to enable him to make his decisions. This was described by the Franks Committee Report (1957) as the "administrative" view (*e*). The courts have held, in cases under the Housing Acts, that the rules of natural justice

---

(*c*) See chapter 6, *post*.

(*d*) For a full account of the procedure at a public inquiry see chapter 16, *post*.

(*e*) Franks Committee report, paras. 262, 263.

must apply to the conduct of the inquiry and that the Minister must not receive information from one party to the inquiry behind the back of the other (*f*). It has always been assumed that (except in relation to development plans, for which there are special provisions (*g*)) the same principle applies to planning inquiries. But the courts have never questioned the Minister's right to obtain information and opinion from other quarters, particularly from other government departments. The administrative school of thought considers it is both proper and reasonable for the Minister to obtain information in this way.

Diametrically opposed to the administrative view is what the Franks Committee called the "judicial" view (*h*). This regards a planning inquiry as a dispute between the local planning authority and the individual: the ensuing decision should be judicial in the sense that it should be based wholly and directly upon the evidence presented at the inquiry.

These two opposing views were considered by the Franks Committee, which came to the conclusion that neither provided a satisfactory analysis (*i*).

> "Our general conclusion is that these procedures cannot be classified as purely administrative or purely judicial. They are not purely administrative because of the provision for a special procedure preliminary to the decision—a feature not to be found in the ordinary course of administration—and because this procedure as we have shown, involves the testing of an issue, often partly in public. They are not on the other hand purely judicial, because the final decision cannot be reached by the application of rules and must allow the exercise of a wide discretion in the balancing of public and private interest. Neither view at its extreme is tenable, nor should either be emphasised at the expense of the other.
>
> If the administrative view is dominant the public inquiry cannot play its full part in the total process, and there is a danger

(*f*) The leading case is *Errington* v. *Minister of Health*, [1935] 1 K.B. 249.
(*g*) Act of 1971, s. 9(4); Sch. 5, para. 6 (4). See chapter 4, *post*.
(*h*) Franks Committee report, paras. 262, 264.
(*i*) *Ibid.*, paras. 272, 273, 274.

> that the rights and interests of the individual citizens affected will not be sufficiently protected. In these cases it is idle to argue that Parliament can be relied upon to protect the citizen, save exceptionally. We agree with the following views expressed in the pamphlet entitled *Rule of Law*. 'Whatever the theoretical validity of this argument, those of us who are Members of Parliament have no hesitation in saying that it bears little relation to reality. Parliament has neither the time nor the knowledge to supervise the Minister and call him to account for his administrative decisions.'
>
> If the judicial view is dominant there is a danger that people will regard the person before whom they state their case as a kind of judge provisionally deciding the matter, subject to an appeal to the Minister. This view overlooks the true nature of the proceeding, the form of which is necessitated by the fact that the Minister himself, who is responsible to Parliament for the ultimate decision, cannot conduct the enquiry in person."

The Franks Committee endeavoured to find a reasonable balance between these two views by applying the tests of openness, fairness and impartiality to the current practice (*k*). The application of these tests led to the conclusion that some reforms were necessary, and the Franks Committee recommended amongst other things that the case for the planning authority should be properly notified in advance and supported at the inquiry (*l*), that the Inspector's report should be available to the parties to the inquiry (*m*), that the Minister should submit to the parties for their observations any factual evidence which he obtains after the inquiry, whatever the source, and that the Minister should give the reasons for the decision (*n*). These recommendations have largely been put into effect, partly by legislation (*o*) and partly by administrative action.

These changes undoubtedly bring current practice much nearer

(*k*) Franks Committee report, paras. 276, 277.

(*l*) *Ibid.*, paras. 280 *et seq.*

(*m*) *Ibid.*, para. 344.

(*n*) *Ibid.*, paras. 347 *et seq.*

(*o*) Tribunals and Inquiries Act, 1971, replacing the Tribunals and Inquiries Act, 1958; Inquiries Procedure Rules, 1974. See chapter 15, *post*.

the judicial school of thought. It should not, however, be thought that they are detrimental to the interests of the administrative school. On the contrary, they should strengthen administration by ensuring that only tested and proven information is relied upon in reaching a decision; insistence upon the giving of reasons should also discourage ill-thought-out decisions.

Judicial determinations.—Examples of judicial determinations by the Minister have been mentioned above (*p*). They involve a decision on a point of law and he must not consider questions of good planning policy. Before making his decision he must give the parties involved an opportunity to be heard though often the parties agree to submit written representations instead (*q*). The Minister's decision may be the subject of an appeal to the High Court (*r*).

The Minister's Responsibility to Parliament

The Minister is responsible to Parliament for the manner in which he carries out his functions under the Planning Acts. Questions may be put to him at Question Time and debates held. Parliament has not the time to exercise any detailed supervision. It was also suggested in the pamphlet *Rule of Law* (*s*) that Parliament lacks the necessary knowledge, but this does not seem to be the case. There have from time to time been important and useful debates, particularly on broader topics such as the conduct of planning inquiries. The Minister's decisions in the "Essex chalkpit" case and over Stansted airport were specifically debated. And it was as a result of questions in Parliament that the Minister decided to "call in" the application in respect of the Monico café in Piccadilly Circus. Moreover, as an alternative to a formal parlia-

(*p*) See this chapter, p. 38, *ante*.

(*q*) Act of 1971, s. 53 (determinations whether planning permission is required); s. 88 (determinations whether acts made the subject of an enforcement notice constitute development), s. 95 (appeals against refusal of certificate of established use).

(*r*) *Ibid.*, ss. 246, 247.

(*s*) See this chapter, p. 42, *ante*.

mentary question, M.P.s often raise matters in correspondence with the Minister.

There are, however, certain inherent difficulties about taking up individual cases with the Minister. Four situations may arise:

1. A planning application has been made to the local planning authority and awaits a formal decision. In this case, there is no particular difficulty. The matter can be freely debated in Parliament and the Minister can "call in" the application giving the parties an opportunity to be heard at a public inquiry.

2. The local planning authority have refused permission, or granted it subject to conditions, and there is an appeal to the Minister. Is it consistent with the principles laid down by the Franks Committee to express opinion in Parliament with the obvious intention of influencing the Minister's decision? A former Lord Chancellor thought not. In the course of a debate in the House of Lords, a peer commented on the merits of an appeal then before the Minister. The Lord Chancellor rebuked him on the ground that the matter was *sub judice* (*t*). The rule that there should be no comment on matters which are *sub judice* comes from the courts of law, and it can be argued that it does not strictly apply to the consideration of a planning application; indeed the Franks Committee mentioned the Minister's responsibility to Parliament as one of the reasons why the judicial view of planning decisions could not be wholly accepted (*u*). But if statements can be made in Parliament with the intention of influencing the Minister's decision, what happens to the principle laid down by the Franks Committee that the Minister should only take into account information and opinion which were given at the inquiry or upon which the parties have had an opportunity to comment? Of course, there can be no objection to discussion after the Minister has made his decision, but then it is too late to be of practical value.

3. The local planning authority have granted permission. In

(*t*) House of Lords debates, Dec. 1, 1960.
(*u*) Franks Committee report, para. 274.

this case there will be no appeal and no inquiry (*a*). There can therefore be no objection to parliamentary discussion but it will be of little practical value unless the Minister is prepared to direct the local planning authority to make a revocation order, but this can be very costly in terms of compensation (*b*).

4. The Minister is called upon to give a judicial determination. Here, it is submitted, the *sub judice* principle must apply.

Parliamentary control may to some extent have been strengthened by the Parliamentary Commissioner Act, 1967. The Commissioner can investigate complaints of maladministration arising from the exercise by the Minister of any of his administrative functions. "Maladministration," however, probably refers to the manner in which the Minister reaches his decision rather than to its substance, and in some cases under the Act of 1971 the courts afford redress against this type of maladministration; unless there are special reasons, the Commissioner must not investigate complaints which can be dealt with by the courts. The Minister's conduct can also be reviewed by the Council on Tribunals.

Local Planning Authorities

At local level, the administration of town and country planning (including many of the initiatives in policy making) is the responsibility of the local planning authorities.

Prior to the re-organisation of local government in 1974, the local planning authority (outside Greater London) was usually the county or county borough council. The Minister, however, could set up joint planning boards; these might be constituted for the area, or part of the area, of two or more counties or county boroughs. In fact, only two such joint boards were set up; these were for the Lake District and Peak District National Parks.

Under the pre-1974 system a county council might delegate

(*a*) The only person who can appeal to the Minister against the local planning authority's decision on an application for planning permission is the applicant himself: Act of 1971, s. 36.

(*b*) For revocation procedure, see chapter 8, *post*.

certain planning functions to borough and district councils, and a joint board might likewise delegate certain functions to its constituent authorities. In 1959 provision was made for the compulsory delegation of certain functions to district councils with populations of over 60,000.

The changes introduced by the Local Government Act 1972, with effect from 1st April, 1974, are substantial. There is now a comprehensive two-tier system of county and district councils throughout England and Wales, except for the Isles of Scilly, the "all-purpose" county boroughs having been abolished. The Act divides England (exclusive of Greater London (*c*) and the Isles of Scilly) into six metropolitan counties and thirty-nine non-metropolitan counties (*d*). The metropolitan counties are divided into thirty-six metropolitan districts with populations ranging from 180,000 to 1,100,000. The non-metropolitan counties are divided into 333 non-metropolitan districts with populations mostly between 65,000 and 120,000.

In Wales (*e*) there are eight counties divided into forty districts (*f*).

The new system has brought important changes in the administration of town and country planning. In most cases the new districts are much larger than the former boroughs and county districts, and it has been considered appropriate to entrust the new districts with direct (instead of delegated) responsibility for many planning matters. The Local Government Act provides that the counties shall act as county planning authorities and the districts as district planning authorities. The Minister may set up a joint board as the county planning authority for the area, or part of the area of two or more counties; and he may also set up a joint board as the district planning authority for the area, or part of the area, of two or more districts (*g*).

(*c*) For Greater London, see p. 282, *post*.
(*d*) Local Government Act 1972, Sch. 1.
(*e*) "Wales" includes Monmouthshire: *Ibid*, s. 20(7).
(*f*) *Ibid*., Sch. 4.
(*g*) *Ibid*., s. 182(1).

The former joint planning board for the Peak District has been reconstituted as the planning authority for the national park (*h*). The Lake District National Park is now wholly within the area of one county—the new county of Cumbria—and the former joint planning board has been converted into a "special planning board" (*i*). The Minister has not so far excercised his power to establish any more joint boards.

The county planning authority will be responsible for the structure plan (*k*) and for certain "county matters" in regard to development control (*l*). These county matters will include mineral workings, development inconsistent with the fundamental provisions of the structure plan or with the provisions of any local plan prepared by the county, development affecting certain principal roads, and any other development prescribed by the Minister (*m*).

The district planning authority will be responsible for preparing local plans for its area, unless reserved to the county planning authority (*n*); the district authority will also be responsible for administering the statutory provisions relating to the control of development, except of course in the case of the county matters referred to above (*o*).

In national parks, however, all planning functions will be exercisable by the county planning authority (or joint board) with only a few minor exceptions (*p*). Where there is no joint or special planning board, however, the county council must appoint a national park committee to exercise all planning functions except those relating to development plans, and the control of development which either conflicts with those plans or straddles the boundary of the park (*q*).

(*h*) *Ibid.*, Sch. 17, para. 1.
(*i*) *Ibid.*, Sch. 17, para. 3.
(*k*) *Ibid.*, s. 183(1).
(*l*) *Ibid.*, Sch. 16, para. 15.
(*m*) *Ibid.*, Sch. 16, para 32.
(*n*) *Ibid.*, s. 183(2).
(*o*) *Ibid.*, Sch. 16, para. 15.
(*p*) *Ibid.*, s. 177(4), (5).
(*q*) *Ibid.*, Sch. 17. paras. 5, 6.

The Local Government Act 1972 has also given formal status in planning matters to the parish councils in England and the community councils in Wales. A parish or community council may notify the district planning authority that they wish to be consulted with regard to all applications for planning permission in their area or with regard to particular types of application (*r*).

Delegation to Officers

Until quite recently it was the almost universal rule in local government that decisions could be taken only by the council itself or by a duly authorised committee. The officers might advise but they could not take decisions even in minor matters.

However, the Act of 1968 introduced for the first time powers under which local authorities might delegate the power of decision-making in planning matters to their officers. These provisions (as re-enacted in the Act of 1971) authorised delegation to named officers of the power to decide upon applications for planning permission, for consent for outdoor advertising, for a determination under section 53 as to the necessity for planning permission, for an established use certificate, and for any approval required by the General Development Order or by a condition attached to a planning permission.

As from 1st April, 1974, these powers have been replaced by a wider much wider power under section 101 of the Local Government Act 1972. This provides that a local authority may arrange for the discharge of any of their functions by an officer of the authority. This must, however, be read subject to any other statutory provisions which in effect preclude delegation; for instance, the adoption of a local plan requires a formal resolution of the local planning authority (*s*).

It is, of course, inevitable that, in the day to day conduct of affairs, landowners and developers should seek information and advice from planning officers. This is a desirable practice so long

(*r*) *Ibid.*, Sch. 16, para 20.
(*s*) Act of 1971, s. 14(1).

as all concerned recognise the position of the planning officer in such matters, where formal authority has not been delegated to him. Local authorities sometimes consider that they are not bound by statements made by their officers in response to requests for information or advice. This view gained some support from the decision in *Southend-on-Sea Corporation* v. *Hodgson* (*Wickford*), *Ltd.* (*t*),

> H. Ltd. wanted to use a certain site in connection with their business. The planning officer informed them in writing that the site had existing use rights for that purpose. The Corporation subsequently served an enforcement notice.
>
> HELD: a public authority cannot be estopped from doing its public duty by any representations made by its officers.

But, in the later case of *Lever* (*Finance*), *Ltd.* v. *Westminster Corpn.* (*u*), the Court of Appeal concentrated on the question whether a statement made by the planning officer was within his ostensible authority.

> Planning permission had been granted for the development of an estate in accordance with a detailed plan. The plaintiff's architect then wished to make certain variations in the lay-out, and the planning officer told him that the proposed variations were not material and that he therefore had no objection to them and no further consent was required.
>
> HELD: a planning permission covered the work specified in the detailed plans and any immaterial variations specified therein; the practice by which the planning officer decided whether a variation was material or not was sensible and should be affirmed; and that, accordingly, if the planning officer within his ostensible authority told the developer that a proposed variation was not material and the developer acted on that, the planning authority could not go back on it.

It is not sufficient that the statement in question should be within the ostensible authority of the planning officer. The plaintiff must show that he has acted upon that statement to his

---

(*t*) [1961] 2 All E.R. 46.
(*u*) [1970] 3 All E.R. 496.

detriment. This was made clear in *Norfolk C.C.* v. *Secretary of State for the Environment* (*a*).

> P. Ltd. applied for planning permission to build an extension to their factory. The planning committee of the county council decided that planning permission should be refused. By mistake the planning officer sent to P. Ltd. a document which was in the form of a grant of permission.
>
> HELD: The county council were not estopped from denying the validity of the permission, because P. Ltd. had not acted upon it to their detriment.

However, the powers now given to planning authorities to delegate decisions to officers will, it is submitted, afford increased scope for applying the doctrine of ostensible authority. There are, however, signs that the Courts may be reluctant to expand the doctrine (*b*).

In considering the application of this doctrine, it should be noted that, where a planning officer acts with express authority, his action will be taken to be that of the local planning authority and will thus be binding on that authority whether or not anyone has acted upon it to his detriment. The doctrine of ostensible authority ls of importance where the statements made by a planning officer are not within his express authority.

The doctrine of ostensible authority was a feature of company law for many years until a recent change in the law made it unnecessary in relation to companies. It protected persons dealing with the officers of a company so far as those dealings were *intra vires* the company; it did not protect dealings *ultra vires* the company. For this purpose, a person dealing with a company was considered to have either actual or constructive notice of its powers, since the memorandum of association could be inspected by the public; but the public could not normally ascertain whether

---

(*a*) [1973] 3 All E.R. 673.

(*b*) See the remarks of LORD WIDGERY, C.J., in *Brooks and Burton* v. *Secretary of State for the Environment* 120 Sol. Jo. 605 and quoted in (1977) J.P.L. 82.

the officers of a company had authority to act on its behalf because these are matters of internal management. It was on this basis that the doctrine of ostensible authority protected a person dealing with an officer of a company, the only exception being where that person had actual knowledge that the officer was acting outside his authority.

The following propositions may therefore be suggested with regard to statements made by an officer of a local planning authority;

(1) For the doctrine of ostensible authority to apply, the matter in question must be *intra vires* the local planning authority.

(2) For this purpose members of the public must be deemed to know what are the powers of a local planning authority since these powers derive from statute law.

(3) But members of the public cannot be expected to know what matters are within the authority of an officer because these are matters of internal management.

(4) A local planning authority will be bound by statements made to a member of the public provided the matter in question is; (a) *intra vires* the authority; (b) the member of the public does not actually know that the officer is exceeding his authority, and (c) that person has acted upon the statement to his detriment.

CHAPTER 4

DEVELOPMENT PLANS

When the Act of 1947 came into force, each local planning authority was given the duty of carrying out a survey of the whole of their area and of preparing a development plan showing "the manner in which [they] propose that land in their area should be used, whether by the carrying out thereon of development or otherwise, and the stages by which such development should be carried out" (*a*). The system thus begun was continued under the Act of 1962. One of the principal features of the plan would be the establishment of "zones" for agriculture, houses, shops, industry and so on, but the plan might also define the sites of specific projects (such as schools, open spaces, new roads) and designate areas of comprehensive development.

It was intended that each planning authority should submit a report of the survey and the draft development plan to the Minister by 1st July, 1951, but in nearly every case an extension of time was necessary. The development plan did not come into force until approved by the Minister, and the amount of detail was such that in most cases some years elapsed before approval was given.

A development plan might be amended at any time. In any event, the local planning authority were required to carry out a fresh survey at least once in every five years after the approval of the plan and submit such proposals for amendment as might be necessary as a result of the survey (*b*). Many plans have been the subject of amendment; having submitted their basic map, an authority might wish to prepare more detailed maps for

(*a*) Act of 1971, Sch. 5, para. 2, repeating the definition in the Acts of 1947 and 1962.

(*b*) Act of 1971, Sch. 5, para. 3(1), re-enacting the corresponding provisions in the Acts of 1947 and 1962.

particular areas or to designate land as an area of comprehensive development.

The form and content of these development plans are governed by statutory provisions deriving, as we have seen, from the Act of 1947. Since then new problems have emerged, and in 1965 the Planning Advisory Group of the Ministry recommended a new type of development plan more suited to the requirements of town and country planning today. Their recommendations were given effect by Part I of the Act of 1968 (now Part II of the Act of 1971). The new type of plan consists of (1) a structure plan outlining the general policy for the area and indicating "action areas" in which comprehensive treatment is envisaged in the immediate future; (2) action area plans; (3) other local plans. The structure plans require the approval of the Minister, but action area and other local plans will not normally require his approval.

The new system is being introduced gradually. The Minister may make commencement orders bringing Part II of the Act of 1971 into force at different times in different parts of the country. He has made a series of orders as a result of which most sections of Part II are now in force throughout the country: these are the sections dealing with the preparation and approval of structure and local plans. When a structure plan has been approved, the Minister may then make an order bringing the remaining sections of Part II into force in that area. Even then the old development plan will continue in force unless and until it is revoked by order of the Minister.

The two types of development plan will now be considered in turn.

Development Plans under the Acts of 1947 and 1962

The Survey

The first step in drawing up the older type of development plan was to carry out a survey of existing conditions and future trends.

(*c*) Act of 1971, s. 21 (1), (4).

The importance of such a survey can hardly be exaggerated. As a former Minister put it, "Without this survey, no plan can be of any real value" (*d*).

To take a simple example: it will be necessary in the plan to allocate land for housebuilding, and for this purpose it is important to know the existing population and what the population is likely to be in, say, twenty years time; in addition, it will be desirable to know how many houses will be needed in that period in connection with slum clearance programmes.

It may therefore be a matter of some surprise to learn that the local planning authority were not required to publish the report of the survey (*e*).

There were no statutory requirements as to the form of the survey, but local planning authorities received a good deal of guidance from the Minister, much of it in the form of circulars (*f*).

Contents of Plans

The contents of the development plans were prescribed partly by provisions in the Act of 1947 and later in the Act of 1962, and partly by the Development Plans Regulations. The relevant provisions of the Acts of 1947 and 1962 are preserved on a transitional basis by Sch. 5 of the Act of 1971.

As we have seen, the development plan is to show the manner in which it is proposed that land in the area shall be used (whether by the carrying out of development or otherwise) and the stages by which the development is to be carried out (*g*). In particular, the plan may (*h*)—

(a) define the sites of proposed roads, public and other buildings and works, airfields, parks, pleasure grounds, nature reserves and other open spaces;

(*d*) House of Commons Official Report, Vol. 432, col. 962.

(*e*) Under the new system, the local planning authority must publish the report of the survey: see p. 59, *post*.

(*f*) Notably circulars 40, 63 and 92.

(*g*) Act of 1971, Sch. 5, para. 1(2) repeating the definition in the Acts of 1947 and 1962. (*h*) *Ibid.*, Sch. 5, para 1(3).

(b) allocate areas of land for agriculture, residential, industrial or other purposes;

(c) designate areas of comprehensive development; these are areas which the local planning authority consider should be developed or re-developed as a whole for any of the following reasons (*i*):

- (i) to deal satisfactorily with extensive war-damage;
- (ii) to deal satisfactorily with bad lay-out or obsolete development;
- (iii) to provide for the relocation of population or industry or the replacement of open space in the course of the development or re-development of any other area;
- (iv) for any other purpose specified in the plan.

Before 1060 the plan might also designate land for compulsory acquisition (*k*). This was considered to be a necessary and desirable step towards compulsory acquisition. It did not obviate the necessity of making a compulsory purchase order—normally under the procedure laid down in the Acquisition of Land (Authorisation Procedure) Act 1946,—but it had important advantages to an acquiring authority.

(1) *Where the authority had alternative powers of acquisition.*—For instance, land might be designated in the development plan as subject to compulsory acquisition for school premises and grounds; in this case, the local authority have powers of compulsory acquisition under the Education Act, 1944, and these powers could be exercised whether or not the land was designated in the

---

(*i*) Act of 1971, Sch. 5, para. 1(4).

(*k*) The plan could designate for compulsory purchase: (i) land required by government departments, local authorities and statutory undertakers for their statutory purposes; (ii) land in or adjacent to an area of comprehensive development; (iii) any other land which the local planning authority considered should be subject to compulsory acquisition in order to ensure that the land be used in accordance with the plan.

development plan. The advantage of designation for the acquiring authority lay in the Minister's power to disregard any objection which amounted in substance to an objection to the development plan (*l*).

(2) *Where the authority had no other powers of acquisition.*—This might happen for instance where land was included in an area of comprehensive development. In this case designation provided the general enabling power without which a compulsory purchase order could not be made.

It was however far from obvious that designation was essential. In 1965, the Planning Advisory Group of the Ministry recommended that the designation procedure should be abolished and that there should be conferred upon local authorities a straightforward power to acquire land compulsorily by means of a compulsory purchase order in order to secure its comprehensive development, redevelopment or improvement; the case for such a compulsory purchase would of course have to be made out by reference to the development plan (*m*). This recommendation was put into effect by the Act of 1968.

Maps and Statements

The older type of development plan consists of a basic map and written statement together with such other maps as may be appropriate (*a*).

The basic map prepared by a county borough before 1974 was to the scale of six inches to one mile; maps to this scale are referred to as "town maps" (*b*). The basic map prepared by one of the former administrative counties was to the scale of one inch to one mile—"county map"—but town maps might also have been prepared for particular areas (*c*) which need not have been urban

---

(*l*) Act of 1972, s. 132(1), re-enacting the Act of 1962, s. 86(1).

(*m*) "Future of Development Plans." Report published by H.M.S.O. 1965.

(*a*) Development Plans Regulations, reg. 4.

(*b*) *Ibid.*, reg. 5.

(*c*) *Ibid.*, reg. 6.

in character (*d*). Prior to 1965 it was necessary to submit a programme map to accompany each county map and each town map; after 1965 it was sufficient to indicate in the written statement the stages by which any proposed development was to be carried out.

In addition maps would be required for special purposes such as (a) areas of comprehensive development (*e*); (b) land defined as the site of a proposed road under section 21(2) (d) of the Highways Act, 1959, or designated under section 206 of that Act ("street authorisation maps") (*f*). All these maps were required to be to scale 1/2,500. Any area shown on a county map might also be shown on an "inset map" to scale 1/2,500 (*g*).

The written statement contained a summary of the main proposals of the development plan together with information on such matters as densities for residential development, green belts, the kind of development which would be permitted in rural areas, how it was proposed to deal with non-conforming users and so on. It also indicated the stages by which any development proposed by the plan should be carried out, and the period covered by the plan; and in relation to any comprehensive development area map a statement of the purposes for which the area was to be developed or redeveloped as a whole (*h*).

The written statement might therefore refer to a fair number of matters, but it was nevertheless a comparatively short document. The information given was usually expressed in a condensed form without any reasoning in support. There is indeed a statutory provision—which is still in force—that, in the event of any contradiction between the maps and the written statement, the latter is to prevail (*i*) nevertheless the older type of development plan can fairly be described as map based.

(*d*) See Circular 59, para. 4.
(*e*) Development Plans Regulations, reg. 8.
(*f*) *Ibid.*, reg. 10. Before 1960 the relevant sections were 47 and 48 of the Act of 1947. See chapter 15, *post*.
(*g*) *Ibid.*, reg. 7.
(*h*) Development Plans Regulations, reg. 14.
(*i*) *Ibid.*, reg. 15.

Development Plan Procedure

The procedure for preparing the older type of development plan, or an amendment to such plan, and for securing the Minister's approval is no longer of practical significance. But a very brief review may be of interest for the purpose of comparison with the procedures for the making of new structure and local plans. (*k*)

The local planning authority were required to consult the district councils concerned (*l*) but there were no statutory requirements for public participation such as apply to the new structure and local plans.

When the final draft of the plan had been approved by the local planning authority, it was submitted to the Minister. (*m*) Notice that the plan had been submitted to the Minister, would then be published in the *London Gazette* and the local press, and opportunity given for objections and representations (*n*).

If any objections or representations were received, the Minister would have to decide whether or not to hold a public local inquiry at which any interested persons might be heard. If he decided to dispense with an inquiry he would have to give objectors the opportunity of being heard by an Inspector (*o*).

Having considered the report of the inquiry on hearing, the Minister might approve the plan with or without modifications, or he might reject it (*p*). The Minister made extensive use of his power to modify a plan, and in some cases this caused hardship to landowners. For instance, land might have been held by an industrial firm for extensions to their factory. In the draft plan the land was zoned as industrial and the owners had no reason to make representations. The Minister might then have changed the zoning to, say, residential without the owners having the oppor-

---

(*k*) See pp. 63 and 73, *post*.

(*l*) Act of 1971, Sch. 5, para. 6(1).

(*m*) Development Plans Regulations, reg. 16.

(*n*) Act of 1971, Sch. 5, para. 6(2). Development Plans Regulations, regs. 2(1) and 17.

(*o*) Development Plans Regulations, 1948, reg. 18.

(*p*) Act of 1971, Sch. 5, para. 2.

tunity of stating their case. This procedure was criticised by the Franks Committee, and as a result the Minister said that he would not in future modify a plan in this way without giving the owners of the land notice of his intention and an opportunity of expressing their views (*q*).

The Minister's decision on the plan was final. There was a very limited right of appeal to the High Court in that the validity of the plan could be challenged on the ground that some aspect was not within the powers conferred by the Act of 1971 or that the applicant had been substantially prejudiced by a failure to comply with the requirements of the Act or Regulations. Any such application to the High Court had to be made within six weeks of the date on which public notice was given of the Minister's decision: thereafter the validity of the plan cannot be questioned in any legal proceedings whatsoever (*r*).

Development Plans under the Act of 1971

As has already been explained, the 1947-type development plans were based on the survey which each local planning authority was required to make. The new structure and local plans are also to be based on a survey. Indeed, the Act of 1971 emphasises the importance of the survey; in contrast to the earlier legislation, it specifies the matters which the survey is to cover, and it also makes provision for publishing the report of the survey.

Each local planning authority must institute a survey of their area "examining the matters which may be expected to affect the development of that area or the planning of its development and . . . to keep all such matters under review" (*a*). These matters are to include *inter alia* the following (*b*):

(*q*) Circular 51/58.
(*r*) Act of 1971, Sch. 6, para. 3. See also *Smith* v. *East Elloe R.D.C.*, [1956] 1 All E.R. 855.
(*a*) Act of 1971, s. 6(1).
(*b*) *Ibid.*, s. 6(3).

(a) the principal physical and economic characteristics of the authority's area (including the principal purposes for which land is used) and their effect on neighbouring areas;

(b) size, composition and distribution of the population (whether resident or otherwise);

(c) communications, transport system and traffic of the area and their effect on neighbouring areas;

(d) such matters as the Minister may prescribe by regulations or may in any particular case direct.

Where necessary the authority must consult with neighbouring planning authorities (*c*).

Structure Plans

The local planning authority are required to submit to the Minister, within a specified period, a report of the survey and a structure plan (*d*).

The structure plan will set out "the local planning authority's policy and general proposals in respect of the development and other use of land in that area (including measures for the improvement of the physical environment and the management of traffic)" (*e*). The structure plan will also indicate "action areas". An action area is one which has been selected for comprehensive treatment in the comparatively near future by means either of development, redevelopment or improvement, or by a combination of these methods (*f*). The concept of the action and is thus wider than that of the areas of comprehensive development under the earlier legislation; in particular, the reference to "improvement" in the definition of action areas indicates a type of activity not mentioned in the statutory definition of areas of comprehensive development (*g*). In their choice of action areas,

(*c*) *Ibid.*, s. 6(4).
(*d*) Act of 1971, s. 7 (1).
(*e*) *Ibid.*, s. 7 (3).
(*f*) *Ibid.*, s. 7 (5).
(*g*) See p. 55, *ante*.

the local planning authority should select only those areas in which it is expected that the programme of treatment can be commenced within a maximum period of ten years (*h*). The detailed treatment of the area will be described in a local plan.

In preparing the structure plan the local planning authority are not to work in isolation; they are specifically required to have regard to current policies for the economic planning and development of the region as a whole (*j*) and they are also required to state how the structure plan relates to the structure plans for neighbouring areas (*k*). The latter requirement is obviously of considerable importance in view of the new emphasis on traffic management, but it will also ensure that neighbouring planning authorities come to terms with each other over such matters as overspill. The local planning authority are also required, in drawing up the structure plan, to have regard to the resources likely to be available (*l*), an emphasis on realities not found in the Acts of 1947 and 1962.

The principle that structure plans ought not to be prepared in isolation has been carried further by the Act of 1972. If two or more local planning authorities wish, they may—if the Minister consents—carry out joint surveys and prepare a joint structure plan for a combined area (*m*).

Form of Structure Plans

The form of the new structure plans is to be quite different from that of the 1947-type plans. The structure plan is to consist of a written statement describing the local planning authority's policy and general proposals (*n*). The written statement is to include a reasoned justification of the policy and general proposals (*o*); and it is to contain or be accompanied by such diagrams, illus-

(*h*) Plans Regs., reg. 11.
(*j*) Act of 1971, s. 7(4) (a).
(*k*) *Ibid.*, s. 7(3) (b).
(*l*) *Ibid.*, s. 7(4) (b).
(*m*) Act of 1971, s. 10(A) added by Act of 1972, s. 1.
(*n*) *Ibid.*, s. 7(3). (*o*) Plans Regs., reg. 9(3).

trations and descriptive matter as may be considered appropriate. The Minister may make regulations as to the precise form of these diagrams etc., or he may give directions to the authority concerned in any particular case; otherwise the matter is left to the discretion of the local planning authority (*p*). It seems likely however, that diagrammatic representations will be freely used instead of the scale maps which were required for the 1947-type plans.

The diagrams are to include a "key diagram" showing, so far as may be practicable, the policy and general proposals formulated in the written statement; insets may be used to show the policy and proposals for any part of the area to which the structure plan relates. The key diagram and insets must not be on a map base (*q*).

The relationship of the diagrams and other illustrative material to the written statement has been explained as follows (*r*):

> "The structure plan is largely concerned with long range policies that look forward over twenty or thirty years, well beyond the period within which land allocations and site definitions can be made. But where the policies are related to particular areas, illustrations can help understanding and simplify verbal descriptions. Diagrams and other illustrations will be useful in explaining the context of the plan . . . . They cannot settle detailed matters of the use of particular sites (which is a function of local plans), and therefore the diagrams will not have ordnance survey bases which would create a misleading impression of precision. A second limitation is that the purpose of the diagrams is to explain or illustrate the proposals in the written statement. It is therefore important that no proposals should appear on them other than those which the statement specifically mentions".

In the event of any contradiction between the written statement and any other document (including maps, diagrams, etc.) forming part of the plan, the written statement is to prevail (*s*).

(*p*) Act of 1971, s. 7(6).

(*q*) Plans Regs., reg. 12. For examples of key diagrams, see *Development Plans Manual*, figs. *1a*, *5a*.

(*r*) *Op. cit.*, para. 5.1.

(*s*) Plans Regs., regs. 3(1), 46(2).

Additional Treatment of Urban Areas

The structure plan will set out the planning authority's broad policy and proposals for the whole of its area. But within a county there may be major planning issues and problems for particular urban areas which need to be treated in a more closely argued and self-contained form than would be possible if they figured only as items in a plan for the whole county.

The Plans Regulations provide that for any such area, the county council may, with the Minister's consent, and shall if he so directs, formulate in addition policy and general proposals specifically for that part in a separate part of the plan (*t*).

This separate part is to be prepared as if it were a structure plan; this means, for instance, that there will be a specific written statement and key diagram for the area with such other diagrams and illustrations as may be appropriate. None the less, it will form part of and must be consistent with the structure plan for the whole of the county.

Procedure (A): Public Participation

A structure plan will not come into force unless and until it is approved by the Minister. The procedure for submitting the plan to the Minister and for obtaining his approval is a lengthy one and is designed, *inter alia*, to give the public an opportunity of commenting upon the structure plan whilst it is still at a formative stage and before it is sent to the Minister.

The main steps in this procedure are to be found in the Act of 1971, as amended by the Act of 1972, and in the Plans Regulations. They may be summarised as follows:

1. Before finally determining the content of the structure plan, the local planning authority must consult with district councils, the development corporation of any new town in the area, and such other authorities and bodies as are considered appropriate. All such authorities and bodies must be given an opportunity to

(*t*) Plans Regs., reg. 8.

express their views and the local planning authority must consider any such views (*a*).

2. During this formative stage the local planning authority must also ensure that adequate publicity is given to the report of the survey, and to the draft structure plan. In addition they must consider what persons, or groups, are likely to want to make representations with regard to the draft plan and ensure that they are made aware of their right to do so. The local planning authority must allow proper time for representations to them and they must consider any representations which are received within that time (*b*). The Minister has power to make regulations prescribing the detailed procedure for publicity and public participation (*c*), but the Minister has said that he prefers to rely mostly on advice rather than statutory control in this regard (*d*).

3. The local planning authority will then be in a position to determine the content of the structure plan and to submit it to the Minister. When submitting the plan to the Minister, the local planning authority must indicate what steps they have taken to comply with the provisions for public participation as mentioned above (*e*). If the Minister is satisfied on this point he will proceed to consider the structure plan; but, if he is not satisfied he must return the plan to the local planning authority with directions for ensuring proper publicity and consideration of representations (*f*).

4. Not later than the date on which the plan is submitted to the Minister the local planning authority are to make copies of the plan available for inspection at various places and each copy is to be accompanied by a statement of the time within which objections to the plan may be made to the Minister (*g*).

(*a*) Plans Regs., reg. 6.
(*b*) Act of 1971, s. 8(1).
(*c*) *Ibid.*, s. 18(1).
(*d*) Circular 44/71, para. 54.
(*e*) Act of 1971, s. 8(3).
(*f*) *Ibid.*, s. 8 (4).
(*g*) *Ibid.*, s. 8(2).

Procedure (B): Examination in Public

When the time for submitting objections has elapsed, the Minister can begin his consideration of the structure plan. He is empowered to reject the plan without formally considering the objections on holding the examination in public referred to below (*h*). This is a useful time-saving provision not found in the procedure for the 1947-type plans, although it will probably not be invoked often.

If the Minister does not reject the structure plan at this early stage, he must consider any objections which have been received and which have not been withdrawn.

Section 9 (3) of the Act of 1971, as originally enacted, required the Minister to give each objector an opportunity of being heard at a public local inquiry or other hearing. The Act of 1972 relieves the Minister of this obligation and substitutes a new section 9 (3). This imposes two duties upon the Minister: first, to consider any objections so far as made in accordance with regulations (*i*): secondly, to hold an examination in public of those matters affecting his consideration of the plan which he considers should be examined in public. "The proceedings are thus designed to put more emphasis on a broad examination of strategic issues while not excluding a consideration of detailed objections" (*k*).

No authority or person—not even the local planning authority which prepared the plan—will have any right to be heard at this examination in public (*l*). But it is difficult to see how in practice there could be any effective examination of the strategic issues if the planning authority were not represented, and it seems inevitable that the Minister should invite them to appear. Moreover the Minister may, and in practice does, invite objectors where their case may assist him in the examination of the plan. Indeed,

---

(*h*) *Ibid.*, s. 9(3), substituted by Act of 1972, s. 3(1).
(*i*) No such regulations have yet been made.
(*k*) House of Lords Debates, vol. 325, col. 762.
(*l*) Act of 1971, s. 9(5) substituted by Act of 1972, s. 3(1).

in the debates on the Bill for the Act of 1972, a Government spokesman went so far as to say:

> ". . . the objections and the grounds for them will clearly be very material in the Secretary of State's consideration of which are the key issues to be examined in public and of those who would take part in the examination" (*m*).

The Minister has power in consultation with the Lord Chancellor to make regulations with regard to the procedure to be followed at the examination in public (*n*). The Minister has, however, chosen not to make regulations at least for the time being. He has instead issued a code of practice (*o*). This code of practice has no statutory force so that the Minister is free to change the procedures from time to time without the necessity of making new regulations. There is probably little harm in that.

The "examination in public" is a novel device in planning law, and it is very different from the traditional form of public inquiry. The Minister's code of practice states that it "will normally be conducted by a small panel . . . consisting of an independent Chairman and two other members" (*p*). One of these would normally be from the regional office of the Department of the Environment, it being assumed that his local knowledge would enable him to promote "relevant discussions". The other member would be a planning inspector from the Department. More significantly, perhaps, the code of practice indicates that the "examination" should take the form of a "probing discussion".

In other words the examination is more inquisitorial in character, that is, the person or persons conducting the examination take the lead in questioning witnesses instead of leaving it in the main to examination and cross-examination by opposing advocates.

(*m*) House of Lords Debates, vol. 326, cols. 746.

(*n*) Act of 1971, s. 9(4) substituted by Act of 1972, s. 3(1).

(*o*) "Structure plans. The Examination in Public", March 1973.

(*p*) The independent chairman has so far been drawn from ranks of Q.C.'s versed in planning matters, retired civil servants from the Department of the Environment, retired county clerks, and in one case a professor of economics.

Naturally, there has been concern over the fact that objectors will have no statutory right to be heard in public. The question is whether this will in practice seriously affect landowners and such bodies as amenity societies. Land allocations and site definitions are not the concern of structure plans but of the local plans, and objectors will have a statutory right to appear at local plan inquiries (*q*). But the policies laid down in the approved structure plan will in many cases effectively determine land allocations; for instance once it is decided as a matter of structure plan policy that there should be a green belt for a certain town, the issues at the local plan inquiry will be marginal ones affecting the precise boundary.

The new procedure will, however, have compensating advantages if it significantly shortens the period between the submission of the structure plan and its approval by the Minister. In particular, the public discussion of alternative strategies and the lack of precise definition in the structure plan may seriously increase the risk of planning blight with consequent hardship to property owners; the sooner planning authorities can get ahead with the local plans, the quicker the uncertainties will be removed.

Procedure (C): Final Stages

The person or persons who have conducted the examination in public will report to the Minister, who will then be able to come to a decision. In so doing he is entitled to take into account any matters which he thinks are relevant (*r*), and he may consult the local planning authority, or any other person without apparently being obliged to consult any other authority or person; this represents a departure for reasons of practical convenience from the rules of natural justice and would not be permitted in the absence of statutory provision (*s*).

(*q*) See p. 74, *post*.
(*r*) Act of 1971, s. 9(2).
(*s*) *Ibid.*, s. 9(7) substituted by Act of 1972, s. 3(1). There was a similar provision in the procedure for the older type of development plan.

The Minister may approve the plan with or without modifications or reservations, or he may reject it (*t*); He must give reasons for his decision (*u*). If the Minister proposes to modify the plan in any material respect, he must give notice accordingly and consider any objections which are then made (*v*). This gives statutory force to the practice in respect of modifications to 1947-type plans (*w*).

When the Minister has approved the plan, public notice will be given in the prescribed manner (*x*) and arrangements will be made for enabling the public to inspect or purchase copies of the plan (*y*).

The Minister's decision on the structure plan is final, except for a limited right of appeal in the High Court (*z*).

Local Plans

The structure plan will be supplemented by a number of local plans. The local planning authority may prepare such plans while they are in course of preparing the structure plan (*a*), but in that case the local plans will not come into force unless and until the Minister approves the structure plan (*b*). When the Minister has approved the structure plan, the local planning authority must consider the desirability of preparing a local plan for any part of their area; and, if they conclude that such a plan is desirable, they must prepare one (*c*). The Minister may, after consulting the local planning authority, direct them to prepare a local plan for any part of their area (*d*).

(*t*) Act of 1971, s. 9(1).
(*u*) Act of 1971, s. 9(8) added by Act of 1972, s. 3(1).
(*v*) Plans Regs., reg. 25.
(*w*) See p. 58, *ante*.
(*x*) Act of 1971, s. 18(1) (b).
(*y*) *Ibid.*, s. 18(1) (g).
(*z*) Act of 1971, s. 242. This is in virtually the same terms as the right of appeal in connection with the 1947-type plans as described at p. 59, *ante*.
(*a*) Act of 1971, s. 11(1).
(*b*) *Ibid.*, s. 12(2).
(*c*) *Ibid.*, s. 11(2).
(*d*) *Ibid.*, s. 11(7), (8), (10).

In any event, a local plan must be prepared for any area included in the structure plan as an action area (*e*); the term "action area plans" has now been given statutory recognition (*f*).

In most cases the local plans will be made by the district planning authority, but in some will be made by the county planning authority. It is the duty of the county planning authority, in consultation with the district planning authorities, to make a "development plan scheme". This scheme designates the authorities (whether county or district) by whom the local plans for each area are to be prepared; it specifies the title and nature of each local plan, sets out a programme for the preparation of the local plans, and specifies those which should be prepared concurrently with the structure plan (*g*). However, to the extent that provision is not made to the contrary by the development plan scheme, the structure plan may provide for the making of local plans by the county planning authority (*h*). If the district planning authority are dissatisfied with the proposals of the county planning authority, they may make representations to the Minister who may amend the scheme or even make a fresh one (*i*).

The development plan scheme is to be kept under review and may therefore be amended (*k*). The initial schemes are made whilst the structure plan is still in course of preparation. This may create difficulties if the draft sructure plan is subsequently altered; presumably, the development plan scheme would be amended.

A local plan may cover any part, however small, of the local planning authority's area, but there is no requirement in either the Act of 1971 or the Plans Regulations that the whole of the county should be covered by local plans. Local plans will serve

(*e*) *Ibid.*, s. 11(6).

(*f*) See the Plans Regs., reg. 15.

(*g*) Act of 1971, s. 10C(2), (3) added by Local Government Act, 1972, s. 183(2).

(*h*) *Ibid.*, s. 10C(5).

(*i*) *Ibid.*, s. 10C(7).

(*k*) *Ibid.*, s. 10C(2).

a variety of purposes, and different plans may be made for different purposes for the same part of any area (*l*). The Plans Regulations classify local plans under three headings: district plans, action area plans and subject plans (*m*).

District plans.—The planning authority may make a district plan for any part of its area (other than an action area), that is, a plan based on a comprehensive consideration of matters affecting the development and other use of land in a particular area (*n*). District plans "differ from action area plans in that they may deal with time spans that are longer, changes that take place at uneven rates and development that occurs over relatively wide areas" (*o*). It seems likely that they will form the background for regulatory rather than positive planning.

Action area plans.—As explained earlier (*p*), an action area is one in which it is intended to carry out in a comparatively short time a positive programme by way of development, redevelopment or improvement or by a combination of these methods. The area concerned will have been indicated as an action area in the structure plan; if the local planning authority wish to initiate an action area programme after the structure plan has been made and approved, they will have to do so by submitting an amendment to the structure plan. The Minister will thus have approved the principle of action area treatment for a given area together with the broad proposals for the area. The local plan for the action area will set out the detailed proposals.

Although there is no statutory requirement to this effect, it is the Minister's intention that the precise boundaries of the action area shall be defined in the local plans and not in the structure plan; the reason for this decision is that this is precisely the sort of detail in which the Minister does not wish to be involved (*q*). It

(*l*) Act of 1971, s. 11(4).
(*m*) Plans Regs., reg. 15.
(*n*) *Ibid.*, reg. 15(1).
(*o*) *Development Plans Manual*, para. 8.2.
(*p*) See p. 60, *ante*.
(*q*) House of Commons Official Report, Standing Committee G, col. 81.

should not be inferred from this that the precise boundaries are not important; on the contrary, they are likely to be highly significant because the implementation of the action area proposals will, in many cases, involve substantial use of the powers of compulsory purchase for planning purposes contained in the Act of 1971 and the Minister will have power to disregard any objection to a compulsory purchase order made under these powers if the objection amounts in substance to an objection to the plan itself (*r*).

Subject plans.—These are designed to enable detailed treatment to be given to particular aspects of planning, and each such plan will take the name of the subject with which it deals (*s*).

It is apparently the Minister's wish that, as far as practicable, local planning matters should be dealt with in either district or action area plans because these will be prepared on a comprehensive basis (*t*). None the less, subject plans are likely to be required for a number of reasons. First, they may be required to define areas in which particular policies apply such as green belts; or where particular legal and administrative procedures apply or where special grant aid may be available such as conservation areas.

Secondly, subject plans will be needed for land defined as the site of a proposed road under section 21 (2) (*d*) of the Highways Act, 1959, or designated under section 206 of that Act (*u*). Thirdly, subject plans will be useful for showing particular planning matters in areas in which there is no immediate need for either a district or action area plan. Such matters may well include mineral workings, reclamation of derelict land, recreation in a river valley or country park.

Form and Content of Local Plans.—Local plans may, therefore, be

---

(*r*) See p. 76, *post.*

(*s*) Plans Regs., reg. 15(3).

(*t*) *Development Plans Manual,* para. 10(1).

(*u*) These plans will correspond to the "street authorisation maps" under the 1947-type development plan: see p. 57 *ante.* See also chapter 15, *post.*

very different in character, but the Act of 1971 and the Plans Regulations contain certain basic directions, which may be summarised as follows:

1. A local plan is to consist of a map—called the "proposals map"—and a written statement. The proposals map is to be prepared on an ordnance survey map base; no scale is prescribed —except for street authorisation maps which are to be scale of not less than 1/2500—and, indeed, different scale maps may be appropriate for different plans (*v*). The requirement that a local plan shall include a scale map is in contrast with the provisions as to structure plans described above (*w*).

2. The plan is to formulate, in such detail as may be considered appropriate, the local planning authority's proposals for the development, or other use of land in the area covered; alternatively, it may show the authority's proposals for any particular class of development or land use in that area. Special emphasis is laid upon measures for improving the physical environment and the management of traffic (*a*).

3. The written statement—like the written statement for a structure plan—is to contain a reasoned justification of the proposals contained therein (*b*).

4. The plan will be accompanied by such diagrams, illustrations and descriptive matter as may be considered appropriate. The Minister may make regulations as to the precise form of these diagrams etc. or he may give directions to the authority concerned in any particular case; otherwise the matter is left to the discretion of the local planning authority (*c*).

5. In drawing up a local plan, the local planning authority must see that it conforms to the structure plan, and they are to have regard to any information and any other considerations

---

(*v*) The Act of 1971, s. 11(3): Plans Regs., reg. 18.
(*w*) See pp. 61–62, *ante*.
(*a*) Act of 1971, s. 11(3).
(*b*) Plans Regs., reg. 16(3).
(*c*) Act of 1971, s. 11(5); Plans. Regs. reg. 18.

which may appear to them to be relevant or which they are required by the Minister to take into account (*d*).

Procedure for Local Plans

In most cases a local plan will not require the Minister's approval, but he has discretion to call in any local plan for his approval. Nevertheless, in each case the local planning authority must adhere to the procedure laid down by the Act of 1971. This procedure is in many (though not all) respects similar to that for structure plans and may be summarised as follows:—

1. The local planning authority must ensure that adequate publicity is given to any relevant parts of the survey (*e*) and to the matters to be included in the local plan. In addition, they must consider what persons or groups are likely to want to make representations with regard to the draft plan and ensure that they are made aware of their right to do so. The authority must allow proper time for representations to be made to them and they must consider any representations which are received within that time (*f*).

2. The local planning authority will then be able to prepare the first draft of the plan. Having done so, they must send a copy to the Minister together with a statement of the steps which they have taken to comply with paragraph 1 above; and, if the Minister is not satisfied on this point, he may give directions to the authority (*g*).

3. At the same time, the local planning authority must make copies of the plan available for public inspection, indicating the time within which objections may be made to the local planning authority (*h*).

4. Subject to the Minister's power to call in the plan for his approval, the local planning authority will then have to consider

(*d*) Act of 1971, s. 11(9).
(*e*) As the survey, see p. 59, *ante*.
(*f*) Act of 1971, s. 12(1).
(*g*) Act of 1971, s. 12(2), (3), (4).
(*h*) *Ibid.*, s. 12(2).

the objections. The local planning authority must arrange for a local inquiry or other hearing into objections which have been submitted in the prescribed manner; where objections have not been submitted in the prescribed manner, it seems that the authority will have a discretion whether or not to hold an inquiry (*i*). If an inquiry or other hearing is held the Inspector will in some cases be appointed by the Minister; in other cases he will be appointed by the authority (*k*), but regulations may be made governing the authority's choice of Inspector (*l*).

5. The Inspector will report to the local planning authority. The report will be published and the authority must give due weight to the Inspector's report and each separate recommendation in their consideration of the objections. They must then prepare and publish a statement of their decisions with reasons (*m*).

6. The local planning authority may then proceed to adopt the plan, either as originally prepared or as modified to take account of objections. If the authority decide to modify the plan, they must give public notice of their intentions and give an opportunity for objections (*n*).

7. The authority's decision is final except that there is a limited right of appeal to the High Court on matters of law and procedure (*o*).

There has been some criticism of the procedure for dealing with objections on the ground that the local authority will be "judge in their own cause". Although this phrase is not wholly appropriate to what is essentially an administrative procedure, there is some force in the criticism. There is a risk that, once they have determined on a particular course of action, the authority will close their minds to possible alternatives as suggested by the

(*i*) Act of 1971, s. 13(1). See also Plans Regulations, reg. 29 and Sch. 3 (Form 7).

(*k*) Regulations are to be made specifying the cases in which the authority may appoint the Inspector: *Ibid.*, s. 13(1).

(*l*) Act of 1971, s. 13(2).

(*m*) Plans Regulations, reg. 33.

(*n*) *Ibid.*, reg. 34.

(*o*) Act of 1971, s. 244 (1), (2).

objectors or as recommended by the Inspector; and, even where the authority have in fact given full consideration to possible alternatives, the public may not feel confident that this has been done. There are, however, safeguards. The Minister can call in the application at any time before the authority formally adopt the plan (*p*); and where it is left to the authority to decide whether or not to adopt the plan, objectors may require the authority to state their reasons for doing so (*q*); there is also the duty referred to above to publish a statement of their decisions on the various objections.

Development Plans: Legal Effect and Implementation

Development plans have important consequences in town and country planning and in compulsory purchase. Before considering these in detail, we must consider what the phrase "the development plan" now means for the purpose of the relevant legislation.

Where s. 20 of the Act of 1971 is in force (*r*), the development plan is to be taken as consisting of :

(a) the structure plan in force for the time being together with the Minister's notice of approval;

(b) any alterations in the structure plan together with the Minister's notices of approval of the alterations;

(c) any local plan applicable to the district with a copy of the local planning authority's resolution of adoption (or the Minister's notice of approval);

(d) any alteration to the local plan together with the resolution of adoption (or the notice of approval).

In other parts of the country the development plan will be taken as consisting of the plan made and kept in force for the time being under the Act of 1971. This plan—"the old development plan"—will not be automatically revoked by the making of

---

(*p*) *Ibid.*, s. 14(3).
(*q*) Tribunals and Inquiries Act, 1958, s. 12; Act of 1971, s. 13(1).
(*r*) See p. 53, *ante*.

structure or local plans under the Act of 1971. Unless revoked by the Minister it will continue in force and be treated as part of the development plan for that area (*s*).

The development plan does not confer any right of development. A developer wishing, say, to build houses in an area zoned for residential development must apply for planning permission even though his proposal accords with the provisions of the plan, and there may be various reasons why permission should be refused, *e.g.* density, design, access. And although permission will probably be refused for development which does not accord with the plan, there may be good reasons why such development should be permitted. In short, the provisions of the development plan are not the only factor which the local planning authority should take into account in deciding upon an application for planning permission (*t*).

Certain specific consequences, however, may result from the development plan, namely:

1. Where it is proposed that land should be acquired by compulsory purchase under section 112 or 113 of the Act of 1971 (*u*), the Minister may disregard any objection to a compulsory purchase order which amounts to an objection to the plan itself (*v*).

2. Where land is rendered unsaleable except at a greatly reduced price by reason of some provision of the development plan, an owner-occupier may be able to serve a purchase notice on the appropriate public authority (*w*).

3. The programming in the development may affect the right to compensation for refusal of planning permission under Part VI of the 1962 Act (*a*).

4. The provisions of the development plan may materially

(*s*) Act of 1971, Sch. 7, paras. 2, 6.
(*t*) See chapter 6, *post*.
(*u*) See p. 77, *post*.
(*v*) Act of 1971, s. 132(1).
(*w*) See chapter 11, *post*.
(*a*) See chapter 19, *post*.

affect the amount of compensation obtainable on compulsory purchase (*b*).

5. In considering whether any land is "development land" for the purposes of the Community Land Act 1975, the authorities concerned are to have regard, *inter alia*, to the provisions of the development plan (*c*).

Before 1974 the grant of working rights to mineral development under the Mines (Working Facilities and Support) Act 1966 was facilitated where the development plan provided that the land was to be used for the winning and working of minerals. This is no longer the law (*d*).

Compulsory Purchase for Planning Purposes

The implementation of the development plan will in some cases depend upon the use of the powers of compulsory purchase for planning purposes contained in the Act of 1971. These powers are likely to be used mainly in connection with areas of comprehensive development under the Act of 1962 and action areas under the Act of 1971.

Section 112(1) of the Act of 1971 provides that a local authority (not necessarily the planning authority) may compulsorily purchase any land in their area:

(a) required to secure the treatment as a whole by development, redevelopment or improvement of the land or the area in which it is situated;

(b) if it is expedient in the public interest that the land should be held together with land so required;

(c) to provide for the relocation of population or the replacement of open space in the course of the redevelopment or improvement of another area;

(d) if it is expedient to acquire the land immediately for a

(*b*) See Land Compensation Act, 1961, s. 16.
(*c*) See chapter 22, *post*.
(*d*) The matter is further explained in chapter 14, *post*. at p. 258

purpose which it is necessary to achieve for the proper planning of the area in which the land is situated.

Section 113 enables the Minister to acquire compulsorily any land necessary for the public service.

Where land is acquired under section 112 the authority may themselves develop the land (e.g. by erecting buildings to let) or they may sell or lease the land for private development (*e*).

There is an important provision in section 123(7) of the Act of 1971. If the authority dispose of any land acquired under section 112 (1) (a), (b) or (c), they are to have regard to the needs of persons who were living or carrying on business or other activities in the area. So far as may be practicable, any such person is to be given the opportunity to obtain accommodation in the area on terms which have regard to the price at which his property was acquired from him (*f*). It does not in terms impose on the local planning authority an obligation to have regard to the possible requirements of displaced residents when drawing up their plans for the development of the area. If they have not done so, it may happen that the authority find that they cannot give the persons concerned an opportunity to acquire accommodation in the area on favourable terms. It is interesting to note that, in exercising their functions under the Community Land Act regarding the acquisition and disposal of land, the authorities concerned have rather more positive obligations (*g*).

The effect of section 123 (7) is further limited in that it does not apply where the authority develop the land themselves or retain it for any other purpose (*h*). Under the general law of compulsory

(*e*) Act of 1971, ss. 123, 124. The Minister's consent will be necessary if the land is not being disposed of at the best price or rent obtainable (section 123(3) applying s. 26 of the Act of 1959) and in certain special circumstances.

(*f*) The effect of the corresponding provisions of the Act of 1962 was considered in *A. Crabtree & Co., Ltd.* v. *Minister of Housing and Local Government* (1965), 17 P. & C.R. 232.

(*g*) See chapter 24, p. 360, *post*.

(*h*) *A.B. Motor Co. of Hull, Ltd.* v. *Minister of Housing and Local Government* (1969), 211 Estates Gazette 289.

purchase, suitable alternative accommodation must be offered to any person who is displaced from residential accommodation in consequence of acquisition by an authority possessing compulsory powers (*i*). Such accommodation, however, will not necessarily be in the same area.

(*i*) Land Compensation Act 1973, s. 39.

CHAPTER 5

DEFINITION OF DEVELOPMENT

The whole system of planning control in this country depends on the definition of development. If a particular operation or change of use involves development as defined in the Act of 1971, it will (with a few exceptions (*a*)) require planning permission. If, however, the operation or change of use does not involve development, no planning permission is required.

For the purpose of the Planning Acts, development is defined (*b*) "as the carrying out of building, engineering, mining or other operations in, on, over or under land, or the making of any material change in the use of any building or other land."

OPERATIONS

It will be seen that there are two "legs" to this definition of development—"operations" and "uses". It is important to grasp the distinction between the two. The essence of an "operation" was explained by Lord PARKER, C.J. in *Cheshire C.C.* v. *Woodward* (*c*); it is some act which changes the physical characteristics of the land, or of what is under it, or of the air above it. "Use" refers to the purpose to which land or buildings are devoted. Unless the context otherwise requires, the word "use" does not include the carrying out of building or other operations (*d*). It follows that permission for the use of land for a particular purpose does not confer the right to erect buildings for that purpose. The point is illustrated by the case of *Sunbury-on-Thames U.D.C.* v. *Mann* (*e*).

(*a*) See chapter 6, pp. 112, 113, *post*.
(*b*) Act of 1971, s. 22(1).
(*c*) [1962] 1 All E.R. 517.
(*d*) Act of 1971, s. 290(1).
(*e*) (1958), 9 P. & C.R., 309.

Mann had been granted permission for the continued use of certain land and buildings as a yard, workshop and stores until 30th October, 1957. In May, 1957, he erected a new building on the site for use in connection with the maintenance and repair of engineering equipment. The council served an enforcement notice requiring the building to be pulled down.

Mann claimed that the erection of the building was permitted by Class IV (1) of the First Schedule in the General Development Order, which permits the erection of buildings required in connection with building operations on adjoining land. HELD: As Mann had permission only for the *use* of the land, he could not bring himself within Class IV (1) which refers to *operations*.

Building Operations

For most purposes of the Act of 1971, the word "building" *includes* "any structure or erection and any part of a building so defined but does not include plant or machinery comprised in a building" (*f*). The use of the word "includes" shows that this is not intended to be a complete definition. Its effect is to extend the ordinary meaning of the word "building" to include structures which would not normally be regarded as buildings such as walls, fences, hoarding, masts. Machinery in the open will be a "building" for the purposes of the Act of 1971 so that its erection will be development, but not if housed in a building.

In *Buckingham C.C.* v. *Callingham* (*g*) it was held that a model village of buildings constructed to scale was a structure or erection and therefore subject to planning control. In *Cooper* v. *Bailey* (*h*) the question was whether advertisements displayed at a garage were erected on a "building". The garage consisted of a central building and petrol pumps with two walls on either side running from the building in a curve towards the road; in front of the walls was a kerb marking the limits of the pull-in. Some advertisement signs were fixed to the kerb or displayed on the concrete between the kerb and the wall. It was held that these advertise-

(*f*) Act of 1971, s. 290(1).
(*g*) [1952] 1 All E.R. 1166.
(*h*) (1956), 6 P. & C.R. 261.

ments were displayed on part of the building or structure of the garage.

It does not follow, however, that anything placed on land is to be treated as a building. Things like caravans and vending machines, which are comparatively easy to move, are not normally regarded as buildings for the purposes of planning control (*i*). And in *Cheshire C.C.* v. *Woodward* (*j*) the Divisional Court held that the Minister was quite entitled to find that the installation of a coal hopper some 16 to 20 feet high and a conveyor was not development.

There is apparently no simple test for determining whether some object or installation is a "building". In *Cheshire C.C.* v. *Woodward* (*k*) LORD PARKER, C.J. drew an analogy with the problem frequently encountered in real property law of deciding what fixtures pass with the freehold, and concluded "the Act is referring to any structure or erection which may be said to form part of the realty and to change the physical character of the land". But in the recent case of *Barvis, Ltd.*, v. *Secretary of State for the Environment* (*l*) the Divisional Court adopted a different approach.

> The appellants—specialists in the erection of precast concrete structures—had erected at their depot a mobile tower crane some 89 feet high which ran on rails fixed in concrete. It had previously been used on contract work and they intended to use it again for contract work when required. The dismantling and re-erection of the crane was carried out by specialists; the whole operation took several days and cost about £2,000.
>
> The Minister—applying *Cheshire C.C.* v. *Woodward*—concluded that the erection of the crane with all that it entailed did

(*i*) The placing of caravans on land may, however, involve a material change in the use of the land. See chapter 6, footnote (h), on page 113, *post*.

(*j*) [1962] 1 All E.R. 517. See also *Bendles Motors, Ltd.* v. *Bristol Corpn.*, [1963] 1 All E.R. 578, in which the court held that the Minister was entitled to find that the installation of a free-standing egg-vending machine in the forecourt of a garage and petrol filling station involved a material change of use and therefore constituted development.

(*k*) *Supra*.

(*l*) (1971), 22 P. & C.R., 710.

alter the physical characteristics of the land and amounted to building, engineering and other operations.

The Divisional Court, in dismissing an appeal against the Minister's decision, thought it unnecessary to go so far. BRIDGE, J. giving the first judgment (*m*) applied criteria suggested in *Cardiff Rating Authority* v. *Guest Keen Baldwin's Iron and Steel Co., Ltd* (*n*), where the qustion was whether under rating legislation certain apparatus was a building or structure. These criteria may be summarised as follows:

(1) A building or structure will be something of such size that it has either been in fact or would normally be built or constructed on the site as opposed to being brought on it ready made (*o*).
(2) It will have some degree of permanence; once installed it will normally remain *in situ* and only be removed by pulling down or taking to pieces.
(3) The question whether the thing is or is not physically attached to the site is relevant but not conclusive.
(4) A limited degree of motion does not prevent it being a structure.

The expression "building operations" is also defined. It *includes* "rebuilding operations, structural alterations of or additions to buildings, and other operations normally undertaken by a person carrying on business as a builder" (*p*). The effect of this very wide definition is cut down by section 22 (2) (a) of the Act of 1971 which excludes from the definition of development "the carrying out of

---

(*m*) It is perhaps worth noting that LORD PARKER, C.J. was a member of the Court and concurred with the judgment of BRIDGE, J.

(*n*) [1949] 1 All E.R. 27.

(*o*) A thing is not necessarily removed from the category of building or structures because by some feat of engineering or navigation it is brought to the site in one piece—[1949] 1 All E.R. at p. 36. And see the recent rating case of *Scaife* v. *British Fermentation Products, Ltd.*, [1971] J.P.L. 711.

(*p*) Act of 1971, s. 290(1).

works for the maintenance, improvement or other alteration of any building, being works which affect only the interior of the building or which do not materially affect the external appearance of the building".

It is sometimes difficult to decide whether work on an existing building are works of maintenance for the purpose of section 22 (2) (a) or not. The difficulty is illustrated by the case of *Street* v. *Essex C.C.* (*q*).

Street was the owner of a building erected in the 1930s. It and neighbouring buildings were of poor quality development. A demolition order was stayed on the basis of Street undertaking what were thought to be repairs in accordance with approval given under the byelaws. Unfortunately, he found it necessary to demolish the existing building down to damp course and to rebuild from there.

The local authority served an enforcement notice alleging that Street had carried out development without planning permission and requiring him to remove what they said was a new building. The Minister upheld the enforcement notice. On appeal to the High Court, it was contended on behalf of Street that the work done did not constitute development; provided the design and some part, however small, of the original structure remained, the operations could be said to be works of maintenance.

HELD: Whether the works could fairly be said to amount to works of maintenance, or were properly called reconstruction, was a matter of fact and degree. In the circumstances the Minister was entitled to hold as a matter of fact that what took place was reconstruction and as such involved development.

These problems do not arise in connection with the restoration of war-damaged buildings because it is expressly provided that section 22 (2) (a) shall not apply to war damage repairs; the result is that any war-damage repairs, however trivial, are development (*r*).

(*q*) (1965), 193 Estates Gazette 537.

(*r*) Planning permission for war-damage repairs is granted, however, by the G.D.O. First Schedule, Class XI, unless (as has been done in a number of instances) it is withdrawn in relation to any premises by a direction under Article 4 of the G.D.O. See chapter 6, p. 120, *post*.

The provision of additional space below ground level, if begun after 6th December, 1968, is also deemed to involve development (*s*).

Engineering Operations

The expression "engineering operations" includes "the formation or laying out of means of access to highways" (*a*); otherwise the expression is to be given its ordinary dictionary meaning and includes building and maintenance of roads, the laying of sewers, water mains and other public utility apparatus.

The following are excluded from the definition of development:

(a) the maintenance or improvement of a road by the local highway authority within the existing boundaries of the road (*b*);

(b) the inspection, repair and renewal of sewers, mains, cables, etc., by a local authority or statutory undertaker (*c*).

Mining Operations

There is no definition of mining operations in the Act of 1971, but the word "minerals" is defined as *including* (*d*) all minerals and substances in or under land of a kind ordinarily worked for removal by underground or surface working (*e*). It is submitted that the expression "mining operation" is to be interpreted in the light of the definition and that it would therefore include quarrying and other surface operations as well as underground mining.

Other Operations

As already explained, the word "operation" in this context means something which changes the physical characteristics of

---

(*s*) Act of 1971, s. 22(2) (*a*).
(*a*) *Ibid.*, s. 290(1).
(*b*) *Ibid.*, s. 22 (2) (*b*).
(*c*) *Ibid.*, s. 22 (2) (*c*).
(*d*) In this case, the word "*includes*" must be interpreted as "*means and includes*".
(*e*) Act of 1971, s. 290(1); peat cut for purposes other than sale is excluded.

the land, or of what is under it or of the air above it (*f*). There is, however, some uncertainty as to the meaning of the phrase "other operations", since it can be interpreted in different ways.

(1) It might be taken as meaning any operation affecting the physical characteristics of the land. But in that case why does section 22(2) specifically refer to building, engineering and mining operations? (*g*).

(2) Another approach would be to try to apply the *ejusdem generis* rule, that is, to limit the phrase to operations of the same class or genus as building, engineering and mining. The difficulty here is to find any common genus to building, engineering and mining (*h*).

(3) There is a rule of interpretation known as *noscitur a sociis*; that is, the meaning of a word can be gathered from the words with which it is associated. If this rule were applied, "other operations" would be restricted to operations similar to building, engineering or mining, but in a less strict manner than would be required by the *ejusdem generis* rule (*i*).

Even on the narrowest interpretation, the phrase "other operations" must obviously include some matters which do not fall within the strict definitions of building, engineering or mining. The removal of topsoil (which under some circumstances would appear to be development (*j*)) is probably an operation of this kind.

Does the demolition of a building fall within the category of

---

(*f*) See p. 80, *ante*.

(*g*) See the remarks of LORD MORRIS OF BORTH-Y-GEST and LORD PEARSON in *Coleshill and District Investment Co., Ltd.* v. *Minister of Housing and Local Government*, [1969] 2 All E.R. 525, at pp. 529 and 543 respectively.

(*h*) See the remarks of LORD GUEST, LORD WILBERFORCE and LORD PEARSON, *ibid.*, at pp. 532, 537 and 543 respectively.

(*i*) See the remarks of LORD PEARSON, *ibid.*, at p. 543.

(*j*) The Agricultural Land (Removal of Surface Soil) Act, 1953, makes it an offence to remove top-soil without planning permission in any case where such operations would constitute development.

"other operations"? For some years it was always assumed that the demolition of a building does not of itself constitute development (*k*), and this view was supported by the judgment of MARSHALL, J. in *Howell* v. *Sunbury-on-Thames U.D.C.* (*l*). But in the case of *Coleshill and District Investment Co., Ltd.* v. *Minister of Housing and Local Government* (*m*) the House of Lords refused to say that demolition was not development and left the issue open.

The company owned a disused ammunition store which they proposed to use for storage. The buildings were surrounded by a concrete blast wall and a grass covered embankment of earth and rubble. They removed the embankment thus creating an eyesore, and the local planning authority served an enforcement notice. The company applied for a determination that the removal of the blast wall would not constitute development, but the local planning authority failed to give a determination within the prescribed period. The company appealed against the enforcement notice and the failure to give a determination. The Minister found as a fact that the blast walls and embankment were an integral part of the building; on this finding he held that the removal of the embankments was an engineering operation, and that the removal of the blast walls would constitute an alteration of the building which would materially affect its external appearance.

It was held that the Minister had not erred in law in reaching these conclusions and his decision would be upheld. Although their Lordships discussed whether demolition by itself might or might not constitute development, they did not need in the circumstances to decide the question.

Thus, demolition of part of a building may be development if it materially affects the external appearance of the building. But what if the building is totally demolished? In *Iddenden* v.

(*k*) See, for example, the Minister's remarks in circular 67.

(*l*) (1963), 15 P. & C.R. 26. In *L.C.C.* v. *Marks and Spencer, Ltd.*, [1953] 1 All E.R. 1095 the House of Lords decided the demolition with a view to redevelopment amounted to "works for the erection of a building" for the purposes of the Act of 1947, s. 78; but, it is submitted, the House of Lords did not say that such demolition constituted development. This case is further explained in chapter 6, at p. 123, *post*.

(*m*) [1969] 2 All E.R. 525.

Secretary of State for the Environment (*n*) the appellants demolished three nissen huts and a lean-to shed. The Court of Appeal decided that their demolition was not development. Lord Denning explained that, whilst some demolition operations might be development (as in the *Coleshill* case (*o*)), the demolition of "buildings such as these" was not development. It is not clear whether Lord Denning intended to imply that the demolition of much larger buildings would be development. There seems to be no logical reason why this should be so, unless the scale of the demolition is such that it might be held to be an engineering operation (*p*).

More recently the Dobry report recommended that the demolition of buildings should be brought within the definition of development (*q*). No action has been taken upon the recommendation, but the demolition of buildings in conservation areas now requires listed building consent (*r*).

CHANGE OF USE

We may now consider the second "leg" in the definition of development—namely "the making of any material change in the use of any buildings or other land". There will be no development unless the change of use is "material"; that is, unless the change is of such a character that it matters having regard to the objects of planning control. As was said in *Marshall* v. *Nottingham City Corpn.* (*s*):

> ". . . if the business of a retail dealer is being carried on in any building, it may be that there is a change of use if, for

(*n*) [1972] 3 All E.R. 883. (*o*) *Supra*.

(*p*) It should not be assumed that the nissen huts were very small buildings. The war-time nissen huts were sectional buildings which could be constructed to any length in multiples of six feet; there were standard widths of 18 feet, 24 feet and 36 feet. They were used for such purposes as army barracks and medical wards and in some cases were later converted to dwellinghouses.

(*q*) "Development Control Review: Report on the Control of Demolition' (G. Dobry, Q.C.,), H.M.S.O., 1974.

(*r*) See chapter 13, *post*.

(*s*) [1960] 1 All E.R. 659, at p. 665, *per* GLYN-JONES, J.

example, the business of a baker is substituted for a different business, for example, that of a grocer; but I am unable to see why or how such a change can be material from any point of view which could legitimately be taken by a planning authority."

In many cases it will be obvious that a change of use is "material" in this sense, *e.g.* where it is proposed to use a dwellinghouse as offices or to station a large number of caravans on a field hitherto used for agriculture. In other cases, however, it is far from easy to decide whether a change of use is material or not. Is there, for instance, a material change of use if a doctor uses two rooms in a dwellinghouse for his practice? Or if a family take in a lodger? If not, in this latter case, would it be material if they took in six lodgers? Is there a material change of use if an existing use is intensified, as for instance in *Guildford R.D.C.* v. *Penny* (*t*) where the number of caravans in a field was increased over a period of years from eight to twenty-seven?

Some help with this problem is given by section 22 of the Act of 1971 which lays down specific rules for certain cases. Apart from these, however, the question whether there is a material change of use must be decided in the light of all the circumstances. We will deal first with the statutory rules laid down in section 22, and then with the general principles applicable to cases not covered by these rules.

The Statuory Provisions: Matters Declared to be a Material Change of Use

The following are specifically declared to involve a material change of use:

(a) the conversion of a single dwellinghouse into two or more separate dwellings (*u*);

(b) the deposit of refuse or other waste materials, including the extension of an existing tip, if the superficial area is

---

(*t*) [1959] 2 All E.R. 111.
(*u*) Act of 1971, s. 22(3) (*a*).

extended or the height is extended above the level of the adjoining ground (*a*);

(c) the display of advertisements on any external part of a building not previously used for that purpose (*b*).

The intention is to make it clear beyond doubt that these changes of use constitute development and so require planning permission. There remain, however, difficulties of interpretation. For instance, what is meant in paragraph (a) by "separate" dwellings?

In *Ealing B.C.* v. *Ryan* (*c*) three floors of a house were each occupied by different families; the kitchen was shared by all the families, and it was inferred that any bathroom and lavatory accommodation was also shared. The Corporation served an enforcement notice requiring the use of the property as two or more separate dwellinghouses to be discontinued and later prosecuted the owners for non-compliance. The magistrates dismissed the case.

On appeal counsel for the Corporation contended that if the people in the house were found to be living separately, the dwellings must be separate. The Divisional Court did not accept this contention. A house might well be occupied by two or more persons, who to all intents and purposes were living separately, without that house thereby being used as separate dwellings. Multiple occupation is not by itself enough to bring the statutory rule into operation (*d*); the existence or absence of any form of physical reconstruction is also a relevant factor; another is the extent to which the alleged separate dwellings are self contained.

The effect of these provisions should not be misunderstood. For instance, multiple occupation of a dwellinghouse may consti-

(*a*) Act of 1971, s. 22(3) (*b*). The proviso to s. 22(3) (*b*) is dealt with in chapter 6 at p. 110, *post*.

(*b*) Act of 1971, s. 22(4). This is not likely to be of much practical significance as all outdoor advertisements require consent under the control of Advertisements Regulations whether their display involves development or not—*see* chapter 12, *post*.

(*c*) [1965] 1 All E.R. 137.

(*d*) See the account of *Birmingham Corpn.* v. *Minister of Housing and Local Government and Habib Ullah*, [1963] 3 All E.R. 668, at p. 101, *post*.

tute a national change of use even though the house has not been converted into separate dwellings; that is a matter to be decided by reference to general principles. A similar point arises with regard to the tipping of refuse and other waste materials. Such tipping may constitute a material change of use even though the superficial area of the existing tip has not been extended, nor the height raised above the permitted level. Thus in *Alexandra Transport Co., Ltd.* v. *Secretary of State for Scotland* (*e*), the Court of Session considered that the backfilling of quarry refuse had been part of the use as a quarry; use thereafter as a "dump" was a material change of use.

The Statutory Provisions: Uses excluded from definition of development.

Certain uses of land are specifically excluded from the definition of development. First, there is the use of a building or other land within a curtilage of a dwellinghouse for any purpose incidental to the enjoyment of the dwellinghouse as such (*f*). It follows that the use of an existing garden shed as a garage for the owner's own car or as additional sleeping accommodation would not be development. But, since the word "use" does not include the carrying out of building operations (*g*), this paragraph does not authorise the erection of a building or shed for these purposes.

Secondly, the use of any land for the purpose of agriculture or forestry, and the use for any of these purposes of any building occupied with land so used, does not involve development (*h*). The use of land for agriculture obviously involves the carrying out of a number of operations such as ploughing; in this context it is submitted that the word use must include such operations as are essential to and inseparable from agriculture, but that it does not include such operations as the erection of farm buildings.

(*e*) (1972), 25 P. & C.R. 97.
(*f*) Act of 1971, s. 22(2) (*d*).
(*g*) See this chapter, p. 80, *ante*; Act of 1971, s. 290.
(*h*) Act of 1971, s. 22 (2) (*e*).

Thirdly, no development is involved by a change of use from one purpose to another within one of the use classes specified in a use classes order made by the Minister (*i*). At present this means the Use Classes Order, 1972. This order sets out eighteen use classes, each of which groups together a number of similar uses. By way of illustration, consideration will be given to some of the more important use classes and the definitions involved.

Class I refers to use as a shop for any purpose except as—(i) a shop for the sale of hot food (*j*); (ii) a tripe shop; (iii) a shop for the sale of pet animals or birds; (iv) a cat's meat shop; (v) a shop for the sale of motor vehicles. For this purpose "shop" is defined with some precision (*k*):

(1) It *means* a building used for the purpose of carrying on of any retail trade or retail business wherein the primary purpose is the selling of goods.

(2) It *includes* a building used for the purpose of—

- (a) a hairdresser;
- (b) undertaker;
- (c) travel agency;
- (d) ticket agency;
- (e) post office;
- (f) receiving office for goods to be washed, cleaned or repaired;
- (g) a building used for other purposes appropriate to a shopping area.

(3) It *does not include* a building used as—

- (a) funfair;
- (b) garage;
- (c) launderette;
- (d) petrol filling station;
- (e) office (*l*);

(*i*) *Ibid.*, s. 22 (2) (*f*).

(*j*) The reference to shops for the sale of hot food replaces the reference in earlier Use Classes Orders to fried fish shops.

(*k*) Use Classes Order, Art. 2.

(*l*) For definition of "office" see Class II below.

(f) hotel, restaurant, snackbar or cafe or premises licensed for the sale of intoxicating liquors for consumption on the premises;

(g) betting shop (*m*).

The effect is that a change from, say, a draper's shop to a hairdresser's is not development because both fall within the same use class. But a change from a draper's shop to a shop for the sale of hot food may be development because the latter is excluded from the use class; it does not follow, however, that this change must be development. The Act of 1971 and the Use Classes Order say that a change from one purpose to another shall not involve development. They do not say that a change from something within a particular use class to something outside it must be development: such cases must be considered in the light of all the facts, having regard to the general principles set out below. We have seen that, in *Marshall* v. *Nottingham City Corpn.* (*n*), it was suggested that a change of use from baker's to grocer's shop would not be material because it would not matter to the planning authority. The Use Classes Order puts the matter beyond all doubt. Class II refers to use as an office for any purpose: "office" *includes* a bank, but not a post office or a betting shop (*o*). Class III refers to use as a light industrial building for any purpose and Class IV to use as a general industrial building for any purpose. Classes V to IX refer to various special industrial uses.

For the purpose of these use classes "industrial building" *means* (*p*) a building (other than a building in or adjacent to and belonging to a quarry or mine and other than a shop) used for the carrying on of any process for or incidental to any of the following purposes, namely:

(a) the making of any article or part of any article (*q*), or

---

(*m*) Use Classes Order, Art. 2.

(*n*) See p. 88 *ante*.

(*o*) Use Classes Order, Art. 2.

(*p*) *Ibid.*

(*q*) "Article" means an article of any description including a ship or vessel.

(b) the altering, repairing, ornamenting, finishing, cleaning, washing, packing or canning, or adapting for sale, or breaking up or demolition of any article, or

(c) without prejudice to the foregoing paragraphs, the getting, dressing or treatment of minerals.

The "process" must be one which is carried on in the course of trade or business, that is something which is an occupation rather than a pleasure (*r*). It seems that a hobby, even though financially profitable, is not a trade or business; this appears to have been taken for granted in the case of *Peake* v. *Secretary of State for Wales* (*s*). But it is not essential to the concept of a business that it should be carried on with a view to making a profit; thus in *Rael Brook, Ltd.* v. *Minister of Housing and Local Government* (*t*) use of a building as a cooking centre by a local authority for the provision of school meals was held to be industrial, so that planning permission was not thereafter required for a change to shirt making.

It might appear from this that the court adopts a liberal approach to the definition of "industrial building". The court has, however, recognised the danger that amateur workshops might be turned over to commercial industrial activity without any control by the planning authority. Accordingly, a relatively severe construction is to be placed on the terms of the Order. There were some important remarks to that effect in *Rael-Brook, Ltd.* v. *Minister of Housing and Local Government* (*u*). More recently, the Divisional Court has emphasised the point in *Tessier* v. *Secretary of State for the Environment* (*v*).

A sculptor used a dutch barn as a studio. In the barn there were six large benches with vices, casting pits, a forge, an anvil and furnaces; stone masonry blocks of up to three-and-a-half tons

---

(*r*) *Rolls* v. *Miller* (1884), 27 Ch.D. 71 *per* LINDLEY, L.J. at p. 88.

(*s*) (1971), 22 P. & C.R. 889. For an account of this case, see p. 102, *post*.

(*t*) [1967] 1 All E.R. 262.

(*u*) *Supra*.

(*v*) (1975), 31 P. & C.R. 161.

would be cut out with drills, grinders, electric hammers and hand chisels. The sculptor also used the studio as a showroom and for lectures.

The Minister held that the use was not industrial, but *sui generis*.

HELD: The Minister was entitled to take the view that an artist, expressing his art form and making articles in the process, even if they were sold, was not making them in the course of a trade or business.

A "light industrial building" is one in which the processes carried on or the machinery installed are such as could be carried on or installed in any residential area without detriment to the amenity of that area by reason of noise, vibration, smell, fumes, smoke, soot, ash dust or grit. A "special industrial building" means one used for the purposes specified in Classes V to IX (*w*). A "general industrial building" is any industrial building which is not light or special (*x*).

A few illustrations must suffice. Many modern factories use electrically powered and virtually noiseless machines; such factories are likely to fall within Class III and a change from one type of factory to another within that use class will not involve development. But a motor repair shop will probably fall within Class IV because of the noise which it is likely to create so that a move from light engineering within Class II to motor repairs may involve development. A move from motor repairs to glue making may also involve development because the latter is within Class IX.

Difficulties sometimes arise where two or more uses are carried on together. For instance, manufacturing firms may carry on light industry in one building and general industry in a neighbouring building. Article 3(2) of the Use Classes Order, provides that where a single undertaking has a group of contiguous or

(*w*) Buildings in these classes include those whose uses the Public Health Acts classify as "offensive trades". Class V was considered in *George Cohen 600 Group, Ltd.* v. *Minister of Housing and Local Government*, [1961] 2 All E.R. 682. Classes V, VI and VII have been re-cast by the Use Classes Order, 1972.

(*x*) Use Classes Order, Art. 2.

adjacent buildings used for two or more uses within Classes III to IX, those uses may be treated as a single class—provided the area occupied by general or special industrial buildings is not substantially increased. This facilitates changes of use within the group of buildings.

Interchangeability is also facilitated by article 3 (3) which provides that a use which is ordinarily incidental to and included in a use specified in the Order is not excluded from that use because it is specified elsewhere in the Order as a separate use. The effect of this may be seen from *Vickers-Armstrong, Ltd.* v. *Central Land Board* (*y*) which was decided on article 3(3) of the Use Classes for the Third Schedule Purposes Order, 1948 (*z*).

> An aviation works included an administration block; it was used partly as offices, but also by designers of blueprints and by draughtsmen, and in it technicians carried out important mechanical tests.
>
> In connection with a claim for compensation the question arose as to whether this building could have been used for general industrial purposes without planning permission.
>
> The Court of Appeal held that the building could have been so used without planning permission. "Looked at as a whole, I should have thought that the appellants' works were clearly used as a general industrial building. It is true that the administration block was not wholly used for the carrying out of an 'incidental' process, but it plainly was, I should have thought, incidental use of the works within article 3 (3) of the Order. That being so, it matters not that it cannot have been said wholly to have been used for the carrying out of processes: offices are clearly incidental to the use of a general industrial building."

It frequently happens that an industrial use is ancillary to a non-industrial use. For example, there may be ovens for baking bread at the rear of a baker's shop; a dentist's house may include a workshop for the manufacture and repair of dentures; garage

(*y*) (1957), 9 P. & C.R. 33.

(*z*) This Order provided a similar set of use classes, but for a different purpose (compensation).

premises may include a building used for repair work. Baking bread, the manufacture and repair of dentures, the repair of motor vehicles are all "industrial". Can it then be argued that in each case there is an "industrial building" which can be used for any other industrial process in the same use class?

This problem is not confined to subsidiary industrial buildings, but may arise under other use classes. Two decisions of the Court of Appeal suggest that where the subsidiary use is ancillary to the main use, it cannot be detached and turned into an independent use.

Thus, in *G. Percy Trentham, Ltd.* v. *Gloucestershire C.C.* (*a*) a firm of building and civil engineering contractors bought a farmhouse, yard and farm buildings. This firm used some of the buildings (which had previously been used for housing farm machinery, etc.) for the storage of building materials for their business. The county council having served an enforcement notice, the firm appealed on the ground that both uses fell within class X relating to wholesale warehouses and repositories. The Court of Appeal considered that the farmer's use of these buildings for housing farm machinery was not use as a repository (*b*); but even if the buildings had been a repository, they could not be severed from the rest of the farmhouse and buildings; one had to look at the unit as a whole.

A similar approach was adopted by the Court of Appeal in *Brazil (Concrete), Ltd.* v. *Amersham R.D.C. and Minister of Housing and Local Government* (*c*). A builders' yard with ancillary buildings had been used for storage in connection with a building contractor's business. In 1962 the premises were bought by R. Brazil & Co., Ltd. and this company obtained planning permission to convert a big shed in the yard to various uses including a carpenter's shop. Brazil (Concrete), Ltd—a subsidiary company—then erected a ready mix concrete plant in the yard. It was

(*a*) [1966] 1 All E.R. 701.
(*b*) [1966] 1 All E.R. 701, at p. 702.
(*c*) (1967), 111 Sol. Jo. 497.

contended on behalf of the company that they were entitled to do this because the big shed was now an industrial building for the purposes of the Use Classes Order, which meant that the land used with it fell within that category by virtue of article 2(3) of the Order; that being so, the company were industrial undertakers and as such entitled by virtue of the General Development Order (*d*) to erect the concrete plant. The Court rejected the basic contention that the big shed had become an industrial building for the purpose of the Use Classes Order; although articles were made in the carpenter's shop, that was incidental to the primary purpose of a builder's yard.

General Principles

Where the statutory rules do not apply, the question whether there is a material change of use must be decided on general principles. As we have seen a change is "material" if it matters having regard to the objects of planning control. In this connection the following points may arise:

(1) In most cases the first question to ask will be whether the change of use will completely alter the character of the land or buildings.

(2) where an existing use is intensified it is necessary to ask whether there has been a complete change in the character of the land or buildings.

(3) If the change of use only partially alters the character of the land or building, it will be necessary to ask whether the change is material for some other reason.

(4) In some cases, the answer may depend on the unit of land or buildings under consideration.

(5) In some cases, it is necessary to consider whether established use rights have been lost or abandoned.

We will consider each of these in turn.

(*d*) G.D.O. Class VIII gives permission for certain types of development by "industrial undertakers" as defined in Art. 2(1). As to Class VIII see Chapter 6, p. 119, *post*.

(1) *Will the change of use completely alter the character of land or buildings?*—The relevance of this test was emphasised in *Guildford R.D.C.* v. *Penny* (*e*). On 1st July, 1948, a field was used as a site for eight caravans. Over the years the number was increased to twenty-seven and the local authority served an enforcement notice. On appeal, the magistrates held that this did not constitute a material change of use and quashed the enforcement notice. The Court of Appeal held that an increase or intensification of use might amount to a material change of use. But in this case the land had been used as a caravan site from first to last, and it could not be said that the magistrates had erred in law in finding that there had been no material change of use. The Court of Appeal was saying in effect that the increase in number was not so great that it was unreasonable for the magistrates to hold that there had been no real change in the character of the site.

It should be noted that the test is the character of the use and not the particular purpose of the particular occupier. This is illustrated by *Marshall* v. *Nottingham City Corpn.* (*f*).

From 1912 to 1957 L. owned a plot of land which he used for manufacturing and selling wooden portable buildings, garages and wooden garden ornaments. The goods were made in a workshop and displayed in the open. There was a hut which he used as an office and from which he conducted sales. After 1939 the business dwindled and by 1957 was moribund though not dead.

In 1957 M bought the land from L so that a company of which she was managing director could use it for selling caravans and wooden portable buildings: the company did not manufacture any goods. The Corporation served an enforcement notice alleging a material change of use by (i) using the land for the display and sale of caravans and wooden buildings: (ii) using the hut as a "sales-shop".

M applied for a declaration of the High Court that there was no material change of use. It was held:

(*e*) [1959] 2 All E.R. 111.
(*f*) [1960] 1 All E.R. 659.

(1) Neither the fact that the company were distributors—not manufacturers—nor the fact that the company sold caravans which L had not sold constituted a material change of use;

(2) there was not such a great increase in the intensity as might constitute a material change;

(3) the hut when used by L was a shop and was also a shop as used by the company, so that the case fell within Class I of the Use Classes Order.

Similar considerations arose in *East Barnet U.D.C.* v. *British Transport Commission* (*g*).

This case concerned some 30,855 sq. yards of land belonging to the British Transport Commission near a railway station. The land was divided into seven parcels. Three parcels comprising nearly 20,000 sq. yds. had been used as coal stacking yards; one parcel of over 10,000 sq. yds. had been vacant for many years; two very small parcels consisted of buildings which had been used as workshops; the seventh parcel was a siding.

At different dates Vauxhall Motors took tenancies of all these parcels, and used the land as a transit depot for the handling and storage of crated motor vehicles nearly all of which were received and despatched by rail. In 1951 they applied for planning permission in respect of two of the parcels (one of them previously used for coal stacking, and the other the unused land) and the council granted permission subject to the condition that the use of all the land for this purpose would cease on 31st May, 1958. The use continued after that date, and the council served enforcement notices.

On appeal, the magistrates quashed the enforcement notices on the ground that the use of the land did not constitute development.

The council thereupon took the case to the High Court. It was held, *inter alia*, that the magistrates were entitled to find that there had been no material change of use. The land had originally been a coal storage depot, the coal being brought in and taken away by rail. There would have been no material change of use if the British Transport Commission had changed the storage from coal to oil. "The mere fact that the com-

(*g*) [1961] 3 All E.R. 878.

modity changes does not necessarily mean that the land is being used for a different purpose nor, as it seems to me, is there any relevance in the fact that the purpose for which the land is used is effected by other hands, in this case by [Vauxhall Motors]" (*h*).

Put shortly, there was no material change of use because the land was used throughout as a storage and transit depot. As regards the unused parcel, the Divisional Court said that it was proper to regard this not as a separate unit of land but merely as an unused portion of the whole unit.

(2) *Where the existing use has been intensified, has there been a complete change in the character of the land or buildings?*—It now seems reasonably clear that an increase or intensification of use may amount to a material change of use. In *Guildford R.D.C.* v. *Penny* (*i*) it was not necessary for the Court of Appeal to give a definite ruling on this point, but both LORD EVERSHED, M.R. and SELLERS, L.J. considered that an intensification of use could amount to a material change. Some subsequent decisions of the Divisional Court confirm this.

The first such case was *Birmingham Corpn.* v. *Minister of Housing and Local Government and Habib Ullah* (*j*).

Habib Ullah purchased two houses which until then had been in single family occupation; he installed several families in each. The corporation served enforcement notices alleging that there had been a material change of use by changing the use of each from single dwelling house to house-let-in-lodgings. The Minister considered that there had been no material change of use since the houses were still residential.

HELD: The Minister had erred in law in saying that because the houses remained residential there could not be a material change of use; whether there had been a material change of use, said LORD PARKER, C.J., was a matter of fact and degree in each case. The court remitted the cases to the Minister for reconsideration.

(*h*) *Per* LORD PARKER, C.J., at p. 885.
(*i*) [1959] 2 All E.R. 111.
(*j*) [1963] 3 All E.R. 668.

Although LORD PARKER did not speak of "intensification of user", it is submitted that this decision is consistent only with the view that intensification of user may be a material change. It must often be very difficult to decide at what point an intensification of user results in a material change, but this difficulty does not affect the general proposition of law.

In the recent case of *Peake* v. *Secretary of State for Wales* (*k*), the Divisional Court expressly treated the matter as one of intensification.

> In 1950 following the grant of planning permission, P built a private garage. From then until 1968 he used it for the repair and servicing of motor vehicles as a spare time activity or profitable hobby. In 1968 he was declared redundant in his full time employment and began working full time at the garage. The local planning authority served an enforcement notice. The Minister, dismissing P's appeal, said that a material change of use had occurred in 1968. P then appealed to the High Court.
>
> HELD: although a change in an activity from part-time to full-time could not of itself amount to a material change of use, the Minister was entitled to conclude as a matter of fact and degree that P's use of the garage prior to 1968 was incidental to its designed use as a private garage and that a material change of use had occurred by intensification in 1968.

Another aspect of the same problem arose in *Wipperman* v. *London Borough of Barking* (*l*). Land was used partly for the storage of building materials and partly for car breaking; later the car breaking was discontinued and the whole of the land was used for the storage of building materials. It was held that the Minister was entitled to find that there was a material change of use as respects the whole of the land and so to uphold an enforcement notice requiring the appellant to cease using the whole for the purposes of storage.

In *Wipperman's case* the whole of the site was treated as one

---

(*k*) (1971), 22 P. & C.R. 889.
(*l*) (1965), 17 P. & C.R. 225.

planning unit, and the court regarded it as immaterial whether the two uses occupied separate parts of the site or were so intermingled as to occupy the whole. Today, having regard to the criteria laid down in *Burdle* v. *Secretary of State for the Environment* (*m*), the court would probably be less ready to assume that the whole site should be treated as one planning unit.

(3) ***Where a change of use does not completely alter the character of the land or building is the change material for any other reason?*—** **It would seem that a change of use will be "material" if it completely alters the character of the land or building.** However, there are many changes of use which only partially alter the character of the land or building. In such cases further questions must be asked. In *Guildford R.D.C.* v. *Penny* (*n*), LORD EVERSHED said that a change of use might be material if it would involve a substantial increase in the burden of services which a local authority has to supply. His Lordship did not mention any specific examples, but it will be obvious that a substantial development, particularly if it be of a residential character will involve the local authority in the provision of additional water supplies, sewerage and street lighting and may involve increased provision for education services, fire services and police. Since planning control is to some extent concerned with the preservation of amenity, it may also be relevant to ask what effect a change of use will have on the neighbourhood. A change of use may well be "material" if it is likely to involve a great increase in the number of persons calling at the premises, or if it is likely to cause a great deal of noise.

It may also be proper to ask what is the purpose of a particular change of use, *e.g.* whether it is incidental to the existing use of the premises or whether it is the establishment of a trade or business. This test must, however, be applied with care. The doctor who uses two rooms in his private residence for the purpose

(*m*) [1972] 3 All E.R. 240. This case is discussed at p. 104, *post*.
(*n*) [1959] 2 All E.R. 111.

of his practice and the family who take in a lodger are both doing so for the purposes of gain, but it is probably true to say that in neither case is there a material change of use (*o*). Planning control is concerned with the use of land and not with personal motives.

(4) *What is the unit under consideration?*—The Act of 1971 refers to a material change in the use of "any buildings or other land". This is vague and in some cases can give rise to difficulty. In *East Barnet U.D.C.* v. *British Transport Commission* (*p*) the question whether there had been a material change in the use of one parcel of land turned on whether that parcel should be regarded as a separate unit of land or merely part of a larger unit. LORD PARKER, C.J., commented that the choice of unit was always a matter of difficulty but "looked at *as a matter of commonsense* in the present case it seems to me that this was merely an unused part of the unit in question" (*q*). In other words there can be no hard and fast rules as to the choice of unit: one must approach the problem in each case on commonsense lines.

In the later case of *Burdle* v. *Secretary of State for the Environment* (*r*), however, the Divisional Court attempted a more precise formulation, and suggested three possible criteria for determining the planning unit. First, whenever it is possible to recognise a single main purpose of the occupier's use of his land, to which secondary activities are incidental or ancillary, the whole unit of occupation should be considered. This would seem to cover the circumstances of the *East Barnet* case. Secondly, it may be equally apt to consider the entire unit of occupation even though the occupier carries on a variety of activities, and it is not possible to say that one is incidental or ancillary to another; *e.g.* a composite use where the activities are not confined within separate and physically distinct areas. Thirdly, within a single unit of

(*o*) See circular 67.
(*p*) [1961] 3 All E.R. 878.
(*q*) At p. 886, author's italics
(*r*) [1972] 3 All E.R. 240.

occupation two or more physically distinct areas may be occupied for substantially different and unrelated purposes. In such a case each area used for a separate main purpose (together with its incidental and ancillary activities) ought to be considered as a separate planning unit.

These criteria are not absolute rules. In *Wood* v. *Secretary of State for the Environment*(s), a conservatory attached to a dwelling-house was used for the sale of produce from a smallholding. The Minister, in considering an appeal against an enforcement notice in respect of this use, treated the conservatory as a separate planning unit. The Divisional Court considered that the Minister had approached the matter in the wrong way. LORD WIDGERY, C.J. said that it could rarely, if ever, be right to dissect a dwelling house and to regard one room in it as a separate planning unit. In other words, the Minister should have considered whether the use of the conservatory for the sale of produce amounted to a material change in the use of the whole of the premises.

LORD WIDGERY'S dictum in *Wood's* case is of considerable importance because of the large number of cases in which the resident occupier of a house uses one or two rooms for the purposes of his profession or business. There may, of course, be a material change of use in such cases, but the question is to be decided by looking at the house as a whole and not in separate parts (*t*).

It seems that LORD WIDGERY'S dictum is not to be extended to buildings other than single dwellings. In *Johnston* v. *Secretary of State for the Environment* (*a*), the Divisional Court considered that in the case of a block of flats in single ownership, but let to separate and different tenants, the planning unit would normally be the individual flat in question.

(*s*) [1973] 2 All E.R. 404.

(*t*) See for instance a decision of the Minister concerning the use of part of a dwelling house by a veterinary surgeon for the purposes of his practice: (1976) J.P.L. 328.

(*a*) (1974), 28 P & C.R. 424.

(5) *Have established use rights been lost or abandoned?* The question of how far established use rights can be lost or abandoned has not yet been fully explored by the courts, but the decided cases show that there are circumstances in which this may happen; these circumstances may be classified under two main heads: (a) extinguishment, and (b) abandonment.

Extinguishment: The phrase "material change in the use of any buildings or other land" suggests a distinction between the use of a building and the use of other land, notwithstanding the general rule that "land" includes any buildings erected on it (*b*). So, if a building is destroyed, any existing use rights attaching to it are extinguished and do not enure for the benefit of the land or of any buildings subsequently erected on it. This is illustrated by *Gray* v. *Minister of Housing and Local Government* (*c*).

> G owned a seaside cafe which was gradually converted to predominantly amusement use. The cafe was destroyed by fire. G applied for and obtained planning permission for "Re-erection of premises known as Gray's Cafeteria". He subsequently used the new building for amusements.
>
> HELD: any use rights attaching to the original cafe buildings were extinguished, that building was destroyed by fire.

Similarly, the erection of a building extinguished any use rights previously attaching to the land, a point illustrated by the recent case of *Petticoat Lane Rentals, Ltd.* v. *Secretary of State for the Environment* (*d*).

> An area of open ground was used as a market on all days of the week. In 1963 permission was granted for erection of a building. The ground floor was to be open, the building being supported on pillars, and was to be used for car parking and a loading area; specific permission was given for the use of the ground floor as a market on Sundays. The building was erected in accordance with the planning permission, and the ground

(*b*) See the definitions of "land" in the Law of Property Act, 1925, s. 205(1) and in the Act of 1971, s. 290(1).

(*c*) (1969), 68 L.G.R. 15.

(*d*) [1971] 2 All E.R. 793.

floor was used for market trading both on Sundays and weekdays.

HELD: the previously existing land had merged in the new building and a new planning unit had been created which had no previous planning history, the use of the ground floor for market trading had not been authorised by the planning permission and was therefore a breach of planning control.

It seems that in this case the building covered the whole of the site; the majority of the Divisional Court preferred to leave open the question of what the position would be if the whole of the land had not been covered by building.

Abandonment: The question whether existing use rights have been abandoned is a difficult one, and can usefully be considered under a number of headings suggested by ASHWORTH, J. in *Hartley* v. *Minister of Housing and Local Government* (*e*).

1. If the sole use to which the land is put is suspended and thereafter resumed without there being any intervening different user, *prima facie* the resumption does not constitute development. As LORD PARKER, C.J. put it in an earlier case (*f*): "It is of course quite plain that a change from A to X and then from X to A does not involve development either way, if X is completely *nil*, no use at all".

There are, of course, some uses of land which by their very nature are intermittent. Thus—

> ". . . a racecourse is perhaps used for a few days three or four times a year, but no one would suggest that it ceases to be used as a racecourse in the closed season, or that a new development occurs on the first day of the next meeting." (*g*)

On the face of it LORD PARKER's dictum goes wider than the case of the intermittent use and may well cover seasonal uses and cases where an activity is closed down and is then resumed after an interval.

(*e*) [1969] 1 All E.R. 309.

(*f*) *McKellan* v. *Minister of Housing and Local Government* (1966), 6th May, unreported.

(*g*) *Hawes* v. *Thornton Cleveleys U.D.C.* (1965), 17 P. & C.R. 22 *per* WIDGERY, J. at p. 28.

2. There may, however, be cases where the period of suspension is so long that the original use can properly be described as having been abandoned. As yet there is no clear authority to this effect apart from a remark by LORD DENNING in *Webber* v. *Minister of Housing and Local Government* (*h*), but the remark was *obiter* and the case concerned a composite use so that it is not altogether clear that LORD DENNING intended it to apply to the discontinuance of a single use.

3. If land is put to a composite use, the cessation of one of those uses does not of itself constitute development; but there may be a material change of use if the remaining use absorbs the remainder of the site, as in *Wipperman* v. *Barking London Borough Council* (*i*).

4. If one of two or more composite uses is discontinued, and thereafter resumed, the question whether such resumption constitutes development is a question of fact to be determined in the light of all the relevant circumstances. These circumstances will include the nature of the uses, what portion of the site was devoted to the discontinued use, what use if any was made of that portion during the period of discontinuance, and how long the discontinuance lasted.

CASES OF DOUBT

There will obviously be many cases in which it is not clear whether an operation or use of land involves development. Section 53 of the Act of 1971 provides a relatively simple and inexpensive procedure for dealing with such cases. Any person who proposes to carry out any operation or to change the use of land may apply to the local planning authority for a determination whether the proposed operation or change of use would constitute development, and if so, whether planning permission is required, having regard to the provisions of the development order. The effect of the words "having regard to the provisions

(*h*) [1967] 3 All E.R. 981.
(*i*) (1965), 17 P. & C.R. 225. And see p. 102, *ante*.

of the development order" was discussed in *Edgwarebury Park Investments, Ltd.* v. *Minister of Housing and Local Government* (*j*), LORD PARKER, C.J., said—

> "this is a method by which the proposed developer may ascertain not only whether what he contemplates is development but also whether it is the sort of development which is covered by the blanket provision in the General Development Order, or is one for which he must apply and get permission."

The appellants in this case, however, attempted to use this procedure to determine whether a decision of Hendon Borough Council amounted to a grant of planning permission, which LORD PARKER, C.J., went on to say was—

> "right outside the contemplation of this provision";

though he added,

> "there can be no conceivable reason for the appellants not being able, if they so desire, to proceed in the courts for a declaration as to the validity of the permission."

The local planning authority must give a determination within two months (*a*). The application may be made concurrently with an application for planning permission if required (*b*).

If the applicant is aggrieved by the determination of the local planning authority, he may appeal to the Minister and will have the right to be heard by a representative of the Minister (*c*). Here again, it is quite common to bring this appeal concurrently with an appeal to the Minister against a refusal of planning permission. There is a further right of appeal from the Minister's decision to the High Court (*d*).

The section 53 procedure applies only to persons who propose to carry out operations or to make a change of use. The procedure is not available where the operations or change of use have already been carried out, nor is it appropriate for deter-

(*j*) [1963] 1 All E.R. 124.
(*a*) G.D.O. 1963, Art. 5 (8).
(*b*) Act of 1962, s. 43 (1).
(*c*) *Ibid.*, s. 23 (1) applied by s. 43 (2).
(*d*) Act of 1971, s. 245.

mining the effect of a purported grant of planning permission (*e*).

It seems that the local planning authority may give a determination which is effective for the purposes of section 53 without a formal application having been made. In *Wells* v. *Minister of Housing and Local Government* (*f*) the plaintiff applied for planning permission; the local planning authority in March, 1963 wrote stating that the proposed works could be regarded as permitted development. WIDGERY, J. said that every planning application had implicit in it an invitation to the planning authority to treat the matter under section 53 if their view of the facts made it appropriate; if they could see at once that planning permission was not required, the sensible and legally appropriate action was to do what was done in March 1963.

A determination under section 53, that no planning permission is required may remain effective, even though the law has been changed before the person concerned has carried out the operations or made the change of use in question. In *English Speaking Union of the Commonwealth* v. *Westminster C.C.* (*g*), the Council determined that a change of use from residential club to hotel would not require planning permission because both uses fell within class XI of the Use Classes Order then in force. The plaintiffs had entered into a building contract for the necessary works, but before these were done and thus before any change of use was made, the Minister made the current Use Classes Order in which residential clubs are excluded. The City Council now contended that there would be a material change of use (*h*), but the plaintiffs were granted a declaration that the section 53 determination remained fully operative.

(*e*) *Edgwarebury Park Investments, Ltd.* v. *Minister of Housing and Local Government*, [1963] 1 All E.R. 124.

(*f*) (1966), 110. So Jo. 889. Affirmed by the Court of Appeal [1967], 2 All E.R. 1041.

(*g*) (1973), 26 P. & C.R. 575.

(*h*) The planning officer's reasons for considering that there would be a material change of use were quoted by PENNYCUICK, V.-C. and make interesting reading; but his Lordship did not in the circumstances have to decide that point.

Another way of ascertaining whether a particular operation or change of use involves development is to apply for a declaratory judgment of the High Court. This method may be used as an alternative to applying for a section 53 determination (*i*) and is also available in those cases to which section 53 does not apply.

(*i*) *Pyx Granite Co., Ltd.* v. *Minister of Housing and Local Government*, [1959] 3 All E.R. 1.

Chapter 6

PLANNING PERMISSION

The basis of planning control in England and Wales is section 23 (1) of the Act of 1971 which provides that "Subject to the provisions of this section, planning permission is required for the carrying out of any development of land" (*a*).

There are certain exceptions to this rule, namely:

(1) *Temporary use existing on 1st July, 1948.* Prior to 6th December, 1968 permission was not required for the resumption of the normal use of land which on 1st July, 1948, was temporarily used for another purpose. If the normal use had not been resumed by 6th December, 1968, permission will be necessary (*b*).

(2) *Occasional use existing on 1st July, 1948.*—Permission is not required in the case of land which on 1st July, 1948, was normally used for one purpose and was also used on occasions for any other purpose, in respect of the use for that other purpose on similar occasions after that date provided the right had been exercised on at least one occasion between 1st July, 1948, and the beginning of 1968 (*c*).

(3) *Land unoccupied on 1st July, 1948.*—Where land was unoccupied on 1st July, 1948, but had before that date been occupied at some time on or after 7th January, 1937, planning permission is not required in respect of any use of land before 6th December, 1968, for the purpose for which it was last used before 1st July, 1948 (*d*).

(*a*) This does not apply to development carried out before "the appointed day", which was 1st July, 1948, the day the 1947 Act came into force: Act of 1971, Sch. 24, para. 12.

(*b*) *Ibid.*, s. 23(2).

(*c*) *Ibid.*, s. 22(3).

(*d*) Act of 1971, s. 23(4).

(4) *Resumption of previous use.*—If planning permission has at any time been granted specifically for a limited period, or by a development order subject to limitations, no permission is necessary to resume the use which was normal before that permission was granted, provided that the "normal use" was not begun in contravention of planning control under Part III of the Act of 1971 or the corresponding provisions of the Acts of 1947 and 1962. Nor is permission necessary to resume the previous lawful use of land when an enforcement notice has been served in respect of any unauthorised development (*e*); the previous use cannot be resumed if it also was begun in breach of planning control—the fact that it was established before 1964 and is therefore no longer subject to enforcement action does not make it lawful (*f*).

There would appear to be little, if any, practical significance for most purposes in the distinction between these classes of development and those matters which are excluded from the definition of development. But the distinction may be of significance in certain cases, since by virtue of section 141 of the Act of 1971 the unexpended balance of established development value will be subject to modification in any case where new development is carried out after 1st July, 1948 (*g*).

Except in the cases noted above (*h*) permission is required under Part III of the 1962 Act for all classes of development. That permission may be granted in three ways:

(a) by a development order made by the Minister;
(b) by being "deemed to be granted" in special cases as provided in the Act of 1971;

(*e*) Act of 1971, s. 23 (5), (6), (8), (9), (10). For development orders, see this chapter, *post*. For enforcement notices see chapter 9, *post*.

(*f*) *L.T.S.S. Print and Supply Services, Ltd* v. *Hackney London B.C.*, [1976] 1 All E.R. 311.

(*g*) See chapter 19, p. 313, *post*.

(*h*) Exceptions (2), (3) and (4) do not apply to the use of land as a *caravan site*, except where there was such use at least once during the two years ending on 9th March, 1960: Act of 1971, s. 23(7).

(c) as a result of an application to the local planning authority. Each of these will now be considered in turn.

PERMISSION UNDER DEVELOPMENT ORDER

This form of permission is provided for by section 24 of the Act of 1971. Development orders made by the Minister may be either general orders applicable (subject to any exceptions specified therein) to all land in England and Wales, or special orders applying only to certain specified land.

The General Development Order

The General Development Order is of general application and by article 3 grants permission for twenty-three classes of development as set out in Part I of the First Schedule to the Order. Many of these classes are sub-divided with the result that for a wide variety of developments there is no need to apply to the local planning authority for permission. This is not the same, however, as excluding these matters from the definition of development. The permissions granted by the Order are in many cases subject to certain limitations and conditions and, if these are not observed, the local planning authority can take enforcement action under Act of 1971 (*i*); and nothing in the General Development Order is to operate so as to permit any development contrary to a condition imposed on any other grant of permission under Part III of the Act. Moreover, the Minister and the local planning authority have certain powers under Article 4 (*j*) to withdraw in specific cases the benefit of a permission granted by the Order: this power has been quite extensively used, but this would not have been possible if the matters in question had been excluded from the definition of development. Lastly, the Minister can at any time make new development orders either extending or restricting the range of permitted developments.

(*i*) See chapter 9.
(*j*) See this chapter, p. 120, *post*.

Of the twenty-three classes of development permitted by the General Development Order, classes I to XI, XVIII, XXII and XXIII are of general interest: the remainder concerns development by public bodies such as local authorities, statutory undertakers and the National Coal Board. The permitted developments are subject to an important restriction: the General Development Order does not authorise any development which involves the formation, laying out or material widening of a means of access to a trunk or classified road, or which creates an obstruction to the view of persons using any road used by vehicular traffic at or near any bend, corner, junction or inter-section so as to be likely to cause danger to such persons (*k*).

Class I. Development within the curtilage of a dwellinghouse.— Paragraph 1 permits the enlargement, improvement or other alteration of a dwellinghouse so long as (*a*) its cubic content (as ascertained by external measurement) is not exceeded by more than 50 cubic metres or one-tenth whichever is the greater subject to a maximum of 115 cubic metres; (*b*) height of the building does not exceed the height of the original dwellinghouse; (*c*) No part of the building projects beyond the forwardmost part of the front of the original dwellinghouse. The erection of a garage, stable, loose box or coach house within the same curtilage is to be treated as an enlargement of the dwellinghouse. This permission is subject to a number of conditions.

Paragraph 2 permits the construction of a porch outside any external door of the house subject to limitations as to size, height and distance from the highway.

Paragraph 3 permits the erection, etc., within the curtilage of a dwellinghouse of any building or enclosure (other than a dwelling, garage, stable, loose box or coach house) required for a purpose incidental to the enjoyment of the dwellinghouse as such, includ-

---

(*k*) G.D.O., Art. 3(3). This restriction does not apply to development permitted by classes IX, XII or XIV. The restriction imposed, Art. 3(3) replaces the "standard conditions" referred to in earlier General Development Orders.

ing the keeping of poultry, pet animals, etc., for the domestic needs or personal enjoyment of the occupants of the house. But the building must not project in front of any wall of the original house which fronts on to the highway; height must not exceed in the case of a building with a ridged roof 4 metres or in any other case 3 metres.

Paragraphs 4 and 5 deal with the construction of hardstanding for vehicles within the curtilage, and with the erection within the curtilage of oil tanks for domestic heating.

Class II. Minor operations.—Paragraph 1 permits the erection of gates, fences, walls or other means of enclosure not exceeding 1 metre in height where abutting on a road used by vehicular traffic or 2 metres in other cases. It also permits the maintenance or alteration of gates, fences, etc., provided the height of 1 metre or 2 metres is not exceeded. In *Prengate Properties, Ltd.* v. *Secretary of State for the Environment* (*l*), the Divisional Court adopted a strict interpretation of the phrase "walls or other means of enclosure"; the erection of a wall such as a free standing wall in the middle of a garden—which does not serve some function of enclosure is not within this paragraph.

Paragraph 2 permits the exterior painting of buildings otherwise than for the purposes of advertisement, announcement or direction. The permission is only required where such painting would materially affect the external appearance of the building: in other cases it will not be development at all (*m*). Perhaps the real value of this paragraph is that by giving permission for external painting it avoids arguments as to whether development is involved.

Class III. Changes of use.—This gives permission for "development consisting of a change of use" to:

(a) use as a light industrial building as defined by the Town and Country Planning (Use Classes) Order, from use as a general industrial building as so defined;

(*l*) (1973), 25 P & C.R. 311.
(*m*) See chapter 5, pp. 83, 84, *ante*.

(b) use as any type of shop from use as:

(i) a shop for the sale of hot food;

(ii) a tripe shop;

(iii) a shop for the sale of pet animals or birds;

(iv) a cats-meat shop;

or

(v) a shop for the sale of motor vehicles.

The phrase "development consisting of a change of use" is significant. The changes of use mentioned above are not excluded from the definition of development by virtue of the Use Classes Order, but they can constitute development only if they amount to a material change of use. As in the case of painting, the real value of Class III is to prevent argument.

Class IV. Temporary buildings and uses.—Paragraph 1 gives permission for the erection or construction on land in, on, over or under which operations, other than mining operations, are being or about to be carried out in pursuance of planning permission granted or deemed to be granted under Part III of the Act, or on adjoining land, or buildings, works, plant or machinery needed temporarily in connection with those operations, for the period of such operations. It is a condition that the buildings, etc., shall be removed at the end of that period.

Paragraph 2 gives permission for the temporary use of land for any purpose on not more than twenty-eight days in any calendar year (*n*), and permits the erection and placing of movable structures on the land for the purposes of that use. This permission is often relied on for such temporary uses as fairs, markets and camping. Caravans have been excluded from Class IV, and the temporary use of land for caravans is now governed by Class XXII.

Class V. Uses by members of recreational organisations.—Certain organisations, such as the Boy Scouts Association, have been granted certificates by the Minister under section 268

(*n*) Not more than fourteen days may be devoted to the purpose of motor car or motor cycle racing or the holding of markets.

of the Public Health Act, 1936, which deals with the control of sites for tents and other movable dwellings. Members of organisations holding certificates under section 268 are permitted by Class V to use land for the purposes of recreation and instruction and to erect or place tents or caravans on the land for that purpose.

Section 268 has been replaced in relation to caravans (but not as regards tents, etc.) by Part I of the Caravan Sites and Control of Development Act of 1960 (*o*); the use of land for caravans by an organisation holding a certificate of exemption under that Act is permitted development by virtue of Class XXII.

Class VI. Agricultural buildings, works and uses.—Paragraph 1 permits the carrying out, on agricultural land of more than 1 acre, of building or engineering operations required for the purposes of agriculture, but not the erection or alteration of houses. This permission is subject to the following limitations:

1. The ground area of the building must not exceed 465 square metres, and if the building would be within 90 metres of another building (other than a house) belonging to the same farm and erected during the last two years, the area of that building must be deducted from the maximum of 465 square metres (*p*).

2. The height of any building within 3 kilometres of the perimeter of an aerodrome must not exceed 3 metres nor 12 metres in any other case (*q*).

3. No part of any building (other than a movable structure) or works must be within 25 metres of the metalled portion of a trunk or classified road.

This permission must also be read subject to the provisions of the Landscape Areas Special Development Order (*r*) which

(*o*) As amended by the Caravan Sites Act 1968, s. 13 (2).

(*p*) Originally there was no limit as to size, and this condition was imposed by the General Development (Amendment) Order, 1960.

(*q*) A general restriction on the height of agricultural buildings was first imposed in 1967.

(*r*) S.I. 1950 No. 729.

applies to certain districts in the counties of Caernarvon, Chester, Cumberland, Derby, Lancaster, Merioneth and Westmorland. In these areas of high landscape value any person proposing to erect an agricultural building in accordance with this permission must give at least 14 days notice to the local planning authority who may require the design and external appearance to be subject to their approval.

Section 290 of the 1971 Act defines agriculture as including: "horticulture, fruit growing, seed growing, dairy farming, the breeding and keeping of livestock (including any creature kept for the production of food, wool, skins or fur or for the purpose of its use in the farming of land), the use of land as grazing land, meadow land, osier land, market gardens and nursery grounds, and the use of land for woodlands where that use is ancillary to the farming of land for other agricultural purposes." In *Belmont Farm, Ltd.* v. *Minister of Housing and Local Government* (*s*), it was held that the breeding and training of horses for show jumping was not agricultural.

Class VII. Forestry buildings and works.—Permission is given for building and other operations (other than the provision or alteration of dwellings) required for forestry and for the formation, alteration and maintenance of private ways. The height of any buildings within 3 kilometres of an aerodrome must not exceed 3 metres, and no part of a building (other than movable structures) or works must be within 25 metres of the metalled portion of a trunk or classified road.

Class VIII. Industrial development.—Permission is given for additions to industrial buildings (by extensions or new erections) but not beyond one-tenth of the cubic capacity of the original buildings. The external appearance of the premises must not be materially affected, and the amount of construction must not be such as to need an industrial development certificate (as explained

(*s*) (1962), 13 P. & C.R. 417.

later in this chapter). Permission is also given for various works and installations on industrial premises.

Article 4 Directions

Article 4 of the General Development Order provides that the Minister or the local planning authority may direct either (i) that all or any of the developments permitted by the Order shall not be carried out in a particular area without specific permission or (ii) that any particular development shall not be carried out without specific permission. Such directions are often referred to as "Article 4 directions". An Article 4 direction by a local planning authority requires the consent of the Minister unless it relates only to buildings listed as being of special architectural or historic interest (*t*) and does not affect certain specified operations of statutory undertakers. Directions relating to Classes I to IV may take effect for six months without the Minister's approval. Notice of a direction affecting an area of land must be published in the *London Gazette* and at least one local newspaper; where the direction is for a particular development, notice must be served on the owner and occupier.

In effect, therefore, an Article 4 direction withdraws the permission by the General Development Order and makes it necessary to apply to the local planning authority for permission. If permission is refused or granted subject to conditions, the owner is entitled to compensation on the footing that permission already granted has been revoked or modified (*u*). Article 4 directions have been extensively used so as to withdraw the permission given under Class XI for war damage rebuilding.

It would seem that an article 4 direction may be made after the development has been commenced but not after it has been completed. In *Cole* v. *Somerset C.C.* (*v*) land, which before the war had formed part of a golf course, had been used since 1950

(*t*) See chapter 12, *post*.
(*u*) Act of 1971, s. 164. See chapter 8, *post*.
(*v*) [1956] 3 All E.R. 531.

as a caravan site for members of the Caravan Club. This use was at that time permitted development under Class V of the General Development Order, 1950. In 1954 the county council served on the owner of the land an article 4 direction approved by the Minister. In 1956 the county council served an enforcement notice requiring the owner to discontinue the use and remove the caravans. On appeal, it was held that neither the Minister nor the planning authority had power under article 4 to withdraw permission which had already been given and acted upon. The enforcement notice was therefore invalid.

Special Development Orders

Planning permission may also be granted by special development order. The New Towns Special Development Order (*w*) grants permission for any development carried out by the development corporation in accordance with proposals approved by the Minister under section 3(1) of the New Towns Act, 1965. This permission extends also to development carried out by persons who bought or leased land for development from the development corporation. For instance, an industrialist moving to a new town often builds his own factory on land bought or leased from the development corporation: the corporation would allocate land for this purpose in an area zoned for this purpose in the "master plan" approved by the Minister and the building plan will almost certainly be subject to the approval of the development corporation. The Special Development Order avoids the necessity of applying to the local planning authority.

In certain cases, however, the development corporation must consult with certain other public bodies, and the Minister has power to make a direction similar to those made under article 4 of the General Development Order.

(*w*) S.I. 1963 No. 1142, as amended by T. & C.P. (New Town Special Development) (Amendment) Order 1965, S.I. 1965 No. 1659.

Permission "deemed to be granted" under the Act

(a) Outdoor Advertisements

The display of advertisements does not of itself constitute development, but the erection of an advertisement hoarding will be development because the hoarding is a "building" (*a*) and the use for the display of advertisements of any external part of a building not normally used for that purpose is a material change of use (*b*). All outdoor advertisements require consent under the Control of Advertisements Regulations (*c*), whether development is involved or not. The Act of 1971 provides that where the display of advertisements in accordance with the regulations involves development, planning permission shall be deemed to have been granted (*d*).

(b) Permission granted before 1st July, 1948

The repeal by the Act of 1947 of all previous planning legislation meant that planning permissions granted under earlier legislation were automatically revoked on 1st July, 1948. However, section 77 of the Act provided that where planning permission had been granted since 21st July, 1943, and the development had not been carried out by 1st July, 1948, permission should be deemed to have been granted under Part III of the Act of 1947 subject to any conditions imposed on the original permission. The effect of this section was preserved by the Act of 1962 and now by the Act of 1971 (*e*).

There was one important qualification. Prior to 1st July, 1948, permission may also have been required under the Restriction of Ribbon Development Act, 1935. If such permission had not been obtained, there is no "deemed" grant of planning permission,

---

(*a*) See the definition of "building" in the Act of 1971, s. 290, discussed in chapter 5, at p. 81, *ante*.
(*b*) Act of 1971, s. 22(4).
(*c*) See chapter 12, *post*.
(*d*) Act of 1971, s. 64.
(*e*) Act of 1962, Sch. 13, para. 7; Act of 1971, Sch. 24, para. 1(3).

and application has to be made to the local planning authority in the ordinary way.

Probably there are not many cases still outstanding, and the deemed permission will have expired on 1st April, 1974, if development was not begun by that date (*f*).

(c) Buildings Unfinished on 1st July, 1948

Section 78 of the Act of 1947 provided that where works for the erection of a building had been begun but not completed before 1st July, 1948, then if the works could lawfully have been completed under previous planning control planning permission should be deemed to have been granted under Part III of the Act of 1947 for the completion of the works. This did not apply, however, if any necessary consent under the Restriction of Ribbon Development Act, 1935, was not obtained. The effect of this section was also preserved by the Act of 1962 and now by the Act of 1971 (*g*).

Here, again, the deemed permission will have expired if development was not begun by 1st April, 1974 (*h*).

The effect of section 78 was considered in *L.C.C.* v. *Marks and Spencer, Ltd.* (*i*). In 1938 permission was granted under the Act of 1932 for the erection of an office building subject to a condition that the works should be completed within eighteen months. The existing buildings were demolished by July 1939, but nothing further had been done. The appellants claimed that the respondents were not entitled to carry out the works for the erection of the building in accordance with the permission deemed to have been granted by section 78. The House of Lords dismissed the appeal on the ground that in the circumstances the demolition of the existing buildings constituted works for the erection of a building which had thus been "begun" but not finished.

(*f*) Act of 1971, Sch. 24, para. 19(1). See chapter 7, p. 167, *post* as to when the development is begun.

(*g*) Act of 1962, Sch. 13, para. 8; Act of 1971, Sch. 24, para. 1(3).

(*h*) See footnote (*f*) above.

(*i*) [1953] 1 All E.R. 1095.

(d) Planning permission deemed to be granted by a Government Department

Where any development by a local authority or statutory undertaker in any case requires authorisation by a government department, that department may direct that planning permission "shall be deemed to be granted"; in other words, authorisation and planning permission are conferred simultaneously instead of separately (*j*).

APPLICATIONS FOR PLANNING PERMISSION

Except in the cases mentioned above application for planning permission must be made to the local planning authority.

Who may Apply

The applicant need not be the owner of an interest in the land, nor is it necessary to obtain the consent of the owner (*k*). But whether he has an interest in the land or not, the applicant must give notice of his application to any other person who has a material interest in that land (*l*)

Publicity for Applications

Normally, it is not necessary for the applicant to give notice to the public or to third parties but there are certain exceptions.

1. In the case of certain kinds of development, section 26 of the Act of 1971 requires the applicant to publish a notice in the local press indicating where members of the public may inspect plans of the proposed development. He must also affix to the land a notice stating that the application is to be made The classes of development to which section 26 applies are prescribed by the Minister and are as follows (*m*):

(*j*) Act of 1972, s. 40; and see chapter 14, page 254, *post*.

(*k*) *Hanily* v. *Minister of Local Government and Planning*, [1952] 1 All E.R. 1293.

(*l*) 1971, s. 27(1) as amended by the Act of 1975, Sch. 10, para. 6.

(*m*) G.D.O., art. 8.

(a) construction of buildings for use as a public convenience.
(b) construction of buildings or other operations, or use of land, for the disposal of refuse or waste materials or as a scrap yard or coal yard or for mineral working;
(c) construction of buildings or other operations (other than the laying of sewers, construction of septic tanks or cesspools serving single dwellinghouses or single buildings in which not more than ten people will normally reside, work or congregate, and works ancillary thereto) or use of land for the disposal or treatment of sewage, trade waste or sludge;
(d) construction of buildings to a height exceeding 20 metres;
(e) construction of buildings or use of land for the purposes of a slaughter-house or knacker's yard, or for the killing or plucking of poultry;
(f) construction of buildings and use of buildings for any of the following purposes—casino, funfair, bingo hall, theatre, cinema, music hall, dance hall, skating rink, swimming bath or gymnasium (not forming part of a school, college or university), Turkish or other vapour or foam bath;
(g) construction of buildings and use of buildings or land as a zoo or for the business of boarding or breeding cats or dogs;
(h) construction of buildings or use of land for motor car or motor-cycle racing;
(i) use of land as a cemetery.

Any member of the public then has the right to make representations to the local planning authority within 21 days of the publication in the local press referred to above (*n*).

2. If any part of the land is included in an agricultural holding the applicant must notify the tenant (*o*) who then has the right to make representations to the local planning authority within 21 days of notification (*p*).

(*n*) Act of 1971, s. 29(2).
(*o*) *Ibid.*, s. 27(3) (b). The tenant for this purpose is the person who was such 21 days before the planning application.
(*p*) Act of 1971, ss. 27(4), 29(3).

3. If any person other than the applicant has a "material interest" (*q*) in the land, the applicant must notify him; if he does not know the names and addresses of all such interested parties he must give notice in the local press (*r*). All such interested persons then have the right to make representations to the local planning authority, within 21 days of the latest notification, or of publication in the local press, whichever is the later (*s*).

In each of these cases, it is the duty of the applicant to give the required notices. In the case of development affecting a conservation area, it is the duty of the local planning authority to give public notice; any member of the public then has the right to make representations within 21 days (*t*).

Industrial Buildings

Before applying for planning permission for certain classes of industrial development a certificate must be obtained from the Department of Industry that the development can be carried out consistently with the proper distribution of industry. An application which is not supported by such a certificate is of no effect and cannot be considered by the local planning authority (*u*).

If the Department grant a certificate, they may impose conditions as to the form of any application for planning permission which is made in pursuance of the certificate (*v*); it seems that the Department might require the application to be restricted to one for temporary permission only, or impose restrictions as to the size of the proposed building. The Department may also

---

(*q*) This means either the freehold or a lease with at least seven years to run: Act of 1971, s. 27(7) as amended by Act of 1975, Sch. 10. para. 6.

(*r*) Act of 1971, s. 27(1) (b–d), (2); and see also subsection (7) as amended by Act of 1975, Sch. 10, para. 6. For a person to be an "owner" for the purposes of notification he must have been such 21 days before the planning application.

(*s*) Act of 1971, ss. 27(4), 29(3).

(*t*) Act of 1971, s. 28. For conservation areas, see chapter 13, p. 242, *post*.

(*u*) Act of 1971, s. 67(1). See also s. 67(5) in regard to applications for retrospective planning permission.

(*v*) Act of 1971, s. 70(1).

impose such conditions as they consider appropriate having regard to the proper distribution of industry (*w*), and these conditions must be attached to any grant of planning permission by the planning authority (*x*). The Department are expressly authorised to impose conditions of a type which would not otherwise be imposed under planning law (*y*); the effect of this provision is uncertain, but it is doubtless intended to enable the Department to disregard certain decisions of the courts as to the type of condition which can properly be attached to a grant of planning permission and in particular to impose conditions restrictive of existing use rights (*z*).

There is no appeal against the refusal of the Department to grant an industrial development certificate; and the Minister is not obliged to entertain an appeal against any conditions which the Department may require to be imposed upon a grant of planning permission (*a*). This control applies to the following classes of industrial development (*b*);

(a) the erection or re-erection (*c*) of an industrial building with a floor space (either by itself or with adjacent buildings belonging to the same undertaking) exceeding the specified limit;

(b) the extension for industrial purposes (*d*) of an industrial building if the floor space (either by itself or with the original buildings) would exceed the specified limit;

(c) a change of use from a non-industrial building to an industrial building.

(*w*) Act of 1971, s. 70(2).

(*x*) *Ibid.*, s. 70(5), (6).

(*y*) *Ibid.*, s. 70(4).

(*z*) See chapter 7, *post*.

(*a*) Act of 1971, s. 71(2).

(*b*) *Ibid.*, ss. 67 and 68; The Town and Country Planning (Erection of Industrial Buildings) Regulations 1966 S.I. No. 1034, provide that all classes of industrial buildings are covered by these sections.

(*c*) Act of 1971, s. 290.

(*d*) An I.D.C. will not be required if the extension is for some other purpose, *e.g.* offices.

The exemption limit specified by the Act of 1971 is 5,000 square feet, but this may be varied (either for the whole of England and Wales or for particular areas) by statutory instrument (*e*). In recent years the exemption limits have been changed on a number of occasions.

The present position is that (i) no certificate is required in the "development areas" as defined in the Development Areas Order, 1966 (*f*); (ii) in the "scheduled areas" the exemption limit is 12,500 square feet; (iii) elsewhere in England and Wales the limit is 15,000 square feet (*g*).

For this purpose "industrial building" is defined (*h*) as a "building used or designed for use—

(a) for the carrying out of any process carried on in the course of trade or business (*i*) any of the following purposes, that is to say,

(i) the making of any article or part of any article, or

(ii) the altering, repairing, ornamenting, finishing, cleaning, washing, freezing, packing or canning, or adapting for sale, or breaking up or demolition of any article, or

(iii) without prejudice to the foregoing paragraphs, the getting, dressing or preparation for sale of minerals or the extraction or preparation for sale of oil or brine,

(b) for the carrying on of scientific research carried on in the course of trade or business".

For the purposes of this definition "building" includes part of a building and "article" means an article of any description including a ship or vessel.

Although, as explained above, the local planning authority cannot consider an application which is not supported by an

(*e*) Act of 1971, ss. 68(1), 69(1) and (2).

(*f*) T. & C.P. (Industrial Development Certificates) Regulations, 1972, S.I., 1972, No. 904.

(*g*) T. & C.P. (Industrial Development Certificates: Exemption) Order, 1976, S.I. 1976 No. 565. The "scheduled areas" are specified in these Regulations and are Greater London and much of south-east England.

(*h*) Act of 1971 s. 66(1).

(*i*) For this purpose, "scientific research" means any activity in the fields of natural or applied science for the extension of knowledge.

industrial development certificate, they must consider whether they would have given permission if the certificate had been obtained. If they would have given permission, they must notify the applicant accordingly and in such a case the absence of an industrial development certificate will not prevent the applicant obtaining compensation under Parts VII and VIII of the Act of 1971 or serving a purchase notice under Part IX (*k*).

Office Buildings

The powers of the Department of Industry in respect of industrial development derive from the Act of 1947. It was not until the passing of the Control of Office and Industrial Development Act 1965, that Whitehall was given similar powers to control office development. These powers, which are now to be found in the Act of 1971, apply to the metropolitan region (*l*) and any other areas to which they may be applied by statutory instrument (*m*). Where these provisions apply, an application for planning permission for the provision of new offices (whether by the erection or extension of buildings or by change of use of existing buildings) must be accompanied by an office development permit from the Department of the Environment (*n*). In issuing a certificate, the Department may impose restrictions similar to these which may be imposed on industrial development certificates (*o*).

Developments not exceeding specified limits of floor space are exempt; the Act of 1971 (re-enacting earlier provisions) specifies a limit of 3,000 square feet, but they may be varied by statutory instrument (*p*).

(*k*) Act of 1971, s. 72. For compensation, see chapters 19 and 20, *post*. For purchase notices, see chapter 11, *post*. Compensation cannot be obtained for a condition imposed in pursuance of the requirements of the industrial development certificate: Act of 1971, s. 147(3).

(*l*) The "metropolitan region" is Greater London together with some neighbouring areas: Act of 1971, s. 85, Sch. 13.

(*m*) Act of 1971, s. 74 (4). (*n*) *Ibid.*, s. 74(1). (*o*) *Ibid.*, s. 77.

(*p*) *Ibid.*, ss. 75, 287. At present the exemption limit is 15,000 square feet. The Control of Office Development (Exemption Limit) Order 1976, S.I. 1976, No. 652.

These provisions as to office buildings were due to expire in 1972, but they have been extended for a further five years (*q*).

Form of Application

The application must be made on a form issued by the local planning authority and must be accompanied by a plan sufficient to identify the land and such other plans and drawings as are necessary to describe the development. The local planning authority may require the applicant to supply such further information as they need for giving a decision (*r*).

In the case of building operations, however, an *outline* application may be submitted with a view to obtaining permission in principle before going to the expense of preparing detailed plans. In this case plans and particulars relating to siting, design, external appearance and means of access need not be submitted, these matters being left for subsequent approval in the event of permission being granted on the outline application.

The local planning authority may decline to entertain an outline application if they consider that the application ought not to be considered separately from siting, design, external appearance and means of access; in this event, the applicant may either furnish particulars of these details or appeal to the Minister as if his application had been refused (*a*). A permission on an outline application is a valid planning permission even though the applicant must obtain further approvals before acting upon it. An outline permission can be revoked only in accordance with the statutory procedures; these normally require the consent of the Minister and the payment of compensation (*b*).

Reference to Applications to the Minister

Normally, the decision on an application for planning permission will be made by the local planning authority. But,

(*q*) Act of 1972, s. 5(1).
(*r*) G.D.O. Art. 5 (1).
(*a*) G.D.O. Art. 5 (2). And see chapter 13, *post*, as to conservation areas.
(*b*) *Hamilton* v. *West Sussex C.C.*, [1958] 2 All E.R. 174.

as mentioned earlier (*c*), the Minister has power under section 35 of the Act of 1971 to "call in" any application for planning permission: that is, to direct that it shall be referred to him for decision. The Minister has, for many years now, directed that all applications for permission for ironstone workings in the Midlands shall be referred to him (*d*); he also gave a similar direction in relation to applications for permission for development within the City of London involving exceptional difficulties (*e*) but this is no longer in force. An application may also be called in because it involves a substantial departure from the development plan, or because of disagreement between the planning and housing authorities over the loss of housing accommodation (*f*).

Where an application is referred to the Minister, the parties have the right to a hearing before an Inspector and this will usually take the form of a public local inquiry (*g*).

Consultations by Local Planning Authority

On receiving an application for planning permission, the local planning authority may have to consult various Government departments and other authorities. Thus, in the case of development affecting trunk roads and certain other major highways (whether existing or proposed) the local planning authority consult the Minister (*h*) who may direct the authority either to refuse permission or to impose conditions. If the proposed development would involve a change from residential to non-residential use, the local planning authority must consult the local housing authority

(*c*) See chapter 3, p. 37, *ante*.

(*d*) The original direction in this behalf is mentioned in "Town and Country Planning 1943–1951" (Cmd. 8204). The latest direction, made in consequence of the recent reorganisation of local government and the changes in county boundaries, was issued in June 1974.

(*e*) S.I. 1948 No. 1460.

(*f*) See below.

(*g*) Act of 1971, s. 35 (5).

(*h*) G.D.O. Art. 11. These provisions apply to (*a*) the formation, laying out or alteration of any means of access to the highway: (*b*) any other development within 67 metres from the middle of the existing or proposed highway.

and, if they do not agree, the application must be referred to the Minister under section 35 (*i*).

Other consultations are prescribed by Article 13 of the General Development Order or by directions made by the Minister under Article 13. Thus, the Minister must be consulted in regard to applications for permission to carry out development of land which is within 800 metres of any royal palace or park and which might affect the amenities of that palace or park, and the Minister would presumably be able to issue a direction to the local planning authority (*k*). In other cases, the local planning authority must consult with some other Government Department or public authority. For instance, the National Coal Board must be consulted in regard to applications for permission to build in coal-mining areas. The Government department or other public authority concerned may make representations to the local planning authority but cannot give directions.

The local planning authority must not grant permission for development involving a substantial departure from the provisions of the development plan without first going through the procedure laid down by the Development Plans Direction, 1975 (*l*).

The procedures laid down in the 1975 Direction give greater freedom to local planning authorities to grant planning permission for development which would conflict with, or which would prejudice the implementation of, the development plan. The procedure varies according to whether the application for planning permission (referred to in the Direction as the "departure application") is a district or a county matter. Where it is a district matter, the district authority must advertise the application in a local newspaper, and a period of not less than 21 days must be allowed for objections. The district authority must consider any objections which are received, and then decide whether to

---

(*i*) The Housing Accommodation Direction, 1952.

(*k*) Power to issue directions restricting grant of planning permission is given to the Minister by G.D.O., Art. 10.

(*l*) The text of the Direction is appended to circular 96/75.

grant planning permission. Except in one case, there is no longer any need, as there was before 1975, for the district authority to notify the Minister. The exception arises where the proposed development is a departure from a provision in a local plan introduced by way of modification by the Minister himself.

Where the application relates to a county matter, the county authority before granting permission must consider whether it would conflict with the structure plan, any provision introduced into a local plan by the Minister, or with a "fundamental provision" of a 1947-type development plan. In that case, if the county authority propose to grant planning permission, they must (in addition to advertising in a local paper and giving opportunity for objections) notify the Minister, who can then decide whether to call in the application.

It seems that the new procedures have been introduced to take account of the new system of structure and local plans, the new system of local government, and a desire on the part of the Minister to be less involved (*m*). Certainly, they give local planning authorities greater freedom than hitherto to grant permission for departures from the development plan. It may be pertinent to ask, however, whether there are sufficient safeguards against the occasional abuse of that freedom, particularly in relation to departures from a local plan.

Consideration by Local Planning Authority

In reaching their decision the local planning authority must, of course, comply with any directions given by the Minister. They must have regard to the views of any Government departments or other public authorities with whom they have been required to consult and to any representations received from interested parties under section 26, 27 or 28 of the Act of 1971 or in pursuance of the Development Plans Direction. In the case of office or industrial development, the local planning authority will have to

---

(*m*) Circular 96/75, para. 1.

take account of any conditions imposed by the Department of Industry, or the Department of the Environment.

The local planning authority must also have regard to the provisions of the development plan and to any other material considerations (*n*). It is an obvious principle that these considerations must be related to the objects of planning legislation. The difficulty is to say precisely what are these objects. In *Stringer* v. *Minister of Housing and Local Government* (*o*). COOKE, J. said that any consideration which related to the use and development of land was capable of being a planning consideration, its materiality depending on the circumstances. Nevertheless, the courts have insisted that there are some limits. It is not a material consideration that planning permission has already been granted for another form of development: a landowner is entitled to make as many applications as his fancy pleases, and the local planning authority must consider each application on its merits (*p*). The question whether the local planning authority should concern themselves with the cost of the proposed development has given rise to a conflict of judicial opinion. In *J. Murphy & Sons, Ltd* v. *Secretary of State for the Environment* (*q*) ACKNER, J. held that the planning authority were not concerned with the cost of developing a site.

Camden London Borough Council proposed to build flats. The site was not ideal because it was bounded on one side by a railway and on another side adjoined Murphy's industrial works. However, the Council considered it could be made suitable although it would be very expensive.

The Minister called in the Council's application for planning permission and held a public inquiry. Murphy's wished to acquire the site to extend their depot and objected that the Council's development would be unduly expensive. The Minister considered that this was irrelevant in deciding whether planning permission should be granted.

(*n*) Act of 1971, s. 29(1). (*o*) [1971] 1 All E.R. 65, at p. 77.
(*p*) *Pilkington* v. *Secretary of State for the Environment*, [1974] 1 All E.R. 283. (*q*) [1973] 2 All E.R. 26.

ACKNER, J. in upholding the Minister said: "The planning authority exercises no paternalistic or avuncular jurisdiction over would-be developers to safeguard them from their financial follies". However in *Sovmots Investments, Ltd.* v. *Secretary of State for the Environment* (*r*), FORBES, J. disagreed, but his remarks were not essential to his decision in that case and were *obiter dicta*.

The local planning authority must, it is submitted, consider each case on its merits. They are entitled to have a general policy with regard to various matters—for example, discouraging building in the green belt—but they must not pursue such policies to the extent of refusing to consider other relevant issues. Thus, in *Stringer* v. *Minister of Housing and Local Government* (*s*), there was an agreement between Cheshire County Council, the rural district council and Manchester University that development in certain areas in the neighbourhood of the Jodrell Bank telescope was to be resisted; the district council, in pursuance of that agreement, refused permission for development of a site in one of those areas. It was held that the agreement was *ultra vires* the planning authority and that there had been no proper determination on the application for planning permission; there would, however, have been no objection to arrangements for consulting the University provided they did not fetter the freedom of the local planning authority to have regard to all material circumstances.

The Local Planning Authority's Decision

The decision of the local planning authority may take one of three forms. They may grant permission unconditionally or they may grant permission subject to such conditions as they think fit or they may refuse permission (*t*). Although the Act of 1971 permits the authority to attach such conditions "as

---

(*r*) [1976] 1 All E.R. 178.
(*s*) [1971] 1 All E.R. 65.
(*t*) Act of 1971, s. 29(1).

they think fit", such conditions must serve some useful purpose having regard to the objects of planning legislation (*u*) and they must not offend against the general law, *e.g.* a condition requiring a payment of money to the planning authority would be invalid (*a*). Within these limits, however, the local planning authority have a very wide discretion (*b*), and in particular they may attach conditions (*c*):

(i) regulating the development or use of any land under the control of the applicant (whether or not it is the land in respect of which the application has been made) provided the condition is reasonably related to the permitted development.

(ii) requiring the permitted works to be removed or the permitted use to be discontinued at the expiry of a specified period, that is, in effect a permission granted for a limited period only.

Sections 41 to 43 of the Act of 1971 (re-enacting provisions first introduced by the Act of 1968) provide that each planning permission shall be subject to a deemed condition that development shall be commenced within five years. These provisions will be considered in more detail in the next chapter (*d*), but it should be noted here that the local planning authority may by express condition fix a period either shorter or longer than five years.

If the local planning authority refuse permission or impose conditions, they must give their reasons in the notice of their decision (*e*). It appears to be the duty of the local planning

(*u*) *Pyx Granite Co., Ltd.* v. *Minister of Housing and Local Government*, [1959] 3 All E R. 1; *Fawcett Properties, Ltd.* v. *Buckingham C.C.*, [1960] 3 All E.R. 503.

(*a*) *A.-G.* v. *Wilts United Dairies* (1922), 91 L.J.K.B. 897.

(*b*) For further discussion on the local planning authority's powers see chapter 7, *post.*

(*c*) Act of 1971, s. 30(1).

(*d*) See p. 166, *post.*

(*e*) G.D.O. Art. 7(4).

authority to give all their reasons and not merely some of them (*f*). But a developer is not entitled to claim that a condition is void merely because the local planning authority omitted to state any reason (*g*).

Time for Giving Decision

Article 7(3) of the General Development Order provides that the local planning authority shall notify the applicant of their decision within two months, unless the applicant agrees in writing to an extension of time (*h*). If the authority do not give their decision within the proper time, the applicant can appeal to the Minister as if permission had been refused (*i*). Appeals are dealt with later in this chapter.

What happens if the local planning authority issue a decision out of time? The point first came up for consideration in *Edwick* v. *Sunbury-on-Thames U.D.C.* (*k*).

> The council served an enforcement notice on *E* requiring him to discontinue the unauthorised use of land for the display and sale of second-hand cars. Before the notice took effect, *E* applied for planning permission and (under the law as it then was) this had the effect of suspending the operation of the enforcement notice pending a decision on the application. More than two years later, the council notified *E* that permission was refused. If this decision were valid, the enforcement notice would have come into effect, but SALMON, J. held that the statutory direction as to the time within which the local authority should give their decision was mandatory and accordingly the notice of decision was invalid.

The law relating to enforcement notices has now been changed, and the circumstances of the *Edwick* case cannot recur in respect of enforcement notices served after 29th August, 1960, but

(*f*) *Hamilton* v. *West Sussex C.C.*, [1958] 2 All E.R. 174.
(*g*) *Brayhead (Ascot), Ltd.* v. *Berkshire C.C.*, [1964] 1 All E.R. 149.
(*h*) G.D.O., Art. 7(3). The special period of 3 months in respect of applications for development affecting trunk roads has been abolished.
(*i*) Act of 1971, s. 37.
(*k*) [1961] 3 All E.R. 10.

SALMON, J.'s reasoning would apply to any decision of a local authority on an application for planning permission. This was not likely to be of any practical consequence where the decision is in the form of a refusal, but might have serious consequences where the decision purports to grant permission.

However, in *James* v. *Minister of Housing and Local Government* (*l*) the Court of Appeal disapproved of the decision in *Edwick's* case and held that article 5(8) of the General Development Order was not mandatory but directory. LORD DENNING, M.R. said that a grant or refusal of permission out of time is "not void, but at most voidable"; by that his Lordship meant that a decision out of time would not be automatically void, but that some interested party would have the right in certain circumstances to treat it as void. In the House of Lords (*m*), the decision of the Court of Appeal was in part overruled, but three of their Lordships disapproved of *Edwick* and the others did not discuss the point; no reference was made to the suggestion that a grant or refusal of permission out of time might be treated as voidable (*n*).

It is clear therefore that a grant or refusal of permission out of time is not void, but the question whether it is voidable has not yet been finally resolved. Even if such a decision is voidable, the opportunities for avoiding it will be limited; for, as LORD DENNING explained, it will be too late to avoid a grant of permission once it has been accepted and acted upon, or if an appeal is lodged against any conditions attached to the permission (*o*). The question might, however, arise in disputes between vendor and purchaser or the assessment of compensation for compulsory purchase.

It is submitted, however, (i) that there is no logical reason for

---

(*l*) [1965] 3 All E.R. 602.

(*m*) *Sub nom. James* v. *Secretary of State for Wales*, [1966] 3 All E.R. 964.

(*n*) In *London Ballast Co., Ltd.* v. *Buckinghamshire C.C.* (1966), 111 Sol. Jo. 36 MEGAW, J. said that a grant or refusal of permission out of time might be voidable: all the circumstances must be looked at.

(*o*) [1965] 3 All E.R. 602, at p. 606.

treating a planning permission as voidable merely because the local planning authority have not complied with the provisions of article 7(4) as to the time within which they should give notice of their decision; (ii) that the purpose of article 7(4) is to fix a period after which in the absence of a decision the applicant can appeal to the Minister. It was also suggested in earlier editions of this book that a grant of planning permission is effective as soon as the local planning authoity make their decision and that the notice required by article 7(4) is merely the documentary evidence. The Divisional Court has held, however, that there is no planning permission until written notice has been given to the applicant (*p*).

Appeals to the Minister

If the applicant is aggrieved by the decision of the local planning authority, or by their failure to give a decision within the proper time, he may appeal to the Minister (*q*). No one else has the right to appeal. Unless the Minister agrees to an extension of time, the applicant should give notice of appeal to the Ministry within six calendar months of receiving the local planning authority's decision or (where the appeal is against their failure to give a decision) within six months of the date by which they should have done so (*r*). The appellant must notify the persons mentioned in section 27 (1) of the Act of 1971 as amended by the Act of 1975 (*s*).

The normal method of hearing an appeal is by means of a public local inquiry at which the appellant, the local authority and members of the public can be heard; a private hearing (at which only the appellant and the local authority would be heard)

(*p*) *R.* v. *Yeovil B.C., Ex parte Trustees of Elim Pentecostal Church. Yeovil.* (1971), 23 P. & C.R. 39.

(*q*) Act of 1971, s. 36(1).

(*r*) G.D.O. Art. 16(1).

(*s*) Act of 1971, s. 36(5). This applies the same procedure as in applications at first instance to the local planning authority. See this chapter, p. 126, *ante*.

may be held where there are special reasons. If the parties agree, an appeal may be dealt with purely by written representations.

Where there is to be an inquiry, the local planning authority must give the appellant a full statement of their case not later than twenty-eight days before the date of the hearing (*t*).

Until recently the Inspector never gave a decision but reported to the Minister whose decision was made known in due course. However, in 1968 Parliament empowered the Minister to make regulations authorising the Inspector to give a decision in certain types of case (*u*). The first regulations (*a*) authorised the Inspector to give the decision in five classes of appeals, but this list has now been extended. The current regulations (*b*) apply to the following appeals:

Appeals relating to development by operations.—

1. The erection, or the enlargement or other alteration, of a building or buildings for use as not more than 60 dwelling-houses.

2. Development for residential purposes of not more than two hectares (4.94 acres) where the application does not specify the number of houses.

3. The erection, or the enlargement or other alteration, of buildings for use for any purpose other than residential purposes or an excepted purpose (*c*), provided the total floor space to be created does not exceed 500 square metres and the area of land does not exceed 8,000 square metres.

4. Construction or widening of means of access.

5. Operations incidental to existing or proposed development of any kind specified in the foregoing or following classes.

(*t*) Inquiries Procedure Rules 1974, rule 6.

(*u*) Act of 1968, s. 21.

(*a*) Town and Country Planning (Determination of Appeals by Appointed Persons) (Prescribed Classes) Regs. 1968, S.I. 1968, No. 1972.

(*b*) Town and Country Planning (Determination of Appeals by Appointed Persons) (Prescribed Classes) Regs. 1972, S.I. 1972, No. 1652, Sch. 1.

(*c*) "Excepted purpose" appears to mean the classes of case excepted from the regulations as described below.

Appeals relating to change of use.—

6. Change of use of a building or buildings to not more than 60 dwellinghouses.

7. Change in the use of a building or buildings for use for or in connection with any purposes (other than residential purposes or an excepted purpose (*c*)), provided the floor space used for such purpose does not exceed 500 square metres and the area of the land does not exceed 8,000 square metres.

8. Change in the use of land to any purpose (other than excepted purpose (*c*)) provided that the area of land involved does not exceed 4,000 square metres.

There are some exceptions; for instance, the Inspector cannot decide the appeal if the development is to be carried out by a local authority or if the development affects a trunk road and the Minister has given a direction (*d*). In any event, the Minister may reserve the decision in any particular case to himself (*e*).

In every other appeal, the previous practice still applies; that is, the Inspector reports to the Minister and his decision is made known in due course by letter. Upon receipt of the Minister's decision the appellant may ask to see the Inspector's report but not before (*f*).

The Minister is empowered to deal with the appeal as if it had to come to him in the first instance (*g*). Amongst other things, this means that in the case of an appeal against a condition attached to a planning permission the Minister can attach other conditions or even refuse permission altogether.

The Minister's decision is final (*h*), except for the possibility of

---

(*d*) *Ibid.*, Sch. 2. And see page 131, *ante*.

(*e*) Act of 1971, Sch. 9, para. 3.

(*f*) Although there was no right in law at that time to see the Inspector's report, the Report of the Franks Committee in 1957 inspired the Minister to agree as a matter of practice to allow appellants to see the Inspector's report *after* his decision was made known. The matter has now been put upon a statutory basis. See the Inquiries Procedure Rules, rule 13.

(*g*) Act of 1971, s. 36(3). In this and the following chapter references to the Minister's decision should be taken as including a decision given by the Inspector. (*h*) *Ibid.*, s. 36 (6).

challenge under section 245 of the Act of 1971. Section 245 enables an application to be made to the High Court on the ground either that the Minister's decision was outside the powers conferred by the Planning Acts or that some procedural requirement of these Acts had not been complied with. It should be possible therefore to question the Minister's decision on the ground that he had taken into account considerations not relevant to planning, that he had imposed or upheld an improper condition or that there was some breach of the rules of natural justice in the handling of the appeal. It seems, however that the right of challenge under section 245 does not apply to decisions of the Minister arising out of an application for the approval of details reserved by an outline permission (*i*).

The application to the High Court may be made by any person aggrieved by the decision or by the local planning authority. "Any person aggrieved" does not mean any member of the public who is annoyed by the Minister's decision, but someone who has suffered some prejudice to his own interests. In *Buxton* v. *Minister of Housing and Local Government* (*k*), SALMON, J. considered that the right to apply to the High Court under section 245 as "a person aggrieved" was limited to the person who appealed to the Minister against the decision of the local planning authority and to any other person with a legal or equitable interest in the land.

> A company had appealed to the Minister against a refusal of planning permission to work a chalk pit. A public local inquiry was held, and four adjoining landowners objected on the ground that the proposed working would cause serious damage to their property. The Inspector accepted the evidence on this point and recommended that the appeal be dismissed. The Minister rejected the Inspector's finding and allowed the appeal.
>
> The four landowners then applied to the High Court under section 31 of the 1959 Act, now section 245 of the Act of 1971.

(*i*) *Turner* v. *Secretary of State for the Environment* (1973), 28 P. & C.R. 123.

(*k*) [1960] 3 All E.R. 408.

HELD: "a person aggrieved" meant a person who had suffered a *legal* grievance, in the sense that he had suffered an injury to some legal right possessed by him; although, in ordinary parlance, the applicants were aggrieved by the Minister's decision, they had not suffered any injury to any legal right and accordingly were not "persons aggrieved".

It seems, however, in the light of later decisions that this is an unduly restrictive interpretation of the words "a person aggrieved". In *A.-G. of the Gambia* v. *N'Jie* (*l*), the Privy Council were concerned with the meaning of these words in an ordinance of the Supreme Court of the Gambia concerning complaints of professional misconduct against members of the Bar. LORD DENNING said:

"The words 'a person aggrieved' . . . do not concern a mere busybody who is interfering in things which do not concern him; but they do include a person who has a genuine grievance because an order has been made which prejudicially affects his interests".

Then in *Maurice* v. *London County Council* (*m*)—a case under the London Building Acts—LORD DENNING referred expressly to SALMON, J's decision in *Buxton* v. *Minister of Housing and Local Government* (*n*) and said: "That narrow view should now be rejected". These remarks of LORD DENNING were *obiter*, but they were followed by ACKNER, J. in the recent case of *Turner* v. *Secretary of State for the Environment* (*o*); in that case both sides accepted that section 27 parties would be "persons aggrieved" for the purposes of section 245, and his Lordship held that persons who had attended the inquiry and made representations by permission of the Inspector were also included. It remains to be seen whether the courts will be prepared to extend the categories of "aggrieved persons" beyond the two classes referred to in *Turner's* case.

(*l*) [1961] 2 All E.R. 504.
(*m*) [1964] 1 All E.R. 779.
(*n*) *Supra*.
(*o*) (1973), 28 P. & C.R. 123.

High Court proceedings under section 245 must be commenced within six weeks of the Minister's decision; thereafter, the decision may not be questioned in any legal proceedings whatsoever.

Planning Inquiry Commissions

The usual type of public local inquiry has not always proved to be the best way of dealing with the issues arising out of the siting of some large development of a national or regional character such as a nuclear power station or an airport. The controversy over Stansted airport is the best known example but there have been others. The matter may come before a public local inquiry in a number of ways; if the development is to be carried out by a government department, there may be a development plan amendment with related compulsory purchase orders, as in the case of the new medical school and hospital at Nottingham (*p*); in other cases there may be an application for planning permission which has been either called in by the Minister or has come to him on appeal. In each case, however, the inquiry is into the merits of a particular site; it is open to objectors to suggest alternative sites but the Inspector cannot go very far in considering whether another specific site would be better because the owners of that site are not before the inquiry and it may be in the area of another planning authority.

Another disadvantage of the usual type of public local inquiry is that the proposed development may raise questions of a scientific or technical character of an unusual kind, and a commission might be better equipped than a single Inspector to deal with these.

The Act of 1971 (re-enacting provisions originally contained in the Act of 1968) attempts to deal with these problems by providing for planning inquiry commissions. Provided there are issues of special national or regional importance or questions of an

---

(*p*) This case came before the High Court in *W. J. Simms, Sons & Cooke, Ltd.* v. *Minister of Housing and Local Government* (1969), 210 Estates, Gazette 705.

unusual scientific or technical character, the responsible Minister may set up such a commission to inquire into and report upon any application for planning permission which has been called in by the Minister or is before him on appeal; any proposal that a government department should direct that permissions should be deemed to be granted for development by a local authority or statutory undertakers; any proposal that development should be carried out by or on behalf of a government department (*q*).

The Commission will carry out its work in two stages. First, it is to investigate the issues involved (*r*). It seems that at this stage it will work on the lines of a Royal Commission by taking written and oral evidence but without affording opportunities for cross-examination (*s*); the Commission may also at this stage arrange for the carrying out of research at the expense of the Minister (*t*). It also seems that the Commission might at this stage suggest alternative sites. The second stage in the procedure is the holding of a public local inquiry on the usual lines (*u*).

The Commission's function is to report to the responsible Minister; the last word rests with him (*a*).

(*q*) Act of 1971, s. 48(1), (2).
(*r*) Act of 1971, s. 48(6) (*a*).
(*s*) House of Commons Official Report, Standing Committee G.
(*t*) Act of 1971, s. 48 (7).
(*u*) *Ibid*., s. 48(6) (b).
(*a*) *Ibid*., s. 48(6), (c).

CHAPTER 7

PLANNING PERMISSION: FURTHER CONSIDERATIONS

EFFECT OF PERMISSION

A grant of planning permission, unless it provides to the contrary, enures for the benefit of the land and of all persons interested in it (*a*). It is thus possible to grant permission for the sole benefit of a particular individual, but in general this is not favoured by the Minister. "The use of such a permission should not be contemplated unless it is quite clear, first that the reason for imposing the condition is a planning reason, and second, that there is no other means by which the desired result can be achieved—where it is desired to avoid the perpetuation of a use allowed on hardship grounds, the better course may be to grant permission for a limited period only" (*b*).

The Minister's policy may be illustrated by a number of cases:

> *M* was the occupier of two buildings *A* and *B*. In building *A* he carried on the business of general motor repairs and maintenance including the specialised work of tuning sports cars and racing engines. Building *B* was used for storage. *M* wished to switch the uses of the two buildings, but the local planning authority refused permission. The Minister considered that the authority were justified in resisting any extension of industrial accommodation in the area concerned, but pointed out that *M* did not intend to extend the volume of his business. He allowed the appeal and granted permission for the use of *B* for repair and maintenance of vehicles subject to conditions (1) that during the currency of the permission building *A* should be used only for storage: (2) that the permission should enure only for so

(*a*) Act of 1971, s. 33(1).
(*b*) Circular 58/51.

long as *M* remained in occupation of building *A*; (3) that on the termination of his occupancy of *A*, the use of *B* for repair and maintenance should cease, and the Minister granted permission for the industrial use of *A* to be renewed (*c*).

In another case the owner of a smallholding applied for permission for a caravan required to accommodate *B* whose help was wanted in the running of the smallholding. The Minister was satisfied that it would take some time to bring the land into production and that there were exceptional difficulties in connection with *B* reaching the smallholding. He accordingly allowed the appeal to the extent of granting permission for a caravan for Mr. and Mrs. B for a period of five years (*d*).

But where a student at a theological college had taken part-time charge of a nonconformist church for the duration of his studies and needed a site for a caravan, the Minister on appeal granted permission for a caravan in the church grounds for a temporary period; it was evidently not considered necessary to make the permission a personal one (*e*).

A planning permission obtained by a planning authority for their own development under the new procedures introduced in 1976 are personal to that authority and do not ensure for the benefit of the land (*f*).

A grant of permission is effective only for the purposes of the Town and Country Planning Acts. It does not relieve the developer of the necessity of complying with other legislation affecting the use and development of land such as the byelaws governing the construction of buildings and streets. Nor does it override restrictions imposed on the land under the general law such as easements or restrictive covenants; although there is machinery for securing the removal or modification of restrictive covenants, the fact that planning permission has been granted

(*c*) [1960], J.P.L. 436.
(*d*) Ministry ref. 2381/40620/122.
(*e*) Ministry ref. 781/40620/29.
(*f*) General Regulations, reg. 4 (7). See further chapter 14, p. 251, *post*.

is normally no ground on which a restrictive covenant can be revoked or modified (*g*).

The grant of a planning permission does not revoke any previous planning permissions which have not been acted upon. Where there are two or more outstanding planning permissions the developer may be able to choose which he will act upon; indeed, in some circumstances, he may be able to rely on one permission as regards one part of the land and on another permission as regards the other part of the land. These points are illustrated by *F. Lucas & Sons, Ltd.* v. *Dorking and Horley R.D.C.* (*h*).

> In 1952 the plaintiffs were granted permission to develop a plot of land by the erection of twenty-eight houses in a cul-de-sac layout; the layout showed fourteen houses on the north side and fourteen houses on the south side of the cul-de-sac. In 1957 the plaintiffs obtained permission to develop the same land by building six detached houses each on a plot fronting the main road; the plaintiffs built two houses in accordance with this permission. They then proposed to proceed with the building of the cul-de-sac and the fourteen houses on the southern side thereof, relying upon the 1952 permission. The council contended that the 1952 permission was no longer valid or effective. The plaintiffs sought a declaration that it was effective and entitled them to carry out all or any of the building or other operations to which it related.
>
> Granting the declaration, WINN, J. said that the 1952 permission was not conditional upon the developer completing the whole of the approved development; it was a permission for any of the development comprised therein.

The learned judge pointed out that section 12 of the Act of 1962 (now section 22 of the Act of 1971) forbids development without planning permission, so it is more natural and more likely to have been the intention to look at any particular development

(*g*) The principal method of obtaining the removal of a restrictive covenant is by application to the Lands Tribunal under the Law of Property Act, 1925, s. 84. Less well known is the power of the county court under the Housing Act, 1957, s. 165, to vary restrictive covenants affecting the conversion of a house into flats; in this case the fact that planning permission has been granted appears to be relevant.

(*h*) (1964), 17 P. & C.R. 111.

to see whether or not it is unpermitted than to look at the contemplated project for the achievement of which the planning authority has granted a planning permission. The practical wisdom of this approach may be seen by the following test:

> "Were it right to say that the grantee of such a planning permission as this 1952 planning permission was only enabled thereby to develop the area of land conditional upon his completing the whole contemplated development, it would be very difficult at any given moment to say whether (assuming that some houses had been built but that not all the sites included in the scheme had been filled) the development already achieved was permitted development or development without permission" (*i*).

In some circumstances, however, the developer may not be able to choose between two planning permissions. In *Slough Estates, Ltd.* v. *Slough B.C.* (*j*) the Court of Appeal held the appellants had abandoned an earlier permission. In any event, the local planning authority can avoid these difficulties, without liability to compensation, by attaching a condition that the later permission is not to be exercised in addition to or in combination with the earlier permission (*k*).

VALIDITY OF CONDITIONS

As already explained (*l*) the power to impose conditions on a grant of planning permission is not unlimited.

The provision in the 1971 Act that the planning authority may impose such conditions "as they think fit" must be read subject to the requirements of the general law. Of these perhaps the most important is the long established rule that statutory powers must be exercised only for the purpose of the statute concerned.

Thus in *Pilling* v. *Abergele U.D.C.* (*m*) the local authority refused a licence for a caravan site under section 269 of the Public Health Act, 1936, on the ground that the caravans would be

---

(*i*) (1964), 17 P. & C.R. 111, at p. 117.
(*j*) [1969] 2 All E.R. 988.
(*k*) *F. Lucas & Sons, Ltd. v. Dorking and Horley R.D.C.* (*ante*).
(*l*) See chapter 6, pp. 135–136, *ante*.
(*m*) [1950] 1 All E.R. 76.

detrimental to the amenities of the locality; it was held that section 269 was concerned with sanitary matters, and that the authority were not entitled to consider questions of amenity.

This principle was specifically considered in relation to planning control in *Pyx Granite Co., Ltd.* v. *Minister of Housing and Local Government* (*n*) and subsequently in *Fawcett Properties, Ltd.* v. *Buckingham C.C.* (*o*).

The latter case provided the House of Lords with the opportunity of considering a number of points relating to the validity of conditions. As a result the following principles appear to have been established—

(1) A condition must "fairly and reasonably relate to the permitted development". That is, it must serve some useful planning purpose.
(2) A condition must not be wholly unreasonable.
(3) A condition may be imposed restricting the user of premises according to the personal circumstances of the occupier.
(4) A condition will be declared invalid on the ground that its meaning is uncertain.

These points will now be considered in turn.

Conditions must Serve some Useful Planning Purpose

In *Pyx Granite Co., Ltd.* v. *Minister of Housing and Local Government* (*p*) the Minister had refused permission for quarrying on certain land belonging to the company and had granted permission on certain other land subject to conditions. The company contended (i) that by reason of certain special circumstances planning permission was not required (ii) that the conditions imposed by the Minister were invalid.

LORD DENNING said that the court would quash a condition if it did not "fairly and reasonably relate to the permitted develop-

---

(*n*) [1958] 1 All E.R. 625; reversed in part, [1959] 3 All E.R. 1.
(*o*) [1960] 3 All E.R. 503.
(*p*) See note (*n*), *supra*.

ment", but in the present case the conditions did fairly and reasonably relate to the proposed quarrying operations. The company appealed to the House of Lords who reversed the decision of the Court of Appeal on point (i). In the circumstances it was not necessary for their Lordships to consider point (ii).

In *Fawcett Properties, Ltd.* v. *Buckingham C.C.* (*q*) the county council had granted planning permission for two cottages in the green belt subject to the condition that "the occupation of the houses shall be limited to persons whose employment or latest employment is or was employment in agriculture as defined by section 119 (1) of the Town and Country Planning Act, 1947 (replaced by section 290 of the 1971 Act), or in forestry, or in an industry mainly dependent upon agriculture and including also the dependents of such persons as aforesaid".

The company contended that this condition was invalid on the grounds *inter alia* that its effect was so wide that it did not fairly and reasonably relate to the permitted development. ROXBURGH, J. declared the condition invalid but was overruled in the Court of Appeal. The case then went to the House of Lords which held that a condition must fairly and reasonably relate to the permitted development, but the present condition satisfied the test, because it served some useful planning purpose—namely, in this case, the protection of the green belt.

A Condition must not be Wholly Unreasonable

Even if conditions serve some useful planning purpose they may be quashed if they are unreasonable. But it is the well settled policy of the courts to interfere only if the condition is wholly unreasonable; that is, such as could find no justification in the minds of reasonable men (*r*). Or, as it was put in another case (*s*),

---

(*q*) [1960] 3 All E.R. 503.
(*r*) *Kruse* v. *Johnson*, [1898] 2 Q.B. 91, at p. 99.
(*s*) *Associated Provincial Picture Houses, Ltd.* v. *Wednesbury Corpn.*, [1947] 2 All E.R. 680, at p. 684.

> "the task of the court is not to decide what it thinks is reasonable but to decide whether the condition imposed by the local authority is one which no reasonable authority acting within the four corners of their jurisdiction could have decided to impose".

It is impossible to give an exhaustive catalogue of what might be considered unreasonable in this sense. But it is clear that it is wholly unreasonable for a local planning authority to impose a condition which requires a developer to take on part of the authority's duties under other legislation. Two cases illustrate this point.

The first of these cases was *Hall & Co., Ltd.* v. *Shoreham-on-Sea U.D.C.* (*t*). The company applied for planning permission to develop some land for industrial purposes. The land adjoined a busy main road, and in granting permission the council imposed a condition requiring the company to construct an ancillary road over their own land along the entire frontage and to give rights of passage over it to and from the adjoining land on either side. The Court of Appeal considered that the condition was unreasonable because it required the company to construct a road and virtually to dedicate it to the public without paying any compensation; "a more regular course" was open to the council under the Highways Act, 1959, that is the council should acquire the land paying proper compensation and then construct the road at public expense.

In *R.* v. *Hillingdon London Borough Council, Ex parte Royco Homes, Ltd.* (*u*) Royco applied for planning permission to develop land for residential purposes. The Council granted permission but imposed conditions, among others, that the houses when erected should be occupied at first by persons on the council's housing waiting list, and should for ten years be occupied by persons enjoying the protection of the Rent Act 1968. The Divisional Court held that these conditions were unreasonable

(*t*) [1964] 1 All E.R. 1.
(*u*) [1974] 2 All E.R. 643.

since they were the equivalent of requiring Royco to take on at their own expense a significant part of the duty of the council as housing authority.

There are grounds for thinking that a condition may be unreasonable if it enables a third party to frustrate the planning permission. In *Kingsway Investments (Kent), Ltd.* v. *Kent C.C.* (*v*) the defendants had granted outline permission subject to the conditions (i) that detailed plans should be submitted to and approved by them before any work was begun; and (ii) that the permission should cease to have effect after three years unless within that time such approval had been notified. The plaintiffs submitted detailed plans, but they were not approved, and the three years ran out. The Court of Appeal, by a majority, held that the second condition was void. DAVIES, L.J., pointed out that the permission might lapse without any default on the part of the plaintiffs; ". . . . the defendants are taking away with one hand that which they have purported to grant with the other and are thus evading the revocation procedure." This, therefore, lends some support to the view that a condition is unreasonable if it puts certain matters out of the control of the developer, but it may be that in the final analysis the learned Lord Justice was basing himself on the point about the revocation procedure. WINN, L.J., held the condition to be invalid on different grounds, but made this significant remark:

> "Nonetheless the characteristic of deprivation of ability to secure by his own efforts full enjoyment of the fruits of the permission granted to him is an important feature of the condition challenged."

The House of Lords—again by a majority—found a somewhat ingenious method of holding the condition valid thereby reversing the decision of the Court of Appeal (*w*). It is submitted, however, that the reasons adduced were entirely consistent with the views quoted above.

(*v*) [1969] 1 All E.R. 601.
(*w*) [1970] 1 All E.R. 70. And see pp. 164, 165, *post*.

There is also the question whether the local planning authority can impose conditions which deprive a landowner of existing use rights. Of course, there will be many cases in which the proposed development cannot be carried out without destroying existing use rights. The problem arises where the local planning authority seek to impose conditions restricting existing use rights which are not necessarily incompatible with the proposed development. The point is illustrated by *Allnatt London Properties, Ltd.* v. *Middlesex C.C.* (*x*). The plaintiffs had applied for planning permission to build an extension to an existing factory. Permission was granted subject, *inter alia*, to two conditions: (i) that the extension should be used only in conjunction with the main building as one industrial unit; (ii) that until 1971 the site should be used only by a person or firm occupying at the date of the permission a light or general industrial building in the county. The combined effect of the conditions was to deprive the plaintiffs of their existing use rights in the main building in that they would not be able to sell it to anyone not complying with condition (ii). GLYN-JONES, J. held that these conditions were void as being unreasonable.

This was followed by the decision of the House of Lords in *Minister of Housing and Local Government* v. *Hartnell* (*y*).

H. had owned a field of 4.7 acres; for several years he had stationed a number of residential caravans on part of this field comprising about three-quarters of an acre. In 1959 there were six caravans. When Part I of the Caravan Sites and Control of Development Act, 1960, came into force he applied for a site licence to station 94 caravans on the whole field. As there was no planning permission in force, the application was treated by virtue of the Act as an application for planning permission. The local planning authority granted permission subject to a condition that not more than six caravans should be stationed on the land at any time. H. appealed and the Inspector reported that

---

(*x*) (1964), 15 P. & C.R. 288.
(*y*) [1965] 1 All E.R. 490.

it had not been established that there were existing use rights for more than six caravans; the Minister dismissed the appeal.

HELD: (1) H. had existing use rights in respect of the smaller area of three-quarters of an acre and these were not limited to six caravans; he was entitled under his existing use rights to bring on to this part of the field such number of caravans as would not amount to making a material change of use. (2) The local planning authority was not entitled to impose conditions depriving H. of these existing use rights.

The Minister had argued that, while the planning authority were not entitled to take away the whole of the owner's existing rights, they were entitled by virtue of the Act of 1960 in relation to caravans to take away without compensation anything short of the whole value by imposing conditions. The House of Lords said that a statute should not be held to take away private rights of property without compensation unless the intention to do so is expressed in clear and unambiguous terms.

On the basis of these authorities it seemed reasonable in earlier editions of this book to suggest that a local planning authority should not attempt to restrict existing use rights by attaching conditions to a grant of planning permission; the more regular course would be for the authority to make an order under section 51 of the Act of 1971, paying compensation accordingly.

However, it now appears that this proposition may not be correct. In the recent case of *Kingston-upon-Thames Royal London B.C.* v. *Secretary of State for the Environment* (z) Lord WIDGERY, C.J. said that there is no principle of planning law which requires a local planning authority to refrain from imposing conditions abrogating existing use rights.

The British Railways Board applied for planning permission for the reconstruction of a railway station. Permission was granted subject to the condition that a certain piece of land should be made available at all times for car parking and should be used "for no other purpose".

A main electric traction cable ran across this piece of land.

(z) [1974] 1 All E.R. 193.

When the Board failed to remove the cable, the Council served an enforcement notice. On appeal the Minister quashed the notice; the condition was *ultra vires* in that it prevented the lawful use of land without compensation.

HELD: the Minister had erred in law, and the case should be remitted to him for further consideration of the merits of the condition.

This decision might appear to be quite contrary to the decision of the House of Lords in *Hartnell* v. *Minister of Housing and Local Government* (*a*), but the Divisional Court considered that that case had been decided on special facts.

As mentioned above, however, the courts will interfere only if the condition is wholly unreasonable. For instance, the courts will not consider whether a condition is unduly burdensome or whether a different condition might not have been reasonable in the circumstances. It might well be asked why the courts should not quash a condition if it is unreasonable in this more general sense. The courts will consider the question of reasonableness or the merits of some action where a statute specifically requires a public authority to act reasonably or where a statute provides a right of appeal to the courts against the decision of a local authority (*b*). But where (as in the case of the Planning Act and many other statutes) there is no specific mention of reasonableness, it is the general policy of the courts not to intervene. Thus, in *Associated Provincial Picture Houses, Ltd.* v. *Wednesbury Corpn.* (*c*), the proprietors of a cinema had applied to the local authority under the Sunday Entertainments Act, 1932, for a licence to open on Sundays. The licence was granted subject to a condition that children under 15 should not be admitted whether accompanied by an adult or not. The plaintiffs sought a declaration

---

(*a*) *Supra.*

(*b*) For example, appeals against certain decisions made under the Public Health Acts go to the magistrates: appeals against repair notices and demolition orders under the Housing Act, 1957, go to the County Court.

(*c*) [1947] 2 All E.R. 680.

that the condition was invalid. The Court of Appeal held that it was lawful for the Corporation to take into consideration matters affecting the well-being and the physical and mental health of children. That, said the court, ended the matter:

> "once that is granted, counsel must go so far as to say that the decision of the authority is wrong because it is unreasonable, and then he is really saying that the ultimate arbiter of what is and is not reasonable is the court and not the local authority. It is just there, it seems to me, that the whole argument entirely breaks down. It is perfectly clear that the local authority are entrusted by Parliament with the decision on a matter in which the knowledge and experience of the authority can best be trusted to be of value" (*d*).

The courts have adopted a similar policy in relation to byelaws made by local authorities. Although it is said that the validity of a byelaw may be questioned on the grounds of unreasonableness, it is clear that a byelaw will only be held to be unreasonable if it is manifestly unjust or oppressive (*e*) or if its application in a particular case would serve no useful purpose (*f*). Byelaws made by local authorities being bodies of a public representative character entrusted by Parliament with delegated authority should be supported if possible (*g*).

The idea that the local authority are likely to be the best judges of what is reasonable has been expressed in a number of cases. It is not, however, the invariable policy of the courts to trust the local authority. For instance, the court will consider whether local authority expenditure is reasonable—even where statute empowers authorities to pay such wages as "they think fit" (*h*)—apparently on the ground that local authorities have a fiduciary responsibility to their ratepayers.

(*d*) *Per* LORD GREENE, M.R., at p. 683.
(*e*) *Kruse* v. *Johnson*, [1898] 2 Q.B. 91.
(*f*) See for instance *Repton School Governors* v. *Repton R.D.C.*, [1918] 2 K.B. 133; and *A.-G.* v. *Denby*, [1925] Ch. 596—both cases concerning the application of building byelaws as to space about buildings.
(*g*) *Kruse* v. *Johnson*, *ante*.
(*h*) *Roberts* v. *Hopwood*, [1925] A.C. 578.

Finally, it may be noted that the courts are no more likely to question the reasonableness of a condition imposed by the Minister on a grant of a planning permission. Indeed, in *Sparks* v. *Edward Ash, Ltd.* (*i*)—a case in which it was contended that certain traffic regulations were unreasonable—the Court of Appeal said that "If it is the duty of the courts to recognise and trust the discretion of local authorities, much more must it be so in the case of a Minister directly responsible to Parliament . . . ."

Conditions Restricting use of Premises according to Personal Circumstances of Occupier

An example is the condition imposed in *Fawcett Properties, Ltd.* v. *Buckingham C.C.* (*k*) restricting the use of the cottages to agricultural occupants. The validity of such conditions was expressly upheld in that case.

It should be noticed that there is a difference in principle between a condition of this type and a personal planning permission. In the one case the permission runs with the land, although subject to a condition as to the persons who may occupy it; in the other, the permission itself is personal and does not run with the land.

Conditions may be Void for Uncertainty

If the language of a condition is so obscure that its effect is uncertain, the court may declare it to be void. Thus in *Fawcett Properties, Ltd.* v. *Buckingham C.C.* (*l*) LORD MORTON of Henryton considered that the condition was so obscurely worded as to be void; the other members of the House were critical of the wording but were prepared to uphold it. It seems that in borderline cases the benefit of the doubt will be given to the planning authority (*m*).

(*i*) [1943] 1 All E.R. 1.
(*k*) See p. 151, *ante*.
(*l*) See p. 151, *ante*.
(*m*) *Crisp from the Fens, Ltd.* v. *Rutland C.C.* (1950), 48 L.G.R. 210.

Special Types of Condition

Conditions Restricting use of Buildings

Section 33 (2) of the Act of 1971 provides that the grant of permission for the erection of a building may specify the purposes for which the building may be used; and if no purpose is specified, the permission is to be construed as including permission to use the building for the purpose for which it is designed.

The effect of this may be considered by reference to industrial buildings. In many cases, it will be appropriate to impose a condition restricting the use of the building to light industry and for this purpose the condition will probably refer to class III of the Use Classes Order. Such a condition is clearly authorised by section 33(2). What is less clear is whether a condition may be imposed limiting the use of the building to one particular manufacture—*e.g.* light engineering—so as to preclude the right to change to any other light industry within class III. The difficulty about such a condition is that it attempts to prevent something which by the terms of the Act of 1971 is not development at all, and it has been argued that planning control cannot restrict matters which do not involve development. On the other hand, it seems reasonable that in permitting development the planning authority should be enabled to impose this type of condition provided it serves some useful planning purpose. The language of section 29(1)—the local planning authority may impose "such conditions as they think fit"—as well as of section 33(2) would appear to support this view. This view of the matter has now been upheld in the recent case of *City of London Corpn.* v. *Secretary of State for the Environment* (*n*). Where such a condition is imposed, application can always be made for permission for the retention of the building or the continuance of the use without complying with the condition (*o*).

(*n*) (1971), 23 P. & C.R. 169.
(*o*) Act of 1971, s. 32(1) (b).

Conditions restricting Permitted Development

A somewhat similar problem arises in connection with conditions restricting the right to carry out development permitted by the General Development Order, 1973. For instance, a planning authority might wish when granting permission for building a new house to impose a condition excluding the right to extend it under class I of the Order. Or, on a grant of permission for mineral working, the authority might wish to impose conditions as to the siting of plant and machinery required for the treatment of the excavated mineral, thus restricting the mineral operator's rights under class XVIII.

Such conditions appear to be authorised by article 3(2) of the General Development Order, 1963, which provides that "nothing in the Article or the First Schedule to this Order shall operate so as to permit any development contrary to a condition imposed in any permission granted or deemed to be granted otherwise than by this Order". Some doubt, however, has been cast as to the meaning of this by LORD PARKER, C.J. in *East Barnet U.D.C.* v. *British Transport Commission* (*p*). In this case, as we have seen (*q*), the Divisional Court upheld a decision of the magistrates that the change of use from a coal stacking yard to a transit depot for crated vehicles did not in the circumstances constitute development. It was also held, that, even if the change did amount to development, the permission of the planning authority was unnecessary because the land was operational land of the British Transport Commission and its use was permitted by class XVIII of the General Development Order, 1950 (replaced by General Development Order, 1963, class XVII). The condition imposed by the local planning authority requiring the use of the land to be discontinued on a certain date was therefore invalid. Commenting on article 3(2) LORD PARKER, C.J. said:

> "It was faintly suggested by counsel for the appellants that a specific condition, such as was imposed in this case on the

(*p*) [1961] 3 All E.R. 878.

(*q*) See chapter 5, p. 100, *ante*

grant of an application, overrode any unlimited permission in a General Development Order. I find myself quite unable to accede to that argument. It seems to me that that provision is covering a case where a specific permission is followed by a General Development Order in unqualified terms. It has been suggested by counsel for the appellants that the position is really the other way round and the Justices are not entitled to quash unless it can be shown that the specific permission was a nullity. Again I cannot accede to that argument."

These remarks appear to be obiter because the permission to which the condition was attached was in fact a nullity and it was therefore unnecessary to decide the effect of article 3(2). None the less, these remarks are important. They appear to mean that article 3(2) applies only to conditions or limitations imposed on a grant of planning permission prior to the date on which the General Development Order, 1950, came into operation. With respect, LORD PARKER'S interpretation does not follow inescapably from the wording of article 3(2), and one is entitled therefore to interpret this provision in the light of other circumstances.

It may be argued in support of LORD PARKER'S interpretation that conditions ought not to be imposed which circumvent the provisions of Article 4 as to the withdrawal or restriction of permitted development on payment of compensation (*r*). On the other hand, there may well be good planning reasons for imposing such a condition and, if it cannot be imposed, the planning authority might well feel that they must refuse permission for what may be called the primary development; for instance, where application is made for permission to work minerals, there may be strong objections on grounds of amenity and the planning authority may quite properly consider that permission must be refused unless they can impose conditions restricting further development by virtue of class XVIII. Moreover, article 3(2) of the 1950 Order (now article 3(2) of the 1973 Order) is a re-enactment of the corresponding provision in the

---

(*r*) See chapter 6, p. 120, *ante*.

repealed General Development Order, 1948, which came into operation on the same date as the Act of 1947. If LORD PARKER'S view is correct, then article 3(2) would apply only to permission "deemed to have been granted" under Part III of the Act of 1947 (or 1971) by virtue of something done before 1st July, 1948. For these reasons it is respectfully suggested that conditions imposed on a valid grant of planning permission can lawfully restrict development permitted by the General Development Order.

Conditions Limiting Period of Permission

As we have seen, conditions may be imposed limiting the period for which permission is granted. The proper form of such a condition is indicated by section 30 (1) (b) of the Act of 1971, namely, it should require the buildings or works to be removed or the use to be discontinued at the expiration of a specified period. This form is not always adopted in practice; for instance, the Minister's decision on an appeal may state that "the Minister hereby gives permission for a period of five years". The effect of such words was considered by the Court of Appeal in *Francis* v. *Yiewsley and West Drayton U.D.C.* (*s*), in which the Minister on appeal granted permission for the retention of some unauthorised caravans "for a period of six months from the date of this letter". It was held that there was an implied condition that the caravans should be removed at the end of the six months period.

On the expiry of a temporary permission, application may be made under section 32 of the Act of 1971 for permission to retain the buildings or works or continue the use in question. Alternatively, the previous normal use of the land may be resumed without applying for permission, provided the previous use was not instituted in breach of planning control (*t*).

(*s*) [1957] 3 All E.R. 529.
(*t*) Act of 1971, s. 23(5), (6).

Conditions relating to Industrial Buildings and Offices

As mentioned in an earlier chapter (*u*) an application for planning permission for industrial development must be supported by a certificate from the Department of Industry, who may impose any condition which they consider appropriate having regard to the proper distribution of industry (*a*). Similarly, where an office development permit is required (*b*), the Department of the Environment may impose such conditions as they consider appropriate in the exercise of their discretion whether or not to issue a permit (*c*).

The precise effect of these conditions is uncertain. Although at first sight they appear to give the Department concerned very wide powers, it seems reasonably clear that that Department may only impose such conditions as they consider are justified in order to secure the proper distribution of industry and employment. Provided this basic requirement is satisfied such conditions, it is submitted, could not be impeached on the ground that they do not serve the purposes of the Planning Acts. It is possible that these provisions also enable the Department to impose restrictions on existing use rights even if a condition to this effect could not normally be attached to a grant of planning permission under the Act of 1971. (*d*).

EFFECT OF STRIKING OUT CONDITIONS

Although it is clear that the courts will in suitable cases declare a condition to be invalid, the effect on the permission is uncertain. Does the permission remain in force shorn of the condition, or does the permission itself fall with it?

(*u*) See chapter 6, p. 126, *ante*.
(*a*) Act of 1971, s. 71 (1).
(*b*) See chapter 6, p. 129, *ante*.
(*c*) Act of 1971, s. 77 (2), (3). In exercising their discretion whether to issue or withhold office development permits, the Department shall have particular regard to the need for promoting the better distribution of employment in Great Britain: *Ibid.*, s. 74(3).
(*d*) See the discussion on this point at pp. 154 *et seq.*, *ante*.

There seem to be three possible answers to this question. There are dicta which appear to suggest that, if a condition is declared void, the permission automatically falls with it. At the opposite extreme there are some dicta which suggest that the permission should always stand. But the weight of opinion appears to be in favour of an intermediate position, that is, that the permission will fall if the offending condition is of fundamental importance but not if it was trivial or unimportant.

In *Pyx Granite Co., Ltd.* v. *Minister of Housing and Local Government*, ROMER, L.J. was of the opinion that "it would not be open for the court to leave the permission shorn of its conditions or any of them" (*e*). But since the Court of Appeal were unanimous in holding that permissions were required and that the condition was proper, the point did not require decision and ROMER, L.J's remarks must therefore be regarded as obiter. The House of Lords subsequently held that permission was not required, so that the validity of the condition did not arise and there was no discussion on the possible effect of invalidating it.

These remarks of ROMER, L.J. were adopted by the Court of Appeal in *Hall* v. *Shoreham U.D.C.* (*f*); in that case, however, it was obvious that the conditions in question were fundamental to the whole of the planning permission, and the council were granted a declaration that the permission was consequently null and void. But in some later cases, the permission has been allowed to stand. Moreover the judgments in that case recognised that it might be permissible to sever an offending condition if it were merely trivial or unimportant. So in *Allnatt London Properties* v. *Middlesex C.C.* (*g*) GLYN-JONES, J. considered himself free in the circumstances of that case to hold that the planning permission should stand, shorn of the offending conditions.

Such was the state of the authorities when the matter came up again in *Kent C.C.* v. *Kingsway Investments (Kent), Ltd.* (*h*).

(*e*) [1958] 1 All E.R. 625. (*f*) [1964] 1 All E.R. 1.
(*g*) (1964), 15 P. & C.R. 288.
(*h*) [1970] 1 All E.R. 70.

The Court of Appeal, having declared the condition void, held that the permission remained in force (*i*). The condition in question related, said DAVIES, L.J., not to the development itself but to matters preparatory or introductory to the permission; it was unimportant to the development itself. WINN, L.J., went further: "if it [the condition] is void it can have no effect on the force of the permission itself".

However, in the House of Lords, the majority of their Lordships held that condition was valid. They nevertheless went on to consider whether the permission would have stood if they had decided that the condition was void. LORD MORRIS OF BORTH-Y-GEST and LORD DONOVAN said that there might be cases in which unimportant or incidental conditions were superimposed on the permission; if such conditions were held to be void, the permission might be allowed to survive. But in the present case the condition was not trivial or unimportant. It would seem therefore that the Lordships did not accept the distinction drawn by DAVIES, L.J. between conditions relating to the development itself and conditions of a preparatory nature. And LORD GUEST seems to have thought that the permission would always fail, even apparently where the offending condition was unimportant.

To sum up: it seems that the correct approach is to consider whether the condition is fundamental to the permission; in other words would the planning authority have granted permission without the condition in question.

ENFORCEABILITY OF CONDITIONS

A condition may be valid having regard to the principles set out earlier in this chapter but it should not be imposed unless it can be properly enforced. The machinery of enforcement is discussed later in this book, but one or two examples of unenforceable conditions may usefully be mentioned here. An obvious example is that of a condition requiring building or engineering

(*i*) [1969] 1 All E.R. 601.

operations to be completed by a specified date. A condition forbidding the felling of trees is difficult of enforcement; although the owner of the land might be called upon to plant new trees, it may be many years before these reach such maturity that the land could be said to be restored to its former condition.

Duration of Permissions

Prior to 1969 a planning permission might remain unused indefinitely unless a condition had been attached requiring work to be commenced within a specified period. Although such conditions might lawfully be imposed (*a*) local planning authorities made little use of them; indeed such conditions might have been invalid if imposed upon an outline permission.

In some parts of the country unused permissions have accumulated to the extent of becoming a serious problem. The local planning authority in such circumstances have no means of knowing whether the land will in fact be developed and, if so, when; at the same time developers may complain that the planning authority are acting unreasonably in refusing permission to develop other land.

The Act of 1968 introduced provisions designed to overcome these problems, and these are now to be found in the Act of 1971. First, where planning permission was granted before 1st April, 1969, it will lapse if development is not commenced before April 1974 (*b*). If the permission was an outline permission, application for approval of any reserved matters must have been made before April 1972 and development must be commenced before April 1974 or within two years of the grant of approval, whichever is the later (*c*); this formula avoids the possibility of injustice arising from delay on the part of the planning authority or the Minister in granting detailed approval.

Every new planning permission will be deemed to be subject

(*a*) Act of 1971, s. 30(3).
(*b*) Act of 1971, s. 41, Sch. 24, para. 18.
(*c*) *Ibid.*, s. 42, Sch. 24, para. 18.

to a condition that development shall be commenced within five years or such other period as the planning authority may expressly impose (*d*). In the case of outline permissions, the deemed condition will be to the effect that application for approval of reserved matters must be made within three years, and that the development must be begun within five years of the date on which the outline permission was granted or within two years of the grant of approval, whichever is the later; here again the planning authority may impose different periods (*e*).

Development will be deemed to have been commenced when a start is made on any of the following "specified operations" (*f*):

(a) any work of construction in the course of the erection of a building;

(b) the digging of a trench which is to contain the foundations, or part of the foundations, of a building;

(c) the laying of any underground main or pipe to the foundations, or part of the foundations, of a building or to any such trench as is mentioned above;

(d) any operation in the course of laying out or constructing a road or part of a road;

(e) any change in the use of any land, where that change constitutes "material development" (*g*).

It will thus be sufficient for instance to start digging a trench for the foundation of a building, and it is easy to imagine that there will be cases in which a trench will be dug and nothing more done for a number of years. If this happens, the local planning authority will be able to serve a "completion notice", stating that the planning permission will cease to have effect if the development is not

---

(*d*) Act of 1971, s. 41.

(*e*) *Ibid.*, s. 42. These time limits will be extended where the planning permission has been suspended under the Act of 1975: see chapter 22, *post*.

(*f*) *Ibid.*, s. 43(1), (2).

(*g*) "Material development" means (a) any development permitted by the General Development Order: (b) certain forms of development falling within Schedule 8 of the Act of 1971: (c) any other development prescribed by the Minister: Act of 1971, s. 43(3).

completed within such period (not less than twelve months) as may be specified. The notice will not take effect, however, unless and until confirmed by the Minister and before confirming the notice he must give to the persons upon whom it has been served, and the local planning authority, the opportunity of appearing at a public local inquiry or other hearing.

CHAPTER 8

REVOCATION OR MODIFICATION OF PLANNING PERMISSION

Although a grant of planning permission is intended, in the absence of conditions to the contrary, to enure permanently for the benefit of the land (*a*), in certain circumstances it may be revoked or modified. The local planning authority may, if they consider it expedient, having regard to the development plan and to any other material considerations, make an order for this purpose; with some exceptions, the order must be submitted to the Minister for confirmation (*b*). The Minister himself may either direct the local planning authority to make an order for this purpose or he may do so himself (*c*). If the order becomes effective, the local planning authority will have to pay compensation for abortive expenditure and for the depreciation in the value of the land (*d*).

It is only comparatively rarely that the Minister or the local authority will consider it desirable to revoke or modify a permission and the liability to compensation may deter an authority from such action even where they consider it desirable.

EXTENT OF POWER TO REVOKE OR MODIFY

The power of revocation or modification applies only to permissions granted on an application under Part III of the Act of 1971. The reference to "an application" excludes any permission

(*a*) See chapter 7, p. 146, *ante*.
(*b*) Act of 1971, ss. 45, 46.
(*c*) *Ibid.*, s. 276.
(*d*) See chapter 20, *post*.

granted by a development order (*e*) and any permission "deemed to have been granted" under Part III by virtue of either section 77 or section 78 of the 1947 Act (as preserved by Schedule 24 of the Act of 1971) or of section 40 or 64, concerning authorisations by government departments and advertisements respectively (*f*).

The power to revoke or modify applies only where the development has not been completed. This is made clear by section 45(4) of the Act of 1971, which reads:

> "The power conferred by this section to revoke or modify permission to develop land may be exercised—
>
> (a) where the permission relates to the carrying out of building or other operations, at any time before those operations have been completed;
>
> (b) where the permission relates to a change of the use of any land, at any time before the change has taken place:
>
> Provided that the revocation or modification of permission for the carrying out of building or other operations shall not affect so much of those operations as has been previously carried out."

If the local planning authority wish to remove or modify development completed in conformity with planning permission they must take action under section 51 (*g*). There are two alternative procedures. First, there is what may be called the standard procedure which involves submitting the order to the Minister for confirmation. Secondly, there is the procedure which may be used where the local planning authority do not expect objections to the order and there is not likely to be a claim for compensation.

The Standard Procedure

The local planning authority submit the order to the Minister,

---

(*e*) A permission granted under the General Development Order, however, may in effect be revoked or modified as a result of an "Article 4 direction" (see chapter 6, p. 120, *ante*).

(*f*) See chapter 6, *ante*.

(*g*) See chapter 10, *post*.

and give notice to the owner (*h*) and occupier of the land and to any other person likely to be affected.

Any person receiving the notice has the right to be heard by a representative of the Minister either at a public local inquiry or private hearing, before the Minister decides whether or not to confirm the order (*i*).

Where the Minister himself makes an order, he must similarly notify the persons affected, and give them an opportunity of being heard before coming to a final decision (*k*).

The validity of the order as confirmed or made by the Minister may be questioned in High Court proceedings under section 242 of the Act of 1971, but not otherwise (*l*).

Procedure for Unopposed Orders

This procedure is available where (*m*):

(a) the owner and occupier of the land and all persons who, in the authority's opinion, will be affected by the order have notified the authority in writing that they do not object to the order; and

(b) it appears to the authority that no compensation is likely in respect of the order.

In these circumstances, the authority publish an advertisement in the local press reciting the above mentioned matters and stating that any person affected by the order may notify the Minister that he wishes to be heard by a representative of the Minister at a public local inquiry or other hearing. A similar notice is to be served on the very persons who have already

---

(*h*) The "owner" means a person, other than a mortgagee not in possession, who (whether in his own right or as trustee) is entitled to receive the rack-rent of the land or, where the land is not let at a rack-rent, would be so entitled if it were so let: Act of 1971, s. 290. And see chapter 11, p. 202, *post*.

(*i*) Act of 1971, s. 45(3).

(*k*) *Ibid.*, s. 276(3).

(*l*) See chapter 6, pp. 141, *et seq.*, *ante*.

(*m*) Act of 1971, s. 46(1). There are a few cases in which this procedure is not available: see sub-s. (6).

indicated that they do not object (*n*). This latter requirement appears at first sight to be quite remarkable; one possible reason is that no compensation can be obtained in respect of an unopposed order made under this procedure, and the individual notices must draw attention to this fact.

The authority must then send a copy of the public advertisement to the Minister, who has the right to call in the order. If at the end of a specified period no person claiming to be affected has requested a hearing and the Minister has not called in the order, it takes effect (*o*).

Land Incapable of Beneficial Use

If the effect of the order is to render the land incapable of reasonably beneficial use the owner may serve a purchase notice under Part IX of the Act of 1971 (*p*).

(*n*) Act of 1971, s. 46(2), (3). General Regs., reg. 25.
(*o*) *Ibid.*, s. 46(4), (5).
(*p*) *Ibid.*, s. 188. For purchase notices, see chapter 11, *post.*

CHAPTER 9

THE ENFORCEMENT OF PLANNING CONTROL

A system of enforcement is required to deal with cases in which development is carried out either without planning permission or in breach of the conditions or limitations attaching to a grant of planning permission. One simple method of enforcement would have been to make a breach of planning control an offence punishable by the courts. With some minor exceptions (*a*), however, Parliament decided not to make a simple breach of control a punishable offence. Instead, the local planning authority are authorised to serve an enforcement notice requiring the owner or occupier of land or premises to remedy the situation. It is when this enforcement notice is ignored that the local planning authority may prosecute the offender.

When this system was introduced by the Act of 1947, it was thought right to insist that the enforcement notice should be served within four years of the breach of planning control. If no enforcement notice were served within that time, the unauthorised development or breach of condition became immune from action; in this way a great many unauthorised changes of use have become the established use of the land. However, in 1968 it was decided to remove this time limit on the service of enforcement notice in respect of unauthorised changes of use (*b*) occurring after the end of 1963 (*c*), whilst retaining the time limit in respect of

(*a*) The display of advertisements without the necessary grant of consent under the Advertisements Regulations and thus without any necessary grant of planning permission is an offence: Act of 1971, s. 109 (1). So, too, is the removal of top-soil in such circumstances as to involve development: Agricultural Land (Removal of Surface Soil) Act, 1953.

(*b*) The four year rule is retained in respect of change of use of any building to single dwellinghouse—see p. 175, *post*.

(*c*) Approximately four years before the introduction of the Bill for the Act of 1968.

building and other operations. The changes thus introduced by the Act of 1968 are now embodied in the Act of 1971.

It is very unusual not to have some time limit in civil proceedings (*d*). As will be apparent from what has been said about material change of use (*e*), there are many cases in which there is genuine doubt as to what use rights attach to land or buildings; the absence to the possibility of enforcement action will make it difficult in many cases to sell property; the system of certification of established uses introduced by the Act of 1968 (and now contained in the Act of 1971) will afford some relief but not in every case (*f*).

ENFORCEMENT NOTICE

Service of Enforcement Notice

The law relating to the service of enforcement notices is highly technical, but it may be reduced to the following rules:

1. The local planning authority must be satisfied that there has been a breach of planning control after the end of 1963 (*g*). There is a breach of planning control if either (*h*):

   (a) development has been carried out without permission; or

   (b) a condition or limitation attached to a grant of planning permission has not been complied with.

2. The local planning authority should not automatically serve an enforcement notice in respect of every breach of planning control. They should be satisfied that it is desirable to serve an enforcement notice having regard to the provisions of the development plan and to any other material considerations (*i*). In effect, the planning authority should ask themselves whether they would have granted planning permission had an application been made to them. If the local authority do not serve an enforcement

(*d*) Cf. the Limitation Acts.
(*e*) See chapter 5, *ante*.
(*f*) See p. 188, *post*.
(*g*) Act of 1971, s. 87(1).
(*h*) *Ibid.*, s. 87(2).
(*i*) *Ibid.*, s. 87(1).

notice the Minister may either direct them to serve an enforcement notice, or he may serve the notice himself (*k*).

3. In the following cases the enforcement notice must be served within four years of the alleged breach of planning control (*l*):

(a) carrying out without planning permission of building, engineering, mining or other operations;
(b) breach of any condition or limitation attaching to planning permission for such operations;
(c) change of use without planning permission of any building to use as single dwellinghouse.

4. The notice must be served on the owner and occupier of the land and on any other person having an interest in the land who in the opinion of the local planning authority would be materially affected (*m*).

Note: "Owner" presumably means the person entitled to receive the rack-rent or would be entitled to receive it if the land were so let (*n*). This would exclude, for instance, the owner of a freehold reversion subject to a lease at less than a rack-rent.

The word "occupier" clearly includes anyone occupying land under a lease or tenancy. And it now seems clear—in spite of some earlier doubts (*o*)—that it may include a licensee. In *Stevens* v. *London Borough of Bromley* (*p*) the Court of Appeal rejected the proposition that an occupier for this purpose must be someone who has an interest in the land; the intention of the legislature was to ensure that anyone who might be prejudiced by an enforcement notice should be served with it.

(*k*) Act of 1971, s. 276 (5).
(*l*) *Ibid.*, s. 87(3).
(*m*) *Ibid.*, s. 87(4).
(*n*) See definition of "owner" in Act of 1971, s. 290, and *London Corpn.* v. *Cusack-Smith*, [1955] 1 All E.R. 302, chapter 11, p. 202, *post*.
(*o*) LORD DENNING, M.R. suggested that a licensee could not be an occupier: *James* v. *Minister of Housing and Local Government*, [1965] 3 All E.R. 602, at p. 605; *Munnich* v. *Godstone R.D.C.*, [1966] 1 All E.R. 930.
(*p*) [1972] 1 All E.R. 712.

Not all licensees will be occupiers for this purpose. Whether they are or not will depend on the circumstances. In *Stevens* v. *London Borough of Bromley* (*q*) a number of caravanners occupied sites under licences from the owner of the land. These caravans were the permanent homes of their owners, and many of them made gardens on the small plots surrounding the caravans; each caravan had mains water and electricity and its drains were connected to a common cesspool. The licences could not be revoked unless one month's notice was given. It was held that the caravanners should have been served with the enforcement notice. Where, however, the arrangements are of a more transitory nature—as in *Munnich* v. *Godstone R.D.C.*(*r*)—licensees will not be regarded as "occupiers" for this purpose, but this was obiter.

There are obvious pitfalls here for the local planning authority. Failure to serve someone who should have been served with the notice may invalidate the notice altogether. No harm is done, however, by serving someone who is not perhaps entitled to be served—except that any person who is served with an enforcement notice has a right of appeal.

5. The notice must specify (*s*):

   (a) the alleged breach of planning control, that is the development said to have taken place without permission or the condition or limitation said to have been broken.

   (b) the steps to be taken to restore the land to its condition before the development took place or to secure compliance with the condition or limitation alleged to have been broken; the local planning authority have some discretion

---

(*q*) *Supra.*

(*r*) See note (*o*), *supra*. The report of this case does not state the degree of transience of the so-called occupiers, but DANCKWERTS, L.J. described them as "birds of passage".

(*s*) Act of 1971, s. 87 (6), (7).

as to what is required and they need not insist on the land being restored to precisely the same condition (*t*).

(c) the period (not less than twenty-eight days) at the expiry of which the notice is to take effect.

(d) a further period within which the notice is to be complied with.

If the rules as to service and content are not complied with, the notice may be a nullity; and, even if it is not a nullity, it may be invalid in which case it may be quashed on appeal. The distinction between "nullity" and "invalidity" is important because it affects the rights of persons on whom the enforcement notice is served. If the notice is a nullity, it is "so much waste paper" (*a*); it is, strictly speaking, not an enforcement notice at all, and the recipient is entitled to ignore it or, if he wishes, he can seek a declaration that it is void. If, however, the notice is invalid, it cannot safely be ignored and (with some possible exceptions) the recipient must exercise his rights of appeal under the Act of 1971 (*b*).

What constitutes a nullity in this context was explained by UPJOHN, L.J. in *Miller-Mead* v. *Minister of Housing and Local Government* (*c*). It seems that a notice will be a nullity if it fails to specify one of the two periods mentioned in paragraph 5 (c) and (d) above. This happened in *Burgess* v. *Jarvis and Sevenoaks R.D.C.* (*d*).

Jarvis had built a number of houses without permission and the local authority served an enforcement notice requiring him to demolish the houses. This notice did not separately specify the period after which it was to take effect. Burgess who was

(*t*) *Iddenden* v. *Secretary of State for the Environment*, [1972] 3 All E.R. 883.

(*a*) *Miller-Mead* v. *Minister of Housing and Local Government*, [1963] 1 All E.R. 459, *per* UPJOHN, L.J.

(*b*) See p. 180, *post*.

(*c*) [1963] 1 All E.R. 459.

(*d*) [1952] 1 All E.R. 592. In the Court of Appeal, all three Lords Justices described the notice as "invalid", but presumably they meant "null" or "void".

the tenant of one of the houses obtained a declaration that the notice was invalid.

A notice will also be a nullity if (*e*):

"on its true construction it was ambiguous and uncertain so that the owner or occupier could not tell in what respect it was alleged that he had developed the land without permission or in what respect it was alleged that he had failed to comply with a condition or, again, that he could not tell with reasonable certainty what steps he had to take to remedy the alleged breaches."

This dictum is illustrated by the recent case of *Metallic Protectives, Ltd* v. *Secretary of State for the Environment* (*f*).

The local planning authority served an enforcement notice alleging breach of a condition in a planning permission that no nuisance should be caused to residential properties in the area by reason of noise, smell, smoke, etc. The enforcement notice required the occupier to install satisfactory sound proofing of a compressor and to take all possible action to minimise the effect created by the use of acrylic paint. On appeal, the Minister accepted that the notice was far too imprecise; he therefore substituted precise requirements.

HELD: the enforcement notice as originally served was so defective as to be a nullity from the start: the Minister could not amend it and it must be disregarded.

A notice will be invalid (but not a nullity) if it alleges that development has been carried out without permission when in fact there has been a failure to comply with a condition or limitation. This is illustrated by *Francis* v. *Yiewsley and West Drayton U.D.C.* (*g*).

In 1949 the owner of the land carried out development by using it as a residential caravan site. He later applied to the local authority for planning permission which was refused. On appeal the Minister permitted the use of the land for a period

(*e*) *Miller-Mead* v. *Minister of Housing and Local Government* (*supra.*) *per* UPJOHN, L.J.
(*f*) [1976] J.P.L. 166.
(*g*) [1957] 3 All E.R. 529.

of six months from the date of his decision (February, 1950). In July, 1952, the local authority served an enforcement notice alleging that the development had been carried out without permission, but took no further steps to secure compliance with the notice. In December, 1955, the owner claimed a declaration that the notice was invalid. The Court of Appeal held that the notice was invalid. On the facts permission had been granted, albeit retrospectively; the notice was thus based on a wholly false basis of fact.

PARKER, L.J. observed that, although the permission contained no express condition that the caravans should be removed at the end of six months, such a condition was implied. It seems, therefore, that the notice would have been valid had it alleged non-compliance with that implied condition.

The case of *Francis* v. *Yiewsley and West Drayton U.D.C.* was decided before the procedure for appeals was altered in 1960. Under the procedure introduced in that year, and now contained in the Act of 1971 (*h*), it would seem that an appeal on these facts would now lie to the Minister and that it would not be possible to apply to the court for a declaration. But the case remains good authority for the proposition that an enforcement notice will be invalid if it alleges that development has been carried out without permission when in fact there has been a failure to comply with a condition or limitation (*i*).

A notice will not be invalid, however, if it refers to failure to comply with a "condition" when a "limitation" is meant or vice-versa (*k*).

A similar problem arose in *Miller-Mead* v. *Minister of Housing and Local Government* (*l*). The local planning authority had served an enforcement notice which recited that certain land had

---

(*h*) See this chapter, p. 181, *post*.

(*i*) *Garland* v. *Minister of Housing and Local Government* (1969), 20 P. & C.R. 93; *Copeland B.C.* v. *Secretary of State for the Environment* (1976), 31 P. & C.R., 403.

(*k*) Act of 1962, s. 177(6). "Limitations", as distinct from "conditions", arise in connection with permitted development under the G.D.O.

(*l*) [1963] 1 All E.R. 459.

been used as a caravan site without the grant of planning permission and requiring the owner to move the caravans. The owner appealed on the ground that he had the benefit of the temporary permission granted by class IV (2) of the General Development Order (*m*) and that the notice was therefore invalid The Court of Appeal held that the recital was not incorrect and that the notice was valid.

Finally a notice will be invalid if the local planning authority do not comply with the rules as to service. Thus in *Caravans and Automobiles, Ltd.* v. *Southall B.C.* (*a*) company A owned the whole of the site used for the display and sale of caravans without planning permission; company A occupied part of the site for this purpose and company B occupied the remainder of the site for the same purpose. An enforcement notice was served on company A but not on company B. It was held that both occupiers should have been served and the notice was invalid. Where more than one person is to be served, the notices must be served on the same day (*b*). Under the Act of 1971 the Minister may disregard the fact that some person who ought to have been served with the enforcement notice has not been served, if neither the appellant nor that person has been substantially prejudiced (*c*).

Rights of Appeal

As originally enacted the Act of 1947 provided two methods by which an enforcement notice might be challenged:

(a) by applying to the local planning authority for planning permission and then appealing, if need be, to the Minister against the planning authority's decision;

(b) by appealing to the local magistrates on certain limited grounds of law. In addition, it was possible under the

---

(*m*) That is class IV (2) as originally enacted and prior to its amendment in 1960; see p. 117, *ante*.

(*a*) [1963] 2 All E.R. 533.

(*b*) *Bambury* v. *London Borough of Hounslow*, [1966] 2 All E.R. 532.

(*c*) Act of 1971, s. 88(4).

general law to apply to the High Court for a declaration on any matter of law.

These provisions were not well designed. They provided considerable opportunities for delay and evasion which were sometimes well exploited; and, owing to ambiguous drafting, there were doubts as to the precise extent of the right of appeal to the magistrates. The Caravan Sites and Control of Development Act, 1960, substituted a right of appeal to the Minister, both on planning and legal grounds, by any person on whom the enforcement notice had been served or by any other person having an interest in the land; these provisions, with some changes in detail, are now to be found in the Act of 1971. The precise grounds of appeal are as follows (*d*):

(a) that permission ought to be granted for the development to which the enforcement notice relates, or the condition or limitation in question should be discharged;

(b) that the matters alleged in the notice do not constitute a breach of planning control;

(c) in a case to which the four-year rule still applies, that that period has elapsed at the date of service (*e*);

(d) in any other case, that the alleged breach of planning control occurred before 1964;

(e) that the notice was not served as required by section 87(4) (*f*);

(f) that the steps required to be taken by the notice exceed what is necessary to remedy any breach of control;

(g) that the period specified in the enforcement notice for complying with the notice is unreasonably short.

The question of where the burden of proof lies in enforcement appeals was discussed in *Nelsovil, Ltd.* v. *Minister of Housing and Local Government* (*g*). WIDGERY, J. said, "I should have thought

(*d*) Act of 1971, s. 88(1).
(*e*) See p. 175, *ante*.
(*f*) See pp. 175, 176, *ante*.
(*g*) [1962] 1 All E.R. 423. See also *Parker Brothers (Farms), Ltd.* v. *Minister of Housing and Local Government* (1969), 210 Estates Gazette 825.

that a person given a right to appeal on certain specified grounds is the person who has to make good those grounds and is the person on whom that onus rests." He also said, "I can see no sort of hardship in requiring that the onus shall lie on the appellant in such a case." In this case the point at issue was whether a material change of use had occurred more than four years before an enforcement notice was served; but the appellants failed to discharge their burden of proof, and the Minister's decision that (in effect) there was no evidence of the changed use dating back four years was upheld by the court.

Procedure on Appeal

An appeal against an enforcement notice is to be made by notice to the Minister stating the grounds of appeal and the facts on which it is based; the notice of appeal must be given within the period specified in the enforcement notice as the period at the end of which it is to take effect; the Minister has no power to extend the time. However, the Court of Appeal has held that it is sufficient to give the Minister notice of intention to appeal within the prescribed period; the grounds of appeal and the facts on which it is based may be furnished within such further time as the Minister may allow (*h*). Once notice of appeal has been given, the enforcement notice is of no effect pending the final determination or withdrawal of the appeal (*i*).

The appellant and the local planning authority have the right to be heard at a public local inquiry or other hearing (*j*).

The Minister may uphold, quash or vary an enforcement notice. In particular, he may grant planning permission for the development to which the notice relates; and he may determine the purpose for which the land may lawfully be used having regard to its past use and any relevant planning permissions (*a*).

(*h*) *Howard* v. *Secretary of State for the Environment*, [1974] 1 All E.R. 644.
(*i*) Act of 1971, s. 88(1), (2), (3).
(*j*) Act of 1971, s. 88(2).
(*a*) *Ibid.*, s. 16(5).

The Minister is empowered to correct any informality, defect or error in the enforcement notice provided it is not material (*b*). Thus, where an enforcement notice in respect of an unauthorised change of use incorrectly alleged that the previous use of the land was for light engineering, the Minister used his power to correct the notice (*c*). It is doubtful, however, whether the Minister could correct a notice which is based on a wholly false basis of fact as in *Francis* v. *Yiewsley and West Drayton U.D.C.* (*d*). And the Minister cannot correct a notice which is a nullity because, strictly speaking, there is no notice to correct.

The Minister's decision on any point of law may be challenged in High Court proceedings at the instance of the local planning authority, of the appellant or of any other person on whom the enforcement notice was served (*e*); and the Minister may at any stage state a case on his own initiative for the opinion of the High Court (*f*).

There is an important provision in the Act of 1971 that the validity of an enforcement notice shall not be questioned in any proceedings whatsoever on any grounds specified in paragraphs (b), (c), (d) or (e) above except by way of appeal to the Minister (*g*). There is one exception to this rule in connection with proceedings taken by the local planning authority to recover any expenses

(*b*) *Ibid.*, s. 88(4).

(*c*) [1964] J.P.L. 429.

(*d*) [1957] 3 All E.R. 529. And see p. 178, *ante*.

(*e*) Act of 1971, s. 246(1).

(*f*) Section 246(1) states that the parties "may, according as rules of court may provide, either appeal to the High Court against the decision on a point of law or require the Minister to state and sign a case for the opinion of the High Court". UNGOED-THOMAS, J. in *Hoser* v. *Minister of Housing and Local Government*, [1962] 3 All E.R. 945, held that this clearly meant the choice of methods to rest with the rules committee of the Supreme Court, which had in fact decided in favour of the former (appeal by motion to the High Court) and not the latter (case stated). The appellants' contention, therefore, that the choice was conferred by the statute upon them that they could compel the Minister to state a case (which they asserted would enable them to appeal on a point of fact—but this is highly doubtful) failed.

(*g*) Act of 1971, s. 243(1). Subject, of course, to the right to test the Minister's decision in the High Court under s. 246.

which they may have incurred in entering upon the land and securing compliance with the notice, a point which is discussed below (*h*).

This provision thus excludes the right which would otherwise be available at common law to by-pass the Minister by applying to the High Court for a declaration on any point of law covered by paragraph (b), (c), (d) or (e). It does not, it is submitted, take away the right to apply for a declaration that the enforcement was a nullity on the grounds explained earlier in this chapter (*i*).

A further point arises out of ground (g) on which appeal may be made under section 88(1). Where an appeal is brought on this ground, the local planning authority sometimes contend that, although the period is rather short, the appellant could have begun to take appropriate steps before the enforcement notice took effect. In *Mercer* v. *Uckfield R.D.C.* (*j*) the Minister accepted this argument and refused to extend the period for complying with the notice. *M* then appealed to the Divisional Court on the ground that the Minister was not entitled to consider the "previous planning history". The court upheld the Minister's right to do so.

It is by no means clear, however, that the court would take this view in every case. In *Mercer's* case *M* had previously applied for planning permission and, when this was refused, had appealed to the Minister. It was only after the Minister had dismissed this appeal that the authority served an enforcement notice. *M* then appealed against the enforcement notice on the ground that planning permission ought to be given for the offending development as well as on the ground that the period for compliance was too short.

In many cases, however, it is not until the appeal against the enforcement notice that the Minister has an opportunity of considering whether planning permission ought to be given. The appellant may also take the point (which did not arise in *Mercer's*

(*h*) See this chapter, pp. 185, 186, *post*.
(*i*) See pp. 177, 178, *ante*.
(*j*) (1962), 14 P. & C.R. 32.

case) that he does not require permission. If he succeeds on either of these grounds the notice will not take effect. It would surely be unreasonable to expect an appellant to start dismantling his development until he knows whether the notice which has been served upon him will ever take effect.

Effect of Enforcement Notice

As already explained (*k*) an enforcement notice requires the person on whom it is served to take specified steps to remedy the breach of planning control. The notice continues to be effective after it has been complied with (*l*).

In *Postill* v. *East Riding C.C.*(*m*) an enforcement notice required the removal of unauthorised caravans from a field; the owner complied with the notice but six months later brought the caravans back. It was held that he had complied with the enforcement notice and could not now be prosecuted for non-compliance.

The effect of this decision has been overruled by section 93(1) of the Act of 1971 (re-enacting provisions originally contained in the Act of 1960) which provides that an enforcement notice is not discharged by the person on whom it was served having complied with it. Furthermore, it is effective against any subsequent owner, provided it has been registered as a local land charge.

Enforcement of Enforcement Notice

Where the enforcement notice has not been complied with, the local planning authority's remedies vary according to the circumstances.

(1) *Failure to comply with requirements other than discontinuance of a use.*—The local planning authority may enter the land and carry out the requisite work themselves at the expense of the

(*k*) See p. 176, *ante*.
(*l*) Act of 1971, s. 93(1).
(*m*) [1956] 2 All E.R. 685.

person who is then the owner of the land (*n*). If the authority's claim for expenses give rise to legal proceedings the owner cannot challenge the validity of the notice on any of the grounds mentioned in paragraphs (b), (c), (d) or (e) of section 88(1) of the Act of 1971, but he may do so if he was not the owner at the time the notice was served (*o*); in any event, he will be able to challenge the claim on the ground that the expenses are excessive.

In addition, the authority may prosecute the person who was the owner at the time the enforcement notice was served, and he will be liable to a fine (*p*). If that person has ceased to be the owner at the time of the prosecution he is entitled to have the new owner brought before the court (*q*). The original owner must be acquitted if he shows that no blame attaches to him; in any event, if any blame attaches to the new owner, he also may be fined (*r*). If after conviction any person fails to take reasonable steps to comply with the enforcement notice, he will be liable to a further fine (*s*). On any such prosecution the validity of the enforcement notice may be questioned except on the grounds mentioned in paragraph (b), (c), (d), or (e) of section 88 of the Act of 1971 (*t*).

(2) *Reinstatement of buildings or works demolished or altered in compliance with an enforcement notice.*—Provided such reinstatement is "development" this is a breach of the original enforcement notice (*a*). The local planning authority, on giving not less than

---

(*n*) Act of 1971, s. 91(1). If the owner is not the person responsible for the unauthorised development he may recover the expenses from the person who is; s. 91(2).

(*o*) *Ibid*, s. 243(1), (4).

(*p*) The maximum fine on summary conviction is £400; on indictment there is no limit to the amount of the fine: *Ibid.*, s. 89(1).

(*q*) *Ibid.*, s. 89(2).

(*r*) *Ibid.*, s. 89(3).

(*s*) The maximum penalty on summary conviction for this subsequent and continuing offence is £50 a day; on indictment there is no limit: *Ibid.*, s. 89(4).

(*t*) *Ibid.*, s. 243(1). See pp. 180, 181, *ante*.

(*a*) Act of 1971, s. 93(3); even if the terms of the notice "are not apt for the purpose".

twenty-eight days notice, may exercise their right to enter the land to secure compliance with the enforcement notice (*b*) and they may also prosecute. Although the original enforcement notice still applies, nevertheless, any requirements in it concerning *demolition* or *alteration* cannot be enforced by prosecution under section 89 as a punishment for the unauthorised reinstatement or restoration work; otherwise a penalty in respect of this work could be imposed twice over, once for doing it and once for failing to undo it (*c*).

(3) *Failure to comply with requirements of an enforcement notice as to discontinuance of use or compliance with any condition or limitation.*—Any person who uses the land or permits it to be used in contravention of the enforcement notice is guilty of an offence (*d*). It will be observed that in this case, it is not only the owner who may be prosecuted; indeed, if he is unable to prevent somebody else—such as a tenant—from acting in contravention of the notice, he will not be guilty of an offence (*e*). Here again, the validity of the notice may not be questioned on any ground mentioned in paragraph (b), (c), (d) or (e) of section 88 unless the person prosecuted has held an interest in the land since before the enforcement notice was served, was not served with an enforcement notice and did not appeal against it (*f*).

Where the enforcement notice merely requires the discontinuance of a use, the local planning authority have no power to enter upon the land to secure compliance with the notice; indeed, that might be impracticable. The difficulties to which this can give rise are illustrated by *A.-G.* v. *Bastow* (*g*). The owner of a caravan site ignored an enforcement notice requiring him to discontinue the use of land as a caravan site. He was prosecuted

(*b*) *Ibid.*, s. 93(3), (4).
(*c*) *Ibid.*, s. 93(5). The maximum penalty is £400.
(*d*) *Ibid.*, s. 89(5). The maximum penalties on summary conviction are £400 and £50 a day thereafter; on indictment there is no limit.
(*e*) A person cannot "permit" another person to do an act unless he has power to forbid him to do the act: *Goodbarne* v. *Buck*, [1940] 1 All E.R. 613.
(*f*) Act of 1971, s. 243(2).
(*g*) [1957] 1 All E.R. 497

and fined; on this occasion he failed to pay the fine and was committed to prison, but he still did not comply with the notice. The Attorney-General acting in the public interest then sought a High Court injunction requiring the defendant to comply with the enforcement notice. The injunction was granted. The advantage of this proceeding was that failure to comply with the injunction would be contempt of court for which the defendant could be committed to prison until he had "purged his contempt".

Certificates of Established Use

The repeal of the four-year rule in relation to changes of use occurring after the end of 1963 removes some of the certainty as to the purposes for which property may lawfully be used. There are two dangers. First, where the change of use took place before 1964, the risk of enforcement action remains because the local planning authority on discovering the change of use may think it occurred more recently. Secondly, the use may have begun after the end of 1963 and the local planning authority erroneously suppose that it requires planning permission. In both cases the owner or occupier of the land would have grounds for a successful appeal if an enforcement notice were served, but to remove the uncertainty sections 94 and 95 of the Act of 1971 (re-enacting provisions originally introduced by the Act of 1968) enable any person interested in the land to take the initiative by applying for a certificate of established use.

The new procedure is most likely to be used when the property is about to be sold and, by referring to any person interested in the land, Parliament has doubtless intended that a prospective purchaser under a conditional contract should be able to make the necessary application (*a*).

For the purpose of the new procedure, a use of land is said to be established if either:

(a) it was begun before 1964 without planning permission and has continued since the end of 1963; or

---

(*a*) See circular 4/69, para 8.

(b) it was begun before 1964 under a planning permission containing conditions or limitations which have not been complied with since the end of 1963 (*b*); or

(c) it was begun after the end of 1963 as a result of a change of use not requiring planning permission and there has been since the end of 1963 no change of use requiring planning permission (*c*).

Application for a certificate should be made to the local planning authority; normally, it will be for that authority to decide whether or not a certificate should be granted, but the Minister may require the application to be referred to him. The local planning authority's decision is a purely judicial one and, if they are satisfied that the applicant's claim is made out, they must grant a certificate.

If the local planning authority refuse a certificate, or if they fail to give a decision within the proper period (*d*), the applicant may appeal to the Minister. When a case comes before the Minister (whether on appeal or a referred application) the applicant and the local planning authority have the right to a public local inquiry or other hearing.

The Minister's powers are wider than those of the local planning authority. He must of course act judicially in deciding whether or not the claim for an established use is made out; but if it is not made out, he may nevertheless grant planning permission for the use in question.

The Minister's decision is final, but may be challenged on grounds of law under section 245 of the Act of 1971 (*e*).

(*b*) It would appear from the reference to "limitations" that the permission may be one granted by development order: see chapter 6, *ante*.

(*c*) It would seem, therefore, that if in, say, 1965, there was a material change of use from A. to B. without permission and there was subsequently a change from B. to C. not amounting to a material change of use, C. will not be "established".

(*d*) The prescribed period is two months unless the applicant agrees to an extension of time: G.D.O. Art 18 (7).

(*e*) See pp. 141 *et seq*., *ante*.

Stop Notices

As we have seen (*f*), the lodging of an appeal suspends the operation of an enforcement notice until such time as the appeal is finally disposed of or withdrawn. In the meantime, the operation or change of use can continue without penalty. The Act of 1968, however, introduced a stop notice procedure which may be used in respect of operations; it cannot be used to stop a change of use.

Once an enforcement notice has been served the local planning authority may issue a stop notice prohibiting the person on whom it is served carrying out or continuing a specified operation (*g*). The notice may be served on any person having an interest in the land or who is concerned with the carrying out of the operation such as a contractor (*h*). Where a contractor discontinues operations because of a stop notice, the developer will be liable to the contractor as in breach of contract (*i*).

There is no appeal against a stop notice, and failure to comply with it is an offence punishable by fine (*k*). But it is not an offence under the stop notice procedure to continue the operation after the enforcement notice has come into effect; and, of course, the stop notice will cease to have effect if the enforcement notice is quashed or withdrawn (*l*).

There is one important safeguard. If the enforcement notice is quashed or withdrawn, the local planning authority may be liable to pay compensation to persons having an interest in the land; this compensation will include any damages payable to contractors (*m*).

(*f*) See p. 182, *ante*.

(*g*) Act of 1971, s. 90(1). Operations for this purpose include the deposit of refuse although this is classified by s. 22(3) as a material change of use: *Ibid.*, s. 90(2), and see p. 89, *ante*.

(*h*) *Ibid.*, s. 90(3).

(*i*) *Ibid.*, s. 90(8).

(*k*) The maximum penalty on summary conviction is £400 and a daily fine of £50; there is no limit on indictment: *Ibid.*, s. 90(5).

(*l*) *Ibid.*, s. 90(4).

(*m*) Act of 1971, s. 177.

The number of stop notices is likely to be small. In the case of building and similar works the issue of an enforcement notice is usually sufficient as the developer is not likely to risk further expenditure pending the outcome of an appeal. In any event, the Minister has asked local planning authorities to be sparing in their use of this new procedure (*n*).

(*n*) Circular 4/69.

CHAPTER 10

MODIFICATION OF EXISTING RIGHTS

The main purpose of planning legislation is, as we have seen, to ensure that land is used in the manner considered best for the public advantage. The principal means by which this is achieved is by the requirement that "development" shall not be carried out without planning permission. This method is only partially effective, for it is dependent upon a would-be developer bringing forward a specific project for the consideration of the local planning authority. More positive action can be taken by using the machinery of comprehensive development areas under the older type of development plan or by means of action areas under the new development plan system introduced in 1968. Comprehensive development is a relatively large scale operation often involving the compulsory acquisition of a large area of land and the financing of redevelopment by a local authority (*a*).

AGREEMENTS UNDER SECTION 52

This section (re-enacting provisions previously contained in the Acts of 1947 and 1962) provides that the local planning authority may enter into an agreement with any landowner for the purpose of restricting or regulating the development or use of the land; since the passing of the Act of 1968, it is no longer necessary to obtain the approval of the Minister. The agreement may be permanent or for a limited period only. Similar powers were contained in section 34 of the Act of 1932 (*b*). Under the Act of 1932, planning control did not automatically apply to the whole country and, pending the preparation of a planning scheme, it

(*a*) See chapter 4, *ante*.

(*b*) Agreements under section 34 were kept in force, on the repeal of the Act of 1932, by the Act of 1947, and in turn by the Act of 1962, and the Act of 1971, (Sch. 24, para. 1).

might well be advantageous both to the local authority and the landowner to secure some agreement as to the future development or use of the land. Under the modern Planning Acts planning control applies to the whole country without the necessity of passing a resolution to prepare a scheme, and this kind of agreement seems less important. In the debates on the Bill for the 1947 Act, the then Lord Chancellor suggested the following as matters which might be dealt with by agreements under section 25 of that Act (*c*):

> "Waiver of claims for compensation for injurious affection in respect of certain lands on condition that no claims were made by the authorities for betterment in respect of development of other land; for gifts of land in consideration of permission to develop other land; for permitting public right of access to private lands in consideration for permission to develop other land; for granting permission to develop or redevelop land on condition that the value of the works was discounted in computing the consideration on a subsequent purchase of the property by the authority."

In some at least of these cases the implication is that planning permission should be granted as part of a bargain under which the landowner accepts a condition which could not lawfully be imposed on an ordinary grant of permission. In some cases this may be reasonable, but there are obvious dangers of abuse. The idea that planning permission can be "bought" seems quite contrary to the general conception of Planning. In practice, the number of agreements made under what is now section 52 is comparatively small (*d*). Agreements have been made to discontinue the sale of petrol from a badly-sited garage upon the opening of a new filling station under the same ownership, to restrict the use of holiday chalets to the summer months and to prevent their being used as permanent residences, and to regulate the use of caravan sites. A particularly interesting agreement

(*c*) House of Lords Official Report, vol. 149, col. 692.

(*d*) The total number of agreements approved by the Minister during the four years 1956–1959 was 83.

related to a windmill in Kent. The windmill was subject to a building preservation order but was falling into disrepair. The county council agreed to carry out the necessary repairs at their own expense in return for undertakings by the owner to restrict the use of property to agricultural and private residential purposes, to keep the mill clean and protect it from damage, and to allow members of the public to visit it (*e*).

Enforcement of Agreements

The local planning authority should have no difficulty in enforcing the agreement against the landowner who entered into it. Agreements by local authorities and other public bodies are normally made by deed and, if this has been done, the agreement will be enforceable even if the landowner has not given any consideration.

There may be difficulty, however, in enforcing the agreement against successors in title to the original owner. For this reason, section 52 provides that the local planning authority may enforce the agreement against persons deriving title from the original owner as if the agreement had been made for the benefit of adjoining land owned by the authority. This means that *restrictive* covenants will be enforceable (*f*). It is doubtful however whether *positive* covenants—that is, those requiring the expenditure of money or labour by the owner—could be enforced against successors in title (*g*).

These difficulties have now been overcome to some extent. Some authorities have obtained local Act powers. Thus section 6 of the Leeds Corporation Act 1966 provides that the Corporation may enter into agreements with developers in respect of certain matters; the Corporation may enforce positive and negative covenants provided the agreement has been entered in the local land charges register.

(*e*) Ministry of Housing and Local Government report, 1957, page 81.
(*f*) *Tulk* v. *Moxhay* (1848), 2 Ph. 774.
(*g*) *Austerberry* v. *Oldham Corpn.* (1885), 29 Ch. D. 750.

Moreover, there is now general legislation regarding the enforcement of covenants in agreements made between local authorities and landowners under various statutory powers. Section 126 of the Housing Act 1974 provides for the enforcement of agreements made between a local authority and a landowner for the purpose of securing the carrying out of works on, or of facilitating the development of, the land concerned. It must, however, be specifically declared that section 126 of the Housing Act is to apply to the agreement; it follows that the provisions of this section will not assist local authorities in enforcing positive covenants in section 52 agreements made before 1974. Here again the agreement must be registered in the local land charges register.

The owner of the land will be able to enforce the agreement both in respect of positive and restrictive covenants since the authority were parties to the original agreement. In the case of agreements entered into before 1st April, 1974—the date on which the new system of local government came into force—the new successor authority will be liable on the covenants by virtue of section 254 (3) of the Local Government Act 1972.

Section 52 provides, however, that nothing in the agreement is to prevent the exercise by the Minister or by the authority of their powers under the Act of 1971 so long as those powers are exercised in accordance with the provisions of the development plan. Although this enables the Minister or the authority to override the agreement to some extent, there is some advantage to the landowner: were it not for this express provision the authority would have complete freedom to exercise its powers under the Act of 1971 since it is a general rule of law that a public body cannot by agreement restrict the future exercise of its statutory powers: indeed, this was so held in relation to agreements under section 34 of the Act of 1932 (*h*).

Powers of other Authorities under Section 52

The power to enter into agreements under section 52 is not

(*h*) *Ransom and Luck, Ltd.* v. *Surbiton B.C.*, [1949] 1 All E.R. 185.

limited to local planning authorities. Agreements may be made between a district council and the owners of land in their district: and, where the local planning authority is a joint board, by a county council or district council.

Orders under Section 51

This section (re-enacting provisions previously contained in the Acts of 1947 and 1962) provides for the modification of existing rights without the local authority having to acquire the land. Compensation must be paid to the owner for the loss of the rights but at least the local authority are spared the added expense of acquiring land for which they would have no particular need. This is a particularly useful method of dealing with the comparatively small but objectional black spot such as "back-garden" industry or a caravan site in the wrong place. Many such uses were of course established at a time when planning permission was not required; in some cases they have arisen since 1948 in contravention of planning control but the local planning authority have failed to serve an effective enforcement notice within the proper time (*i*).

The local planning authority may take action under section 51 if they consider it desirable for the planning of their area, including considerations of amenity: regard is to be had to the development plan and to any other material considerations. An order may be made (*k*):

(a) requiring any use of land to be discontinued or imposing conditions on the continuance of the use; or

(b) requiring any buildings or works to be altered or removed.

The local planning authority may be prepared to sanction some other development of the land: if so, they may include in the order a grant of planning permission for that purpose (*l*).

If the Minister considers that the local authority ought to

(*i*) See chapter 9, p. 173, *ante*.
(*k*) Act of 1971, s. 51(1).
(*l*) *Ibid.*, s. 51(2).

have made an order he may either make the order himself or require the authority to do so (*m*).

An order of the local planning authority does not become effective unless and until it is confirmed by the Minister (*n*). Before the Minister can confirm the order, the owner and the occupier of the land must be given an opportunity of being heard—usually at a public inquiry (*o*). If the order is made by the Minister he will give the persons affected a similar opportunity of being heard before he comes to a final decision (*p*).

The Minister may confirm the order with or without modifications (*q*) and he may include in the order a grant of planning permission for some other purpose (*r*). The validity of the order may be challenged not later than six weeks after the Minister's confirmation in High Court proceedings under section 245 of the Act of 1971 but not otherwise (*s*).

If the order relates to the use of the land, failure to comply is an offence punishable by fine (*t*). But if it requires the removal or alteration of buildings or works the remedy is for the local planning authority to carry out the requirements of the order and recover the cost from the owner (*u*).

If the effect of the order is to render the land incapable of reasonably beneficial use the owner may serve a purchase notice under Part IX of the Act of 1971 (*v*).

(*m*) *Ibid.*, s. 276(2) (b).
(*n*) *Ibid.*, s. 51(4).
(*o*) *Ibid.*, s. 51(6).
(*p*) *Ibid.*, s. 276(3).
(*q*) *Ibid.*, 51(4).
(*r*) *Ibid.*, s. 51(5) (b).
(*s*) See chapter 6, pp. 141 *et seq.*, *ante.*
(*t*) The maximum fine on summary conviction is £400 with a daily fine of £50 if the offence continues thereafter; there is no maximum fine on indictment: Act of 1971, s. 108(1).
(*u*) Act of 1971, s. 108(2).
(*v*) See chapter 11, *post.*

CHAPTER 11

PURCHASE NOTICES

Although planning control often prevents the landowner putting his land to the most profitable use, normally his only remedy—and this is not always available—is to claim compensation under Parts VII and VIII of the Act of 1971 (*a*). This is reasonable enough: in the normal case, there remains a profitable use for the land, and the owner can either continue to use it for this purpose or sell the land to someone else at a reasonable price. To take an obvious example: however disappointing a refusal of planning permission for building development may be to the owner of agricultural land he can continue to use it for agriculture or sell it to someone who is prepared to use it for agriculture; in such cases compensation should be an adequate remedy.

There are however some cases of hardship in which the Planning Acts recognise the need for some further remedy. For instance, there may be no profitable use for the land unless planning permission can be obtained for its development; a common example is the site of a building destroyed by war damage or by fire. Such land is said to have become incapable of reasonably beneficial use, and Part IX of the Act of 1971 enables the owner in certain circumstances to serve a purchase notice requiring the appropriate local authority to purchase his interest.

Hardship may also arise where land is designated, say, in the development plan for some purpose which will ultimately involve its compulsory acquisition. The designation does not render the land incapable of reasonably beneficial use, but the threat of compulsory purchase may make it virtually unsaleable. This

---

(*a*) See Chapters 18 and 19, *post*.

hardship also is remedied to some extent by Part IX of the Act of 1971 which enables certain owner-occupiers to serve a purchase notice in these circumstances.

ADVERSE PLANNING DECISIONS (*b*)

Sections 180 to 187 of the Act of 1971 apply where planning permission has been refused or granted subject to conditions as a result of an application to the local planning authority, and any owner of the land claims that certain basic requirements have been satisfied—namely,

(a) the land has become incapable of reasonably beneficial use in its existing state; and

(b) if permission was granted subject to conditions, that the land cannot be rendered capable of reasonably beneficial use by carrying out development in accordance with these conditions;

(c) in any case (*i.e.* whether permission was refused or granted subject to conditions) that the land cannot be rendered capable of reasonably beneficial use by carrying out any development for which permission has been granted or for which either the local planning authority or the Minister have undertaken to grant permission.

The expression "beneficial use" was explained by WIDGERY, J. in *Adams and Wade, Ltd.* v. *Minister of Housing and Local Government* (*c*) as follows:

> "The purpose of section 129 [of the Act of 1962] (*d*) is to enable a landowner whose use of his land has been frustrated by a planning refusal to require the local authority to take the land off his hands. The reference to 'beneficial' use must therefore be a reference to a use which can benefit the owner or a prospective

(*b*) These provisions were originally laid down in s. 19 of the 1947 Act, to which amendments were made by the Acts of 1954 and 1959; they were then re-enacted in the Act of 1962, and now in the Act of 1971.

(*c*) (1965), 18 P. & C.R. 60.

(*d*) Act of 1971, s. 180.

owner and the fact that the land in its existing state confers some benefit or value upon the public at large would be no bar to the service of a purchase notice".

In many cases, therefore, the test will be an economic one—is the land in its existing state capable of yielding a reasonable return to its owner? In some cases—for example the site of a former building—it will usually be quite clear that there is no beneficial use in this sense. Where this is *some* beneficial use, it will be necessary to decide whether that use is reasonably beneficial. In the event of dispute, this will be largely a question of fact for the Minister, and the court is not likely to interfere with the Minister's findings if he has applied the right tests. Thus, in *General Estates Co., Ltd.* v. *Minister of Housing and Local Government* (*e*), the company owned a site of about eleven acres. About half was let to a sports club at a rent of £52 a year; the rest was vacant but could be let for grazing at about £20 a year. The Minister concluded on these facts that the land had not become incapable of reasonably beneficial use. The company applied to the High Court under section 179 of the Act of 1962 (now section 245 of the Act of 1971) for an order to quash the Minister's decision. The application was dismissed; it could not be said that the Minister's findings were so perverse as really to be outside his powers.

In deciding what is a reasonably beneficial use it may be helpful to compare the value of the land in its existing state with the value it would have if developed in accordance with planning permission. There have been some expressions of doubt as to whether comparisons of this sort are legitimate. Thus in *Brookdene Investments, Ltd.* v. *Minister of Housing and Local Government* (*f*) FISHER, J. asked:

> "How can a use which would involve the carrying out of a development be relevant to an inquiry as to whether land has become incapable of reasonably beneficial use *in its existing state*?"

(*e*) (1965), 194 Estates Gazette 202.
(*f*) (1970), 21 P. & C.R. 545.

The cases have not entirely resolved these doubts. But it is clear that comparisons of this kind can be made only within fairly narrow limits. Section 180 (2) of the Act of 1971 provides that for the purpose of deciding whether the basic conditions for the service of a purchase notice have been satisfied no account is to be taken of the possibility of any "new" development (that is, development outside the scope of the *existing use* of the land). This, however, merely prevents the owner claiming that his land has become incapable of reasonably beneficial use by comparison with its profitability if he could get permission for new development. In other words, it is not sufficient for the owner to show that his existing use of the land is substantially less profitable than it would be if he were given permission for new development.

Does it follow that land is incapable of reasonably beneficial use if in its existing state it is of substantially less value than it would be if permission were granted for Schedule 8 development? The question came before the Divisional Court in *R.* v. *Minister of Housing and Local Government, Ex parte Chichester R.D.C.* (*g*).

A piece of coastal land of about 2½ acres was subject to considerable erosion, and a large sum of money would be required to prevent further erosion. There were fourteen bungalows on part of the land, and the remainder was divided into seventeen plots which were let as caravan sites during the summer under temporary planning permissions. The owner applied for permission to develop the land for residential purposes; on this being refused he served a purchase notice. The Minister confirmed the notice on the ground that "the land in its existing state and with the benefit of temporary planning permissions—is of substantially less use and value to its owner than it would be if planning permission had been granted (without limitation as to time) for the rebuilding of the buildings which formerly stood there and have been demolished since January 7th, 1937."

The Chichester R.D.C. applied to the High Court for an order to quash the Minister's confirmation of the purchase notice.

(*g*) [1960] 2 All E.R. 407.

> HELD: the reason given by the Minister was not valid because the question was whether "the land has become incapable of reasonably beneficial use in its existing state" and not whether the land was of less use to the owner in its present state than if developed.

The Divisional Court did not, however, go so far as to say that there should be no comparison of the value of the land in its existing state with the value which it would have after Schedule 8 development. Where the Minister erred in the *Chichester* case was in accepting the comparison with Schedule 8 as conclusive. The correct approach seems to be that approved, albeit somewhat reluctantly, by FISHER, J. in *Brookdene Investments, Ltd.* v. *Minister of Housing and Local Government* (*h*)—namely, that a comparison with Schedule 8 values may be made; but, if it is made, it must be made along with other relevant facts, and it is for the Minister to decide in each case how much weight is to be given to such comparison.

"Any Owner"

A purchase notice may be served by "any owner of the land" who considers that the above conditions are satisfied. Section 290 of the Act of 1971 provides that unless the context otherwise requires the word "owner" is to mean—

> "a person, other than a mortgagee not in possession, who, whether in his own right or as trustee for any other person, is entitled to receive the rack-rent of the land or, where the land is not let at a rack-rent, would be so entitled if it were so let."

Although rack-rent is not specifically defined, this definition clearly excludes the owner of a reversion expectant on the termination of a long lease at a ground rent. For this reason, it was contended in *London Corpn.* v. *Cusack-Smith* (*i*) that the context required a different meaning for the word "owner".

(*h*) *Supra.*
(*i*) [1955] 1 All E.R. 302.

Land in the City of London was held by *H* on 99 years' lease at a ground rent. Following the destruction of the buildings *H* disclaimed liability for the rent under the Landlord and Tenant (War Damage) Act, 1941, until the premises were rebuilt. Planning permission was subsequently refused for rebuilding and *H* served a notice under section 19 of the Act of 1947 requiring the Corporation to purchase his interest; this notice was confirmed by the Minister.

Subsequently the freeholders served a notice requiring the purchase of their interest, but the Corporation contended that the freeholders were not within the definition of owner in section 119 (1) of the 1947 Act (now section 290 of the Act of 1971). The House of Lords (reversing a decision of the Court of Appeal) held that the word "owner" must be given the meaning ascribed by section 119 (1).

The hardship in this case occurred because the lessees had exercised their right under the Act of 1941 to suspend payment of the ground rent and the Corporation had refused to permit rebuilding: a similar situation might arise where a building is destroyed by fire, and the lease contains a clause permitting abatement of the ground rent. In other cases, however, there will be less hardship, because the freeholder will be entitled to the ground rent even if the lessee's interest is acquired by a public authority.

Procedure

In these cases of adverse planning decisions, a purchase notice is served on the council of the county or district (*k*) in which the land is situate. If the council are willing to comply with the purchase notice, or if they have found another local authority or statutory undertaker who are willing to comply with it, they serve a notice to that effect; the authority in question are then deemed to have served notice to treat for the interest of the owner who served the notice.

(*k*) Act of 1971, s. 180, amended by Local Government Act 1972, Sch. 16, paras. 37, 38.

If the council are not willing to comply with the notice and have not found another authority or statutory undertaker who would be willing to comply with it, the council must within three months forward the purchase notice to the Minister at the same time notifying the owner. If the Minister considers that the basic requirements are satisfied, he will either—

(a) confirm the notice, in which case the council are deemed to have served notice to treat;

(b) grant permission for the development in respect of which the application was made: or, if permission was granted subject to conditions, amend the conditions so far as is necessary to render the land capable of reasonably beneficial use;

(c) grant permission for some other development of either the whole or part of the land (*l*);

(d) substitute another local authority or statutory undertaker for the council on whom the notice is served, in which case that authority or statutory undertaker are deemed to have served notice to treat.

A special situation arises where the land forms part of a larger area for which planning permission has been given; there may be a condition that the particular piece of land in question is to remain undeveloped or is to be laid out as amenity land, or the application for permission may show that this was contemplated. In these circumstances, the Minister may in his discretion refuse to confirm the notice (*m*).

Whatever action the Minister proposes to take he must give notice to the person who served the purchase notice, to the council on whom it was served, to the local planning authority,

---

(*l*) If he considers that this would make it capable of reasonably beneficial use: Act of 1971, s. 183(3).

(*m*) Act of 1971, s. 184 re-enacting a provision originally introduced by the Act of 1968 and designed to deal with the position revealed in *Adams and Wade, Ltd.* v. *Minister of Housing and Local Government* (1965), 18 P. & C.R. 60.

and to any other local authority or statutory undertaker whom he proposes to substitute for the council. Any of these parties then has the right to be heard by a representative of the Minister either at a public local inquiry or other hearing. This procedure also applies where the Minister decides not to confirm a notice on the ground that the basic requirements have not been satisfied, but not apparently if he decides that the purchase notice should not be confirmed on the ground that the person who served it is not an "owner".

The Minister must give his decision during the "relevant period"; that is, nine months from the date of service of the purchase notice or within six months of the date on which a copy of the purchase notice was forwarded to him, whichever is the earlier. If he fails to do so, or if he fails to take any of the other courses of action open to him (see (b) and (c) above), the purchase notice is deemed to have been confirmed (*n*).

Application of Purchase Notice procedure to certain other forms of Planning Control (*o*)

Sections 188 to 191 of the Act of 1971 apply the above procedure, with suitable modifications, to cases where planning permission has been revoked or modified under section 45, or where the local planning authority has made an order under section 51 (requiring a use to be discontinued or any building or works to be altered or removed), or where any tree preservation order or advertisement regulations so provide. A purchase notice may also be served in appropriate circumstances where listed building consent is refused, or granted subject to conditions, or is revoked or modified.

(*n*) Act of 1971, s. 186(2), (3); in *Ealing B.C.* v. *Minister of Housing and Local Government*, [1952] 2 All E.R. 639, the Minister purported to modify a purchase notice, but since his modification was void, the original notice was "deemed to be confirmed" after six months.

(*o*) See chapters 8, 10 and 12 for these special forms of planning control.

Adverse Planning Proposals: Blight Notices

Blight notices relate to land which has become difficult to sell because of "planning blight", that is, the threat of compulsory purchase implicit in some planning proposal. The scheme was first introduced by the Act of 1959, but it has been considerably extended since then: there are now far more cases in which a blight notice can be served, and the conditions have been relaxed. There are, however, two important limitations. First, only certain classes of owner-occupier can serve a blight notice. Secondly, at least some part of the owner-occupier's land must be under threat of compulsory purchase; the scheme affords no protection to the person whose land is depreciated in value by a threat of compulsory purchase hanging over neighbouring land.

A blight notice may be served in respect of a hereditament or agricultural unit consisting wholly or partly of land falling within any of the following cases.

1. Structure Plans

Land indicated in a structure plan either as (*p*):

(a) land which may be required for the purposes of any of the functions of any government department, local authority or statutory undertakers or of the National Coal Board; or

(b) land which may be included in an action area.

A blight notice under this heading may be served at any time after the plan has been submitted to the Minister, but not after the plan has been withdrawn for any reason (*q*).

A blight notice cannot be served under this heading after a local plan has come into force allocating land for any of the purposes mentioned in sub-paragraph (a) above (*r*).

2. Local Plans

Land allocated by a local plan for the purposes of any of the

(*p*) Act of 1971, s. 192(1) (a).
(*q*) Land Compensation Act 1973, s. 68(4), (5).
(*r*) Act of 1971, s. 192(2).

functions mentioned in paragraph 1(a) above (*s*). The blight notice may be served at any time after the local planning authority have formally published the plan, but not after it has been withdrawn for any reason (*t*).

3. Land Affected by Resolution of Local Authority or Directions of Minister

Land earmarked by resolution of local authority or by a direction of the Minister as land which may be required for the purposes of any functions of a Government department, local authority or statutory undertaker (*u*).

4. Compulsory Purchase Orders

Land subject to a compulsory purchase order, but notice to treat has not yet been served (*a*).

The blight notice may be served at any time after the compulsory purchase order has been submitted to the appropriate Minister for confirmation; or, in the case of compulsory purchase by a government department, after the draft order has been published. If subsequently the compulsory purchase order is not confirmed (or, in the case of a government department, the order is not made) a blight notice cannot thereafter be served (*b*).

5. Compulsory Purchase under Special Act

Land authorised to be acquired by special Act (*c*).

6. New Towns

Land within an area designated as the site of a new town. The blight notice may be served at any time after the draft designation order has been published. If subsequently the Minister decides

(*s*) *Ibid.*, s. 192(1) (b).
(*t*) Land Compensation Act 1973, s. 68(4), (5).
(*u*) *Ibid.*, s. 71.
(*a*) Act of 1971, s. 192(1) (j). A compulsory purchase order ceases to have effect if notice to treat is not served within three years of the date on which the order became operative: Compulsory Purchase Act 1965, s. 4.
(*b*) Land Compensation Act 1973, s. 70.
(*c*) Act of 1971, s. 192(1) (i).

not to make the designation order, or modifies it so as to exclude the land in question, a blight notice cannot thereafter be served (*d*).

7. Slum Clearance

Land which is either (a) included in a clearance area under Part III of the Housing Act 1957, or (b) is land surrounded by or adjoining a clearance area which the local authority have determined to purchase (*e*).

8. General Improvement Area

Land indicated by information published under section 31 of the Housing Act 1969 as land which the local authority propose to acquire as part of a general improvement area (*f*).

9. Highway Proposals in Development Plan

Land indicated in a development plan (otherwise than in paragraph 1 or 2 above) as required for the construction or improvement of a highway (*g*).

In this context the expression "development plan" means, it is submitted, a plan approved by the Minister or, in the case of a local plan, one formally adopted by the local planning authority.

10. Orders or Schemes for Trunk or Special Roads

Land indicated in an order or scheme under the Highways Acts 1959 to 1971 for the construction, alteration or improvement of a trunk or special road, or under section 22 of the Land Compensation Act 1973 for mitigating the adverse effects of a trunk or special road (*h*).

11. Compulsory Purchase Order under Highway Land Acquisition Powers

Land subject to a compulsory purchase order under section 47 of the Highways Act 1971 for the acquisition of rights over

(*d*) Land Compensation Act 1973, s. 72.
(*e*) *Ibid.*, s. 73.
(*f*) Act of 1971, s. 192(1) (h).
(*g*) *Ibid.*, s. 192(1) (c).
(*h*) Act of 1971, s. 192(1) (d); Land Compensation Act 1973, s. 74.

highway land, but notice to treat has not yet been served (*i*). The blight notice can be served at any time after the order has been submitted to the Minister for confirmation; or, where the order is proposed by the Minister, after the draft order has been published. If the order is subsequently not confirmed or, in the case of a draft order is not made, a blight notice cannot thereafter be served (*k*).

12. Land Affected by New Street Orders

Land affected by an order made under section 159 of the Highways Act 1959 or section 30 of the Public Health Act 1925 regarding the minimum widths of new streets or highways declared to be new streets (*l*).

13. Land Affected by Suspension of Planning Permission under the Community Land Act 1975

A blight notice may be served under this heading at any time during which a planning permission is suspended under the Act of 1975 (*m*).

14. Land in Disposal Notification Area

A blight notice may be served in respect of such land if either (a) the authority concerned have served counter-notice of intention to purchase or (b) that authority have failed to serve counter-notice (*n*). It follows that a blight notice cannot be served if the authority concerned have served a counter-notice indicating that they do not intend to purchase (*o*).

These categories of land are referred to in the Act of 1971 as land of the specified descriptions (*p*).

Since the passing of the Land Compensation Act 1973, it is

(*i*) Act of 1971, s. 192(1) (g).
(*k*) Land Compensation Act 1973, s. 70.
(*l*) *Ibid.*, s. 76.
(*m*) Act of 1975, s. 22(6). For the provisions as to suspension of planning permission, see chapter 23, *post.*
(*n*) Act of 1975, s. 23 (8).
(*o*) For disposal notification areas, see chapter 22, p. 344, *post.*
(*p*) Act of 1971, s. 192(6).

possible in many cases to serve a purchase notice much earlier than was previously allowed. Before 1973 a purchase notice could not be served in respect of the blighting effect of a development plan or a compulsory purchase order until the development plan or compulsory purchase order had been approved by the Minister. Now it is possible to serve a purchase notice as soon as a development plan proposal or a compulsory purchase order has been submitted to the Minister. Owners of property may of course be seriously affected by the blighting effect of draft proposals, and there is some fear that the procedures for public participation will increase the risk of blight: but owners of property in this position cannot serve a blight notice (*q*).

Who may serve Notice

A purchase notice under these provisions may be served by a person having an interest "qualifying for protection" (*r*) namely (*s*).

(a) the resident owner-occupier of any hereditament;

(b) the owner-occupier of any hereditament with a net annual value not exceeding the prescribed limit—at present £2,250 (*t*);

(c) the owner-occupier of an agricultural unit.

For this purpose "owner-occupier" includes a lessee with at least three years to run as well as a freeholder. "Resident owner-occupier" is defined as "an *individual* who occupies the whole . . . of the hereditament" (*u*); and for this reason in *Webb* v. *Warwickshire C.C.* (*v*) the Lands Tribunal held that the interest must be a strictly personal one abating on death with the result that a personal representative could not serve a blight notice.

(*q*) For the procedures for the making and approval of development plans, see chapter 4, pp. 64, 73, *ante*.

(*r*) Act of 1971, s. 193(1).

(*s*) *Ibid.*, s. 192(3), (4), (5).

(*t*) The present limit is prescribed by the Town and Country Planning (Limit of Annual Value) Order 1973, S.I. 1973 No. 425.

(*u*) Act of 1971, s. 203(3).

(*v*) (1971), 23 P. & C.R. 63.

The effect of this decision has been somewhat modified by the Land Compensation Act 1973. Section 78 provides that a personal representative may serve a blight notice if the deceased owner would have been entitled to serve such a notice at the date of his death. It is a further condition that one or more individuals (to the exclusion of any body corporate) shall be beneficially interested in the proceeds of sale.

"Hereditament" means the land comprised in a hereditament included in the valuation list for rating purposes. As agricultural land is not included in the valuation list, the Act speaks in this connection of an agricultural unit, and this means land which is occupied as a unit for agricultural purposes (*w*).

In certain circumstances a mortgagee of such an interest may serve a blight notice (*x*).

It will be appreciated that a blight notice can only be served in respect of business and other essentially non-residential premises if the net annual value does not exceed £2,250 or if the owner occupies some part of the premises as a dwelling. Investment owners have been excluded because—

> ". . . the value of an investment is affected by many factors. It would be well nigh impossible to determine whether the value of an investment property had changed because of some blighting effect of local authority proposals or because of some change in the market. Local authorities might therefore find themselves forced to buy an interest in property which had not really been blighted by their proposals. Moreover, the time when the interest in property was offloaded on the local authority would be likely to depend, not upon any genuine need to realise capital, in order to enable a man to find a new roof for his head, as in the other case, but merely because at that particular date the changes in the market were such that the money might be more profitably invested in something else" (*a*).

In *Essex C.C.* v. *Essex Incorporated Congregational Church*

(*w*) Act of 1971, s. 207(1).

(*x*) *Ibid.*, s. 201.

(*a*) Speech of Lord Chancellor on 27th April, 1959 (House of Lords Debates: vol. 215, cols. 1041–1042).

Union (*b*), the House of Lords had to consider an appeal concerning an attempt to serve a purchase notice in respect of a church and church hall. The actual decision was that, in the circumstances, the Lands Tribunal had at the outset no jurisdiction to decide whether the respondents' interest in the property was "qualified for protection" by purchase notice, and consequently that the Court of Appeal and the House of Lords had no jurisdiction either. The Lands Tribunal and Court of Appeal had, however, considered that they possessed this jurisdiction, and had decided that since the property was marked "exempt" in the rating list this included it in the category of premises with a net annual value not exceeding the prescribed limit. The House of Lords stated that this decision, though there was in any case no jurisdiction to give it, was wrong.

Service and Effect of Notice

The purchase notice is to be served on the "appropriate authority"—namely, the Government Department, local authority or other body who are likely to acquire the land (*c*).

The person serving the notice is known as the claimant and he must serve a notice in the prescribed form (*d*). This will state that the whole or some part of the hereditament or agricultural unit is land of one of the "specified descriptions", (*e*) that the claimant is entitled to an interest which qualifies for protection in the hereditament or unit, that he has made reasonable efforts to sell that interest, and that he has been unable to sell it except at a price substantially lower than he might reasonably have expected but for the threat of compulsory purchase.

In the case of a hereditament, the notice must require the appropriate authority to purchase the whole of the claimant's interest. This applies even if part only of the hereditament

(*b*) [1963] 1 All E.R. 326.
(*c*) Act of 1971, s. 205(1).
(*d*) For the prescribed form, see the General Regulations.
(*e*) *I.e.* the categories listed at pp. 206, *et seq.*, *ante*.

is land of one of the specified descriptions; only where the claimant does not own the whole can the notice refer to less than the whole hereditament and even then it must require the authority to take the whole amount owned by the claimant (*f*).

In the case of an agricultural unit, the rules are different. The threat of compulsory acquisition may extend only to a small part of the farm and might not cause difficulty in selling the farm as a whole. If, however, the effect is to render the farm unsaleable at a reasonable price, a blight notice may be served in respect of the "affected area", that is, so much of the farm as is land of one of the specified descriptions (*g*). If the claimant can show that the whole or a part of the "unaffected area" would not be viable as a separate unit, then that land may also be included in the blight notice (*h*).

If the appropriate authority are not willing to purchase the land they may within two months serve a counter notice specifying their objections (*a*). There are in effect three main grounds on which the authority may object—

(1) that the conditions laid down in the Act of 1971 have not been satisfied;

(2) that they do not intend to acquire any part of the hereditament or (in the case of any agricultural unit) any part of the affected area;

(3) that they do not intend to acquire any part of the hereditament or any part of the affected area within the next fifteen years, but this only applies where the blight arises from the provisions of the structure plan or in certain cases in which the land is indicated in the development plan for the construction or improvement of a highway.

In the case of an agricultural unit the authority may also object

---

(*f*) Act of 1971, s. 193(1), (2).
(*g*) *Ibid.*, s. 207(1).
(*h*) Land Compensation Act 1973, s. 79.
(*a*) Act of 1971, s. 194.

on the ground that they propose to acquire part only of the affected area (*b*). The claimant may require the objections to be referred to the Lands Tribunal; unless the objection falls within class (2) or (3) above, it is for him to satisfy the Tribunal that the objection is not well founded. If the Tribunal are satisfied the objection is not well founded, they will declare the notice valid. If the authority upholds an objection that the authority intend to acquire part only of the affected area the Tribunal will declare the notice valid in relation to the part only (*c*).

If no counter-notice has been served or if the notice has been declared valid, the appropriate authority will be deemed to have served notice to treat in respect of the hereditament or (in the case of an agricultural unit) either the affected area or such less area as the authority intended to acquire in any event (*d*).

(*b*) Act of 1971, s. 194(2) (c).
(*c*) *Ibid.*, s. 195.
(*d*) *Ibid.*, s. 196.

Chapter 12

SPECIAL FORMS OF CONTROL

One of the objects of town and country planning is the preservation and enhancement of amenity—that is, the pleasant features of town and countryside. This is achieved partly through the control of development as described in earlier chapters; that is, the planning authority may refuse permission for development which would be detrimental to amenity or they may attach conditions designed to safeguard amenity. In addition to this general power of control planning legislation provides a number of special forms of control which are mainly concerned with preserving or improving the pleasant features of the town and country. Provision is made for the preservation and planting of trees; preservation of areas and buildings of special architectural and historic interest; control over the display of outdoor advertising; the proper maintenance of waste land; and the disposal of abandoned vehicles and other refuse.

Tree Preservation

The felling of trees is not development as defined in the Act of 1971, but where it is considered desirable in the interests of amenity the felling or lopping of trees or woodlands can be controlled by making tree preservation orders under section 60 of the Act. A tree preservation order may apply to a single tree, a group of trees or to a substantial woodland. It may prohibit the felling, lopping, uprooting, wilful damage or wilful destruction of the trees without the consent of the local planning authority; and in the case of woodlands, it may contain provisions as to the replanting of any area which is felled in the course of forestry operations permitted under the order (*a*).

(*a*) Act of 1971, s. 60(1), as amended by Act of 1974.

It seems that a tree may be "wilfully destroyed" by negligence as well as deliberate intent. In *Barnet London Borough Council* v. *Eastern Electricity Board* (*b*), contractors laying electric cables damaged the root systems of six large trees all of which were subject to a tree preservation order; as a result, the life expectance of the trees was shortened and they had been rendered less stable and a potential danger. The council prosecuted the Board but the magistrates dismissed the case on the ground that the reduction of the life expectancy of the trees by an uncertain period could not amount to destruction.

The Divisional Court, however, held that a person wilfully destroyed a tree if he inflicted on it so radical an injury that in all the circumstances any reasonable forester would decide that it must be felled.

A tree preservation order will normally be made by the local planning authority (*c*) **but in exceptional cases the Minister may make an order** (*d*). Before February 1969, all tree preservation orders made by the local planning authority required the confirmation of the Minister; orders made since that date need not be confirmed by the Minister if there are no objections (*e*).

There are restrictions on the making of tree preservation orders where a Forestry Dedication Covenant is in force or where the Forestry Commissioners have made a grant under the Forestry Acts. In these circumstances an order may be made only if there is not in force some working plan approved by the Forestry Commissioners and they consent to the making of the order (*f*). Moreover, a tree preservation order cannot prohibit the cutting down of trees which are dying or dead or have become dangerous, nor may it prohibit felling which is necessary to comply with a statutory obligation or to abate a nuisance (*g*).

(*b*) [1973] 2 All E.R. 319.
(*c*) Act of 1971, s. 60(1).
(*d*) *Ibid.*, s. 276.
(*e*) *Ibid.*, s. 60(4).
(*f*) *Ibid.*, s. 60(7).
(*g*) *Ibid.*, s. 60(6).

In making and administering a tree preservation order the planning authority are concerned solely with considerations of amenity; they are not concerned with such matters as the economic value of the trees. Control over felling in the interests of the national economy was introduced, however, by the Forestry Act, 1951 (now the Forestry Act, 1967). Under that Act it is an offence to fell any tree without the consent of the Forestry Commissioners, except in certain specified cases (*h*). The cutting down of a tree may therefore require the consent of the local planning authority under a tree preservation order and/or the consent of the Commissioners under the Forestry Act, 1967.

Making the Order

A tree preservation order made since 16th February 1969 is to be in the form (or substantially the form) prescribed by the Tree Preservation Regulations (*i*). The position of the trees or woodlands must be defined on a map attached to the order (*k*). In order to prevent felling before the order can be confirmed, the local planning authority may include in the order a direction under section 61 of the Act of 1971 that the order shall take effect provisionally on a specified date and this direction will continue in force for a maximum of six months (*l*).

Notice that the order has been made must be served on the

(*h*) The exceptions are to be found partly in the Forestry Act, 1967, s. 9, and partly in the Forestry (Exceptions from Restriction of Felling) Regs., 1951. They include the cutting down of small trees and felling which is necessary for the purpose of carrying out development in accordance with planning permission.

(*i*) Before that date there was no prescribed form, but the Minister had published a model form; although the model form had no legal effect, the Minister was not likely to approve an order which departed from the model on any matter of substance: T. & C.P. (Tree Preservation Order) Regulations 1969, S.I. 1969 No. 17; T. & C.P. (Tree Preservation Order) (Amendment) and (Trees in Conservation Areas) (Exempted Cases) Regulations 1975; S.I. 1975 No. 148.

(*k*) Tree Preservation Regs., reg. 4.

(*l*) Section 8 of the Town and Country Amenities Act 1974 added a new s. 61A in the Act of 1971 in which further provision is made for the protection of trees in conservation areas.

owners and occupiers of the land affected by the order and on any other person known to be entitled to work minerals in the land or to fell any of the trees (*m*). Any of these persons has the right to make objections and representations within twenty-eight days by notice in writing to the Minister (*n*). If no objections or representations are made within that period, the local planning authority may after a further fourteen days confirm the order as an unopposed order (*o*). If there are objections or representations the Minister will have to consider them before deciding whether to confirm the order (*p*). If the order is confirmed whether by the Minister or (as an unopposed order) by the local planning authority, its validity can be questioned in High Court proceedings under section 245 of the Act of 1971 (*q*).

Consents under the Order

The procedure for obtaining consent to fell or top trees protected by a preservation order varies according to whether the Forestry Act, 1967, also applies.

If the Forestry Act, 1967, does not apply, the procedure will be that laid down in the tree preservation order and this procedure will be modelled on the provisions of the Act of 1971 for obtaining planning permission. Application for consent must be made to the local planning authority, and the authority may refuse consent or grant it either unconditionally or conditionally (*r*). The authority must give their decision within two months. If they fail to do so, or if the applicant is aggrieved by their decision he may appeal to the Minister who will deal with the matter in the same way as an appeal against refusal of planning permission.

If the Forestry Act, 1967, applies, application is made to the

(*m*) *Ibid.*, reg. 5.

(*n*) *Ibid.*, regs. 5 and 7.

(*o*) *Ibid.*, reg. 6.

(*p*) *Ibid.*, reg. 8. There is no obligation on the Minister to hold a public inquiry.

(*q*) See chapter 6, pp. 141, *et seq.*, *ante.*

(*r*) The conditions may require the replacement of any tree or trees on the site or in the near vicinity.

Forestry Commissioners. If the Commissioners propose to grant a licence, they must consult the local planning authority; if that authority objects, the application will be referred to the Minister who will deal with it as if it had been referred to him under section 35 of the Act of 1971. If the Commissioners propose not to grant a licence, they need not consult the local planning authority and the applicant has no right of appeal, though he may have a right to compensation under the Forestry Act. The Commissioners may decide not to deal with the application themselves but to refer it to the local planning authority in which case the procedure laid down in the tree preservation order applies (*s*).

If the matter comes before the Minister in any of the ways mentioned above, his decision may be challenged in High Court proceedings under section 245 of the Act of 1971 (*t*).

The local planning authority may revoke or modify any grant of consent under the tree preservation order. The procedure is similar to that described in an earlier chapter for the revocation or modification of planning permission (*u*). The planning authority will be liable to pay compensation for abortive expenditure.

Compensation

No compensation is payable for the making of a tree preservation order, but compensation may be payable for damage or expenditure resulting from a refusal of consent or for the imposition of conditions (*v*).

Replacement of Trees

As we have seen, a tree preservation order may contain provisions as to the replanting of any area felled in the course of forestry operations permitted under the order. In the case of trees not forming part of a woodland, the local planning authority

(*s*) Forestry Act, 1951, s. 13.
(*t*) See chapter 6, pp. 141 *et seq.*, *ante*.
(*u*) See chapter 8, *ante*.
(*v*) See *Cardigan Timber Co.* v. *Cardiganshire C.C.* (1957), 9 P. & C.R. 158.

in granting consent to fell may impose conditions as to the replacement of the trees (*a*).

Further provisions as to the replacement of trees not forming part of a woodland are contained in section 62 of the Act of 1971 (re-enacting provisions originally introduced by the Civic Amenities Act, 1967). This section applies where a tree is removed or destroyed in contravention of the preservation order or is removed or destroyed or dies at a time when its cutting down is authorised without express consent because it is dead or dying or dangerous. In these circumstances the owner of the land must plant another tree of an appropriate size and species at the same place as soon as he reasonably can—unless, on his application, the local planning authority dispense with the requirement. The new tree will be subject to the original preservation order.

Enforcement

The effective enforcement of tree preservation orders has caused some difficulty. The Act of 1947 provided that contravention of a tree preservation order should be an offence punishable by fine, and this was re-enacted in the Act of 1962; the penalties were small and were not always an effective deterrent. Some early tree preservation orders provided for the service of enforcement notices requiring replanting, and this might well have proved an effective deterrent, but in 1953 the Minister advised local authorities that it was doubtful whether these enforcement provisions could be validly included in preservation orders. However, when the Civic Amenities Act, 1967, was passed penalties were increased and express provision made for enforcement notices.

The relevant provisions are now to be found in sections 102 and 103 of the Act of 1971 and may be summarised as follows:

1. If any person contravenes a tree preservation order by

(*a*) There is no express provision to this effect in the Act of 1971 or in the prescribed form of tree preservation order, but reference to such conditions is made in article 7 of the prescribed form and in s. 103(1) of the Act.

cutting down or wilfully destroying a tree, or topping or lopping it in such a manner as to be likely to destroy it, he may be charged under section 102 and may be fined £250 or twice the value of the tree, whichever is the greater.

2. Any other contravention of a tree preservation order is an offence punishable by fine not exceeding £50; if the contravention is continued after conviction, the offender is liable to a daily fine of £2.

3. If a landowner fails to comply with the requirements of section 62 as to the replacement of trees, he is not guilty of any offence but the local planning authority may serve an enforcement notice under section 103 requiring him to plant a tree or trees of such size and species as may be specified in the notice. An enforcement notice under section 103 may also be served if a landowner fails to comply with any conditions of a consent given under a tree preservation order requiring the replacement of trees, although this might also be an offence under section 102. An enforcement notice under section 103 must be served within four years, and there is a right of appeal to the Minister.

Planting of New Trees

The provisions so far described are concerned with the preservation of existing trees and their replacement when felled or destroyed. The Civic Amenities Act introduced for the first time provisions designed to secure the planting of new trees. These provisions are now contained in section 59 of the Act of 1971. Under this section it is the duty of the local planning authority when granting planning permission for any development to consider whether it would be appropriate to impose conditions for the preservation and planting of trees and to make tree preservation orders in connection with the grant of planning permission.

Buildings of Special Interest

There have recently been some substantial changes in the law regarding buildings of special architectural or historic interest.

Prior to 1969, such buildings were protected in two ways. First, the local planning authority or the district council might, subject to the approval of the Minister, make a building preservation order prohibiting the demolition or alteration of the building without the consent of that authority; before approving the order, the Minister had to consider any objections made by interested persons and, if need be, hold a public local inquiry; and, if the authority refused consent under the order for demolition or alteration, there was a further right of appeal to the Minister. Secondly, the Minister might compile lists, or give his approval to lists compiled by other persons or bodies, of buildings considered to be of special interest; there was no provision for objections by the owner or occupier of the building. So long as a building was included in such a list it was an offence to demolish or alter the building without first giving notice to the local planning authority who could then consider whether to make a preservation order.

This system was changed by the Act of 1968 with effect from 1st January, 1969. The provisions as to building preservation orders were repealed and instead it became an offence to demolish or alter a listed building without first obtaining "listed building consent" from the local planning authority or the Minister. Buildings subject to preservation orders under the old law are now deemed to be listed.

The system thus introduced by the Act of 1968 is continued under the Act of 1971, but there are also some additional provisions in the Acts of 1972 and 1974.

Listing of Buildings

By section 54 of the Act of 1971 the Minister may compile lists, or give his approval to lists compiled by other persons or bodies, of buildings considered to be of special architectural or historic interest. In considering whether to list a building the Minister may consider not only the building itself but also: (a) the contribution which its exterior makes to the architectural or historic interest of a group of buildings and, (b) the desirability of preserving any features fixed to the building or contained within its curtilage (*b*); the reference to features undoubtedly includes chattels such as portrait panels and carvings inside the building provided they have been affixed to the premises so as to become part thereof (*c*).

The fact that a building has been listed is to be entered in the register of local land charges (*d*) and the local council must also give individual notice to the owner and occupier (*e*). As before, there is no provision for objections by owners and occupiers at this stage; but, on appeal to the Minister against a refusal of listed building consent, the appellant may contend that the building is not of special architectural or historic interest and ought to be excluded from the list (*f*).

The purpose of listing is to give guidance to local planning authorities in the performance of their functions under the Planning Acts as well as to prohibit demolition or alteration (*g*); this means that the local planning authority will be expected to give special consideration to listed buildings in deciding whether to give planning permission for nearby development and in the preparation of plans for comprehensive development, etc.

There appear to be no restrictions on the types of building which may be included in such lists, but the prohibition on demolition or alteration does not apply to ecclesiastical buildings nor to ancient monuments (*h*). Moreover, in view of the wide

---

(*b*) Act of 1971, s. 54.
(*c*) *Corthorn Land and Timber Co., Ltd.* v. *Minister of Housing and Local Government* (1965), 63 L.G.R. 490.
(*d*) Act of 1971, s. 54(6).
(*e*) *Ibid.*, s. 54(7).
(*f*) See p. 226, *post*.
(*g*) Act of 1971, s. 54(1).
(*h*) Act of 1971, s. 56(1). A building used by a minister of religion wholly or mainly as a residence from which to perform the duties of his office is deemed for this purpose not to be an ecclesiastical building; this special provision overrides the decision of the Court of Appeal in *Phillips* v. *Minister of Housing and Local Government*, [1964] 2 All E.R. 824.

meaning given to the word "building" in section 290 of the Act of 1971 (*i*), it would seem that such structures as village pumps, lych gates and milestones may be included in such lists.

Listed Building Consent

Section 55 of the Act of 1971 makes it an offence to execute, without first obtaining listed building consent any works for the demolition of a listed building or for its alteration or extension in a manner which would affect its character as a building of special architectural or historic interest. In addition, where it is proposed to demolish a building, notice must be given to the Royal Commission on Historical Monuments to enable them to inspect and record details of the building. It is not necessary to apply for consent for works urgently necessary in the interests of safety or health or for the preservation of the building, but notice must be given to the local planning authority as soon as possible.

It is noteworthy that, apart from demolition, the prohibition applies only to works which affect the character of the building as one of special architectural or historic interest. This is a stronger phrase than that used in the definition of development where reference is made to works "which materially affect the external appearance of a building". It is submitted that regard must be had to the reasons why the building has been listed as one of special interest. Thus painting a building in a different colour may be held to involve a material alteration in its external appearance, but in most cases would probably not affect its character as a building of special architectural or historic interest. On the other hand facing a half-timbered building with stucco or roughcast might well be regarded as affecting its special architectural interest. There is no formal machinery by which the owner or occupier of a building can secure a formal determination as to whether his proposed works would affect the character of

---

(*i*) See chapter 5, p. 81, *ante*.

the building (*k*). In the last resort, the question will be one of fact for the Minister on appeal against an enforcement notice or for the magistrates on a prosecution. The commonsense course, however, in cases of doubt would be to discuss the matter with the planning authority or to apply for listed building consent.

In many cases works for the alteration or extension of a listed building will constitute development for which planning permission is required; or, if they do not of themselves require planning permission, they may form part of a larger scheme which does require permission. The grant of planning permission does not of itself obviate the need for listed building consent. However, if a planning permission is so framed as expressly to authorise the works, the permission will operate as a listed building consent; it should be noted that a permission granted by development order (*l*) is never sufficient for this purpose. In all other cases, listed building consent must be expressly obtained; in particular such consent is always required for the demolition of a listed building.

Procedure for Obtaining Consent

The procedure for obtaining listed building consent is modelled on that for obtaining planning permission, but there are some additional requirements as to publicity and consultation with the Minister which illustrate the importance which is now attached to the preservation of buildings of special interest.

Any person may apply for listed building consent; but, if the applicant is not the estate owner of the fee simple nor entitled to a tenancy, he must notify the estate owner and every tenant with at least ten years to run (*m*).

The application should be made on a form obtainable from the

(*k*) The Minister is under no statutory obligation to consider the point if taken on an appeal against refusal of listed building consent, but there appears to be nothing in law to prevent his doing so.

(*l*) Act of 1971, s. 55(2). For permission granted by development order, see chapter 6, p. 114, *ante*.

(*m*) Listed Building Regs., reg. 5.

local planning authority (*n*). If the application involves either the demolition or (with minor exceptions) the alteration of a listed building he must advertise the application stating where plans may be inspected; a notice to the same effect must also be displayed on or near the land. Any member of the public then has a period of 21 days in which to make representations (*o*). The Minister has directed that in the case of demolition, the local planning authority must notify certain national organisations (*p*).

The Minister may give directions calling in the application (*q*); in any event, if the local planning authority propose to grant consent, they must notify the Minister of their intention, and he then has a minimum period of 28 days in which to consider whether or not to call in the application (*r*).

If the Minister does not call in the application, the local authority may grant consent with or without conditions or they may refuse consent (*s*). If consent is refused or granted subject to conditions, the applicant may appeal to the Minister (*t*); so too, if the authority fail to give a decision within the prescribed period (*u*). The Act expressly provides that the grounds of appeal may include a claim that the building is not of special architectural or historic interest (*v*); this is of considerable importance because, as noted earlier in this chapter, the owner or occupier cannot object to the listing of his building. Where a case comes before the Minister (whether on appeal or on calling in) the applicant and the local planning authority have the right to a hearing (*a*). The Minister's decision is final except that it can

(*n*) *Ibid.*, reg. 3.
(*o*) *Ibid.*, reg. 4.
(*p*) The direction is contained in circular 61/68, para. 8.
(*q*) Act of 1971, Sch. 11, para. 4.
(*r*) *Ibid.*, Sch. 11, para. 5. The Minister may dispense with this requirement in certain cases: *ibid.*, Sch. 11, para. 7.
(*s*) *Ibid.*, s. 54(5).
(*t*) *Ibid.*, Sch. 11, para. 8(1).
(*u*) Act of 1971, Sch. 11, para. 9. The prescribed period is two months Listed Building Regs., reg. 3(4).
(*v*) *Ibid.*, Sch. 11, para. 8(2).
(*a*) *Ibid.*, Sch. 11, paras. 4(4), 8(4).

be challenged in High Court proceedings under section 245 of the Act of 1971 (*b*).

Revocation and Modification

A listed building consent may be revoked or modified. The local planning authority may if they consider it expedient having regard to the development plan and any other material considerations make an order for this purpose (*c*). The Minister may direct the local planning authority to make such an order or he may make the order himself (*d*). It is to be noted, however, that the power to revoke or modify only applies where the works authorised by the listed building consent have not been completed (*e*).

In the normal case, the local planning authority must submit the order to the Minister for confirmation, and he will if need be hold a public local inquiry or other hearing before deciding whether or not to confirm the order (*f*). But there is an alternative procedure which may be used where the local planning authority do not expect objections or a claim for compensation (*g*).

Where listed building consent is revoked or modified, the local planning authority are liable for compensation for abortive expenditure and for any other loss or damage directly attributable to the revocation or modification (*h*).

Enforcement

The demolition or alteration of a listed building without consent, or in breach of the conditions attached to consent, is an offence punishable by fine and/or imprisonment: it is similarly

(*b*) *Ibid.*, s. 242(3) (k). See chapter 6, pp. 141, *et seq., ante.*
(*c*) *Ibid.*, Sch. 11, para. 10(1).
(*d*) *Ibid.*, Sch. 11, para. 11(1).
(*e*) *Ibid.*, Sch. 11, para. 10(4).
(*f*) *Ibid.*, Sch. 11, para. 10(2) (3).
(*g*) *Ibid.*, Sch. 11, para. 12.
(*h*) Act of 1971, s. 172. The claim for compensation should be made to the local planning authority within six months of the date of the order, but the Minister may extend this time. Listed Buildings Regs., reg. 7.

an offence to demolish a listed building without giving notice to the Royal Commission on Historical Monuments (*i*).

In addition, the local planning authority may serve a "listed building enforcement notice" specifying the steps to be taken for restoring the building to its former state or for securing compliance with the terms and conditions of listed building consent (*k*). The notice is to be served on the owner and occupier of the building and on any person having an interest in the building which is materially affected by the notice (*l*). Any of these persons may appeal to the Minister on a number of specified grounds; these grounds include: (a) that the building is not of special architectural or historic interest and (b) that the matters complained of do not constitute a contravention of section 55, for instance that they do not affect the special character of the building (*m*). There is a further right of appeal to the High Court on matters of law (*n*).

Failure to comply with an enforcement notice is an offence punishable by fine not exceeding £400 on summary conviction or an unlimited fine on indictment (*o*). The local planning authority may also carry out the work themselves and recover the cost from the owner of the land (*p*).

Compensation and Purchase Notice

Refusal of listed building consent or the imposition of conditions may have two serious consequences for the owner of the building. It may cause him substantial loss at least in the sense of preventing him realising some development value; and where the land has become incapable of reasonably beneficial use, it may prevent him from rendering it capable of beneficial use. These possibilities are recognised to some extent by the Act of 1971.

(*i*) Act of 1971, s. 55(5).
(*k*) *Ibid.*, s. 96(1).
(*l*) *Ibid.*, s. 96 (3).
(*m*) *Ibid.*, s. 97(1).
(*n*) *Ibid.*, s. 246.
(*o*) *Ibid.*, s. 98(1)
(*p*) Act of 1971, s. 99(1).

The Act gives no general right of compensation for refusal or conditional grant of listed building consent. Compensation is payable, however, where the following conditions are satisfied (*q*):

(a) the Minister, either on appeal or on a called-in application, has refused consent for the alteration or extension of the building or has granted it subject to conditions;
(b) the works do not constitute development or, if they do, are development permitted by development order (*r*);
(c) the value of the claimant's interest is less than it would have been if consent had been granted unconditionally.

There is thus no compensation for refusal of consent to demolish a listed building.

If the land has become incapable of reasonably beneficial use, the owner may be able to serve a "listed building purchase notice" on the planning authority. This procedure is available where listed building consent has been refused or granted subject to conditions or revoked or modified, and the owner claims that the following conditions are satisfied (*s*):

(a) that the land has become incapable of reasonably beneficial use in its existing state (*t*);
(b) if consent was granted subject to conditions (or modified by the imposition of conditions) that the land cannot be rendered capable of reasonably beneficial use by carrying out the works in accordance with these conditions;
(c) in any case (i.e., whether consent was refused or granted subject to conditions or revoked or modified) that the land cannot be rendered capable of reasonably beneficial use by carrying out any other works for which listed building consent has been granted or for which the local

---

(*q*) *Ibid.*, s. 171(1).
(*r*) For permission by development order, see chapter 6, p. 114, *ante*.
(*s*) Act of 1971, s. 190(1).
(*t*) For the significance of this phrase see chapter 11, p. 199, *ante*.

planning authority or the Minister has undertaken to grant consent.

The procedure for the service of such purchase notices and the powers of the Minister are similar to those for purchase notices in connection with refusal of planning permission (*u*).

Building Preservation Notice

A building preservation notice may be served to protect a building which is considered to be of special architectural or historic interest but which has not yet been listed as such (*v*). The notice remains in force for a maximum period of six months (*a*), and whilst it is in force the building is protected in the same way as if it had been listed (*b*).

Before serving the notice the local planning authority must request the Minister to consider the listing of the building. They then serve notice on the owner and occupier explaining the position (*c*). In cases of urgency, they may affix a notice to the building itself instead of serving notice on the owner and occupier (*d*). The notice ceases to have effect as soon as the Minister decides to list the building or tells the local planning authority that he does not intend to list it. If he does not reach a decision within six months the notice automatically lapses (*e*).

Application for listed building consent may be made whilst the building preservation notice is in force. And if consent is refused or granted subject to conditions a claim for compensation may be submitted, but the compensation will not be paid unless and until the building is listed (*f*).

If the Minister decides not to list the building or allows the building preservation notice to lapse, the local planning authority

---

(*u*) See chapter 11, p. 203, *ante*.
(*v*) Act of 1971, s. 58(1).
(*a*) *Ibid.*, s. 58(3).
(*b*) *Ibid.*, s. 58(4).
(*c*) *Ibid.*, s. 58(1).
(*d*) *Ibid.*, s. 58(6), added by the Act of 1972.
(*e*) Act of 1971, s. 58(3).
(*f*) *Ibid.*, 173(2).

are liable to compensation in respect of loss or damage directly attributable to the making of the building preservation notice, and it is specifically provided that this compensation shall include damages payable for breaches of contract caused by the necessity of discontinuing or countermanding works to the building (*g*).

Repair and Acquisition of Listed Buildings

The listing of a building does not impose any obligations on the owners or occupiers for the repair of the building, But, if the building is not kept in a reasonable state of preservation, either the Minister or a local authority may acquire the building by compulsory purchase (*h*). The Minister may compulsorily acquire any adjacent buildings required for preserving the listed building (*i*). The power of compulsory purchase does not extend to ecclesiastical buildings and ancient monuments (*k*).

Before starting the compulsory purchase the Minister or the local authority must have served at least two months previously a repairs notice on the owner (*l*) of the building specifying the works considered necessary for the proper preservation of the building (*m*). The Act does not expressly state that neither the Minister nor the authority can proceed with compulsory purchase if the repairs are carried out, but it is submitted that this is the case.

In making a compulsory purchase order, the Minister or the authority must go through the procedure laid down in the Acquisition of Land (Authorisation Procedure) Act, 1946, and the owner and any lessees will have the usual rights of objection under that Act (*n*). In addition, there is right of appeal to the magistrates on the ground that reasonable steps are being taken

(*g*) *Ibid.*, s. 173(3), (4).
(*h*) *Ibid.*, s. 114(1).
(*i*) *Ibid.*, s. 114(2).
(*k*) *Ibid.*, s. 114(3).
(*l*) The word "owner" would appear to have the meaning given by the Act of 1971, s. 290. See p. 202, *ante*.
(*m*) *Ibid.*, s. 115(1).
(*n*) Act of 1971, s. 114(5).

for properly preserving the building; if the magistrates are satisfied on this point, any further proceedings on the compulsory purchase order will be stayed (*o*).

There are two bases of compensation for the compulsory acquisition of a listed building. Under what may be called the standard basis, it may be assumed for the purpose of assessing compensation that listed building consent would be granted for the demolition of the building or for any works for its extension except works for which listed building consent has been previously refused or granted subject to conditions so as to give rise to a claim for compensation (*p*). But the effect of this assumption has been severely reduced by the Act of 1974 which provides that, for the purpose of assessing compensation, the only planning permissions which would be granted would be for development falling within Schedule 8 of the Act of 1971.

The Act of 1974 thus places the owner of a listed building in a less favourable position than other owners whose land is compulsorily acquired. Of course, the owner of a listed building need not ask for compensation to be assessed on the basis of assumptions about demolition and redevelopment; he can claim if he wishes the value of his building as it stands.

There is also a penal basis of compensation. The amount of compensation will be reduced where the building has been deliberately allowed to fall into disrepair for the purpose of justifying its demolition and the redevelopment of the site or any adjoining land. In these circumstances the acquiring authority may include in the compulsory purchase order a "direction for minimum compensation". There is a right of appeal to the magistrates, who may quash the direction for minimum compensation. In any event, the Minister must be satisfied that the direction is justified. Where a direction for minimum compensation is confirmed, it is to be assumed in assessing compensation that planning permission would not be granted for development

(*o*) *Ibid.*, s. 114(6).
(*p*) *Ibid.*, s. 116.

of the site and that listed building consent would not be granted for demolition or alteration of the building (*q*).

OUTDOOR ADVERTISING

The Act of 1947 brought all outdoor advertising under the control of the planning authorities; that is to say, consent is now required for any outdoor advertisement even if its display does not involve development. This system of control is now continued by the Act of 1971. Advertisements displayed prior to 1st July, 1948, were also brought under control, the local planning authority being empowered to "challenge" any such advertisement by requiring the persons responsible for its display to make application for its retention. Provision is also made for areas of special control in which only certain limited classes of advertising are permitted, and the planning authority has no power to grant consent for anything outside these classes.

The system of advertising control is embodied in regulations made by the Minister under section 63 of the Act of 1971 (*r*). The definition of advertisement for the purposes of the Act and of these regulations is extremely wide and includes much else besides ordinary commercial advertising, as follows:

> "any word, letter, model, sign, placard, board, notice, device or representation, whether illuminated or not, in the nature of, and employed wholly or partly for the purposes of, advertisement, announcement or direction, and (without prejudice to the preceding provisions of this definition) includes any hoarding or similar structure used, or adapted for use, for the display of advertisements . . . ." (*s*).

Thus the legend "Samuel Short, Family Butcher" on a shop fascia, or "John Jones, Dental Surgeon" on a door plate will be

---

(*q*) Act of 1971, s. 117.

(*r*) The current regulations are the Control of Advertisements Regulations 1969 to 1975.

(*s*) Act of 1971, s. 290. The definition in the regulations is identical except that memorials and railway signals are specifically excluded.

advertisements as well as the large poster advertising a well-known national product. So will road traffic signs and election posters. The Regulations do not apply, however, to the following (*t*):—

(a) advertisements on enclosed land not readily visible from land outside the enclosure or from any part of the enclosure to which there is public right of access;

(b) advertisements inside a building unless the advertisements are illuminated and visible from outside or unless the building is one used principally for the display of advertisements;

(c) advertisements on vehicles;

(d) advertisements incorporated in and forming part of the fabric of the building, other than a building used principally for the display of advertisements or a hoarding;

(e) advertisements displayed on articles for sale or pumps etc. for dispensing articles for sale providing the advertisement relating to the article for sale is not illuminated and does not exceed 0.1 square metres in area.

Principles of Control

The powers of control conferred by the Act of 1971 are to be exercised only in the interests of amenity and public safety (*a*).

There is an express ban on any condition amounting to censorship of the subject matter of any advertisement; and the consent is to be the use of the site rather than for particular advertisements. There is however one exception: where application is made for the display of a particular advertisement, the authority may consider its contents so far—but only so far—as is necessary from the point of view of amenity and public safety (*b*).

It is clear from all this that the planning authority is not entitled to consider such controversial questions as the economic value or social desirability of advertisements, nor even the sub-

(*t*) Advertisements Regs., reg. 3.
(*a*) Act of 1971, s. 63(1), Advertisements Regs. reg. 5(1).
(*b*) Advertisements Regs., reg. 5(4).

stantial rates payable to the local authority in respect of many commercial advertisements.

In considering questions of amenity, the local planning authority are to consider the general characteristics of the locality, and special consideration is to be given to features of historic, architectural, cultural or similar interest. Under the heading of public safety they are to consider the safety of persons using any road, railway, canal, harbour or airfield likely to be affected by the display of advertisements; and in particular whether they are likely to obscure or hinder the interpretation of traffic signs, etc. (*c*).

Deemed Consent

All advertisements within the scope of the Regulations require consent before they can lawfully be displayed, but certain advertisements are deemed to have received consent under the Regulations themselves:

(1) "Existing advertisements"—advertisements displayed on 1st August, 1948, received a period of grace, provided they complied with certain conditions (*d*); the period of grace expired long ago, and such advertisements may now be "challenged" by the local planning authority (*e*).

(2) Advertisements falling within any of the "specified classes" set out in regulation 14. These advertisements may be challenged by the local planning authority; and the Minister may direct that regulation 14 is not to apply in any particular area or in any particular case. The specified classes cover a wide range of advertisements, including functional advertisements of local authorities, statutory undertakers and public transport undertakers (*f*); professional name plates, etc. (*g*); church notice

(*c*) ***Ibid.***, reg. 5(2).
(*d*) ***Ibid.***, reg. 11.
(*e*) ***Ibid.***, reg. 16.
(*f*) Advertisements Regs., reg. 14, Class I.
(*g*) ***Ibid.***, Class II (b).

boards (*h*); temporary advertisements with regard to the sale or letting of premises; the sale of goods or livestock, and various local events (*i*); and advertisements displayed on business premises with reference to the business carried on or the goods sold on the premises (*j*). In the last case it was a condition prior to 1970 that the highest part of the advertisement should not be more than fifteen feet from ground level, but there was no restriction on the number and size of the advertisements; As from 1st January, 1970, the conditions are (a) that no such advertisements may be displayed on the wall of a shop unless the wall contains a shop window; and (b) the highest part of an advertisement must not be above the bottom of any first floor window in the wall on which it is displayed. Also from 1st January, 1970 there are restrictions on the display of advertisements on the forecourt of business premises (*k*). Posters advertising proprietary goods may be displayed provided they are sold or supplied on the premises.

(3) Election notices, statutory advertisements and traffic signs (*l*). These cannot be challenged by the local planning authority (*m*).

(4) Advertisements for which the period of express consent has expired. An express consent will normally be for a limited period; provided the planning authority did not impose a condition to the contrary when granting consent, the advertisement may continue to be displayed at the expiry thereof subject to the right of the authority to challenge it (*n*).

(*h*) *Ibid.*, Class II (c).
(*i*) *Ibid.*, Class III.
(*j*) *Ibid.*, Class IV.
(*k*) *Ibid.*, Class V.
(*l*) *Ibid.*, reg. 9.
(*m*) *Ibid.*, reg. 16.
(*n*) Advertisements Regs., reg. 13.

(5) Advertisements relating to travelling circuses and fairs—subject to certain conditions these may be displayed on unspecified sites for a limited period (*o*).

Express Consent

Unless an advertisement has deemed consent under the Regulations, application must be made to the local planning authority for express consent (*p*). The authority may grant consent subject to certain standard conditions and any other conditions they think fit or they may refuse consent (*q*); the standard conditions require advertisements to be kept clean and tidy and in a safe condition (*r*). Consent cannot be given for a period of longer than five years without the approval of the Minister; the planning authority may grant consent for a shorter period, but they must state their reasons for so doing (*s*).

If the local planning authority refuse consent or attach conditions, the applicant may appeal to the Minister, but the Minister may refuse to entertain an appeal against the standard conditions or a condition limiting the consent to five years (*t*).

The proposed display may involve development as defined in section 22 of the Act of 1971. It is not necessary to apply for planning permission—this is deemed to be granted by the consent under the Regulations (*u*).

The Regulations contain provisions for the revocation or modification of consent similar to those in the Act of 1971 for the revocation of planning permission (*a*).

(*o*) *Ibid.*, reg. 23.
(*p*) *Ibid.*, reg. 17 as amended by the 1974 Regulations, reg. 2(b) S.I. 1974 No. 185.
(*q*) *Ibid.*, reg. 19.
(*r*) *Ibid.*, 1st Schedule.
(*s*) *Ibid.*, reg. 20.
(*t*) *Ibid.*, reg. 22.
(*u*) Act of 1971, s. 64. See chapter 6, p. 122, *ante*.
(*a*) Advertisements Regs., reg. 24, 25.

Enforcement of Control

Any person who displays an advertisement in contravention of the Regulations is guilty of an offence punishable by a fine not exceeding £100 and a daily fine of £5 (*b*). The persons displaying an advertisement are deemed to include not only the person who puts it up, but also the person whose land it is displayed on and the person whose goods or business are advertised; in the latter two cases, however, it is a defence to show that the advertisement was displayed without knowledge or consent (*c*).

Areas of Special Control

The Act of 1971 provides for the definition of areas of special control which may be "either rural areas or areas other than rural areas which appear to the Minister to require special protection on the grounds of amenity" (*d*). The language is curious since the purpose of defining a special area (whether rural or not) will be the protection of amenity rather than public safety. Perhaps the meaning is that rural areas may be freely defined as areas of special control, but there must be some really pressing reason for imposing special control in an urban area. The effect of special control is that only the following classes of advertisement may be displayed (*e*):

(a) *without express consent*

(i) advertisements of the classes specified in regulation 14 (*f*);

(ii) election notices, etc., as specified in regulation 9;

(iii) advertisements inside buildings.

(iv) advertisements as to travelling circuses and fairs.

(b) *with express consent*

(i) structures for exhibiting notices of local activities;

(*b*) Act of 1971, s. 109(2).

(*c*) *Ibid.*, s. 109(3). *John* v. *Reveille Newspapers, Ltd.* (1955), 5 P. & C.R. 95.

(*d*) Act of 1971, s. 63(3).

(*e*) Advertisements Regulations, reg. 27.

(*f*) See p. 235, *ante*. The conditions for the specified classes are in some cases more stringent than in areas not subject to special control.

(ii) announcements or directions relating to nearby buildings and land, *e.g.* hotels and garages;
(iii) advertisements required for public safety;
(iv) advertisements which would fall within one of the specified classes but for infringing the conditions as to height, number or illumination.

If the local planning authority consider that any area should be made subject to special control, they make an order to this effect. The order will require the Minister's confirmation and, if there are any objections, the Minister will hold a public inquiry before deciding whether or not to confirm the order (*g*).

MAINTENANCE OF WASTE LAND

Section 65 of the Act of 1971 (originally section 33 of the Act of 1947) enables the local planning authority to deal with any "garden, vacant site or other open land" which is in such a condition that it seriously injures the local amenities. In any such case, the authority can serve a notice on the owner or occupier requiring him to take the steps specified in the notice for abating the injury. Subject to a right of appeal to the local magistrates (*h*), failure to comply with the notice is a punishable offence and the planning authority may also enter upon the land and carry out the work at the expense of the defaulter (*i*).

The expression "garden, vacant site or other open land" was considered by the Court of Appeal in *Stephens* v. *Cuckfield R.D.C.* (*k*).

The plaintiff was the owner of a piece of land on part of which he had erected a sawmill; the rest of the land was used as a

---

(*g*) Act of 1971, s. 63(4); Advertisements Regulations, 2nd Sched.

(*h*) Act of 1971, s. 105. Section 106 gives both the appellant and the local planning authority a right of appeal from the magistrates to the Crown Court.

(*i*) *Ibid.*, s. 104 (offence) and s. 107 (execution of work and recovery of expenses).

(*k*) [1960] 2 All E.R. 716.

sawmill yard. In 1955 the use as a sawmill was abandoned and the land let to carbreakers who used the yard as well as the old sawmill for carbreaking. In 1957 the council served a notice under section 33 of the 1947 Act stating the condition of the open land within the curtilage was causing serious injury to the amenity of the district and requiring the removal from the land of all cars, car bodies and machinery.

HELD:—Whether a piece of land was properly described as a "garden" "vacant site" or "open land" was a question of fact to be determined in all the circumstances of each case. The phrase "open land" did not necessarily include all unbuilt land not surrounded by other buildings: on the other hand, an open space was not necessarily excluded because it was surrounded by a fence and might therefore be described as part of the curtilage, *e.g.* a spacious park surrounding a mansion house. But in the present case the land could not properly be described as open land for the purposes of the section, and the notice was quashed.

The Court of Appeal thus refused to lay down hard and fast rules, but they evidently gave some weight to the fact that the land was used for business purposes some part of which business was carried on in a building surrounded by the land in question.

It should not be assumed from this that use of land for business purposes will exclude the section. In *Britt* v. *Buckinghamshire C.C.* (*l*), the local planning authority considered that serious injury to amenity arose from the presence on some open land of old motor vehicles; notice was served on *B* under section 33 of the Act of 1947. On an appeal by *B* to the High Court, it was held that the notice was valid; the section applied where the injury to amenity arises from the use to which land is put as well as where it arises from the condition of the land.

If a local authority consider that any land in their area is derelict, neglected or unsightly, they have power under the National Parks and Access to the Countryside Act, 1949, to carry out work to bring the land into use or to improve its appearance; these

(*l*) [1963] 2 All E.R. 175.

powers apply throughout England and Wales and not only in national parks (*m*).

Abandoned Vehicles and other Refuse

When Parliament enacted the Civic Amenities Act, 1967, to strengthen the powers of planning authorities with regard to the conservation of areas and buildings of special interest and with regard to tree preservation, the opportunity was taken to introduce new provisions as to the disposal of abandoned vehicles and other refuse. These provisions, which are to be found in Part III of the Civic Amenities Act, do not strictly speaking form part of planning law and procedure; but, since they are concerned with the preservation of amenity, they deserve a brief mention. Broadly speaking, Part III deals with the growing problem of abandoned vehicles and other refuse by (a) requiring local authorities to establish places where local residents may deposit refuse, other than business refuse, free of charge; (b) making it an offence to abandon a motor vehicle, or any other thing brought there for the purpose, on any land in the open air without lawful authority; and (c) giving local authorities powers and duties in relation to abandoned vehicles and other refuse.

(*m*) National Parks and Access to the Countryside Act, 1949, s. 89 as amended by the Local Authorities (Land) Act 1963, s. 6.

CHAPTER 13

CONSERVATION AREAS

Conservation areas are a comparatively recent innovation. Prior to 1967, the emphasis was on the preservation of individual buildings as distinct from areas. Of course, under general planning powers, the local planning authority might, when considering an application for planning permission, consider the effect of the proposed development on the character of the surrounding area, and it would be wrong to belittle what had been done by many authorities to prevent unsuitable developments. But until 1967 no positive duty had been laid upon local planning authorities to take specific steps to safeguard the character of areas of special architectural or historic interest.

The Civic Amenities Act 1967 imposed such a duty for the first time: local planning authorities were required to determine which parts of their areas were of special architectural or historic interest, the character or appearance of which it was desirable to preserve or enhance, and to designate such areas as conservation areas. The relevant provisions of the Civic Amenities Act were subsequently re-enacted in the Act of 1971, but they have been considerably extended by the Acts of 1972 and 1974.

Designation of Conservation Areas

The Act of 1974 has substituted a new section 277 of the Act of 1971. Under this new section it is the duty of the local planning authority—that is, for this purpose, the district planning authority (*a*)—to determine from time to time which parts of their area should be treated as conservation areas. The Minister

(*a*) Act of 1971, s. 277(10).

may direct local planning authorities from time to time to review the past exercise of their functions in this respect and to consider whether new areas should be designated.

Although the duties imposed by section 277 are those of the district planning authority, the county planning authority or the Minister may designate conservation areas (*b*); the Minister will probably do this only in exceptional cases (*c*).

The procedure for the designation of a conservation area is comparatively simple. The district planning authority must consult the county planning authority; they then formally determine—presumably by resolution of the council—that a specified area is a conservation area. The Minister's approval is not required, but the local planning authority must give him formal notice of the designation of any area as a conservation area, and they must publish notice in the *London Gazette* and the local press; notice must also be entered in the local land charges register (*d*). There are no provisions for the making of objections or representations at this stage by interested parties (*e*). It seems that the local planning authority may subsequently cancel the designation of an area as a conservation area (*f*).

Conservation Area Plan

The designation of a conservation area has a number of direct legal consequences: special procedures for applications for planning permission, control of demolition of buildings and felling of trees, stricter controls over outdoor advertising. These matters are discussed later in this chapter.

(*b*) The powers of county planning authorities in this respect derive from the Local Government Act, Sch. 16, para. 48. The Minister's powers derive from the Act of 1971, s. 277(4).

(*c*) Circular 147/74, para. 5.

(*d*) Act of 1971, s. 277(7), (9).

(*e*) See, however, the provisions mentioned below for the calling of a public meeting to consider the local planning authority's detailed proposals for safeguarding and enhancing the conservation area.

(*f*) Act of 1971, s. 277(7).

In addition, the local planning authority are now required to prepare proposals for the preservation and enhancement of the character and appearance of the conservation area (*g*). This is a new requirement introduced by the Act of 1974 and is apparently intended to apply to conservation areas designated before the passing of that Act as well as to new conservation areas. The Minister may give directions to local planning authorities as to the time within which such proposals are to be prepared (*h*).

The proposals must be published and submitted to a public meeting in the area concerned; and, before finalising the proposals, the local planning authority must have regard to any views expressed by persons attending that meeting (*i*). In addition to these statutory requirements as to public participation, the Minister has recommended local planning authorities to consult various bodies such as local amenity societies (*k*).

The proposals put forward by the local planning authority are likely to involve the use of various powers under the Planning Acts, *e.g.* listing of buildings of special architectural or historic interest (*l*), the making of article 4 directions to restrict permitted development (*m*), and the making of discontinuance orders to remove or modify non-conforming uses (*n*). There is nothing to prevent the local planning authority putting forward schemes which would involve the use of powers given by other statutes: for instance, they might propose a traffic regulation scheme under the Road Traffic Regulation Act 1967.

The effective treatment of a conservation area may also involve issues which ought to be dealt with in the context of the development plan (*o*), and for that reason the preparation of a local plan

---

(*g*) Act of 1971, s. 277B(1).
(*h*) *Ibid.*, s. 277B(2).
(*i*) *Ibid.*, s. 277B(3).
(*k*) Circular 147/74, para. 17.
(*l*) See chapter 12, p. 222, *ante*.
(*m*) See chapter 6, p. 120, *ante*.
(*n*) See chapter 10, p. 196, *ante*.
(*o*) See the Minister's remarks on this point in circular 53/67.

may well be desirable (*p*); this would of course involve the formal procedures for the making and adoption of local plans (*q*).

Control of Demolition

The local planning authority may well see fit to protect some of the buildings in a conservation area by listing them as being of special architectural or historic interest under section 54 of the Act of 1971 (*a*). There will, however, be many buildings in a conservation area which do not merit listing, but their demolition might detrimentally affect the general appearance of the conservation area. Section 277 A of the Act of 1971 (*b*) prohibits (with some exceptions) the demolition of any building in a conservation area without listed building consent. This new control does not apparently extend to works of alteration, but it probably does prohibit the demolition of part of a building without consent (*c*).

The local planning authority have power to prosecute and to serve an enforcement notice for breach of section 277 A as in the case of listed buildings (*d*). If consent to demolish is refused, the owner may be able to serve a purchase notice (*e*).

Section 277 A does not apply to ecclesiastical buildings (*f*) or ancient monuments. Furthermore, the Minister may make a direction exempting certain classes of building (*g*). He has in fact made a direction exempting some twelve classes of building: these include inter alia small buildings of up to 115 cubic metres,

---

(*p*) *Development Plans Manual*, para. 10.3.
(*q*) See chapter 4, *ante*.
(*a*) See chapter 12, p. 222, *ante*.
(*b*) Section 277A was introduced by the Act of 1974.
(*c*) The word "building" includes part of a building: Act of 1971, s. 290 (1). It is therefore permissible to treat part of a building as a separate building. In any event demolition of part of a building may be a building operation requiring planning permission: see chapter 5, p. 87, *ante*.
(*d*) See chapter 12, p. 227, *ante*.
(*e*) See chapter 12, p. 229, *ante*.
(*f*) See chapter 12, p. 223, *ante*
(*g*) Act of 1971, s. 227A (1).

and buildings which the owner is required to demolish as a result of a statutory order (*h*).

Trees in Conservation Areas

Under section 61 A of the Act of 1971 (*i*), anyone who wishes to cut down, top, lop, uproot, wilfully damage or wilfully destroy (*k*) any tree in a conservation area must give notice of intention to the local planning authority. The authority then have six weeks in which to consider making a tree preservation order. The person concerned must not proceed with his intentions during this period of six weeks unless the authority have given specific consent in the meantime.

The Minister has power to specify exemptions from section 61 A. Some five cases are currently exempted by the Tree Preservation Amendment Regulations.

Advertisements in Conservation Areas

Section 63 of the Act of 1971 (as amended by the Act of 1974) provides that the Minister may make regulations prescribing the classes of advertisements which may be permitted in conservation areas. It seems that the intention is that in conservation areas there should be a strict control of outdoor advertising similar to that which operates in areas of special control (*l*).

Financial Assistance for Conservation Areas

By definition any conservation area is of some special architectural or historic interest (*m*). If the Minister considers that any conservation area is of *outstanding* (*n*) architectural or historic

(*h*) Circular 147/74, para. 15.
(*i*) Section 61A was introduced by the Act of 1974.
(*k*) For "wilful destruction" of a tree, see the account at p. 216, *ante* of *Barnet London Borough Council* v. *Eastern Electricity Board*, [1973] 2 All E.R. 319.
(*l*) For areas of special control see chapter 12, p. 238, *ante*.
(*m*) Act of 1971, s. 277.
(*n*) Presumably therefore this means rather more than "special".

interest, he may after consultation with the Historic Buildings Council, make a grant or loan with a view to the preservation or enhancement of the character of the area (*o*). This might include, for example, acquiring a piece of land to open up a view of an interesting group of houses or improving the line of a terrace, or even generally brightening up the area.

(*o*) Act of 1972, s. 10.

CHAPTER 14

SPECIAL CASES

CROWN LAND

It is a general rule of English law that the Crown is not bound by a statute unless the statute so provides, either expressly or by necessary implication (*a*). Thus, where Parliament intends that a particular statute shall not apply to the Crown, it is normally unnecessary to make any specific provision to that effect. In passing the Act of 1947, the intention of Parliament was that planning control should not apply as a matter of law to the Crown, but since it is possible under the English system of land tenure for the Crown and private persons to hold interests in the same land, it was necessary in the Act of 1947 to make special provision as to Crown land.

"Crown land" is defined (*b*) as any land in which an interest belongs to Her Majesty in right of the Crown or of the Duchy of Lancaster or the Duchy of Cornwall, or belongs to a Government Department or is held in trust for Her Majesty for the purposes of a Government department. The boards of nationalised industries and other public corporations—such as the British Broadcasting Corporation and the new town development corporations—are not Government departments and cannot claim the privileges of the Crown (*c*). The National Health Service is in a somewhat different position, all the land and buildings are vested in the Minister of Health and are thus "Crown land" (*d*).

(*a*) *Magdalen College, Cambridge Case* (1615), 11 Co. Rep. 66 b.

(*b*) Act of 1971, s. 266(7).

(*c*) The British Transport Commission, a nationalised body, was held not to be a Crown servant in *Tamlin* v. *Hannaford*, [1949] 2 All E.R. 327.

(*d*) National Health Service Act, 1946, ss. 6 and 58.

The application of the Act of 1971 to Crown land is as follows (*e*):

1. A development plan may include proposals relating to the use of the land.
2. A Government department does not require planning permission in order to carry out development on land in which they have an interest and no enforcement notice can be served on the department. Other persons having an interest in Crown land and wishing to carry out development are subject to planning control; and, if the appropriate authority agree (*f*), an enforcement notice may be served on any such person.
3. Buildings on Crown land may be listed as buildings of special architectural and historic interest, but a Government department does not require listed building consent to demolish or carry out works on such buildings, and no listed building enforcement notice may be served on the department. Any other person having an interest in the land must obtain listed building consent; and, if the appropriate authority agree, a listed building enforcement notice may be served on any such person.
4. The powers of compulsory purchase for planning purposes conferred by the Act of 1971 may be exercised in relation to any interest in the land, other than a Crown interest, provided the appropriate authority agree.
5. The owner of an interest in Crown land may serve a purchase notice provided the appropriate authority agree.

Although Government departments are exempt from planning control, they are expected to consult local planning authorities

(*e*) Act of 1971, s. 266; Sch. 6, para. 5.

(*f*) The "appropriate authority" is defined in s. 266 (7) of the Act of 1971, and means the particular government department which controls the land in question, or the Crown Estates Commissioners, or the Duchy of Lancaster, or the Duchy of Cornwall, according to circumstances (with the Treasury deciding any disputed cases).

before carrying out major development. The arrangements for such consultation have been reviewed and the new arrangements are set out in circular 80/71. Government departments will consult the local planning authority in respect of any development for which a private developer or a local authority would require specific permission, and also in respect of development in motorway service areas and similar developments in connection with trunk roads (*g*); and, even where consultation would not be required on this basis, Government departments will notify the local planning authority of proposals likely to be of special concern, e.g. development affecting conservation areas. Proposals for development by Government departments will usually be given publicity in the same way as for private developments, and opportunity given for representations by members of the public.

The local planning authority cannot veto development by Government departments; but, where there is disagreement, the matter may be referred to the Minister and he may hold a public inquiry. Such inquiries have been held in the past into the use of land by service departments; proposals for nuclear power stations; and, because of the feelings of local residents, into proposals for prisons and mental homes.

All these arrangements are, of course, subject to modification where national security is involved.

Development by Local Authorities and Statutory Undertakers

Local authorities and statutory undertakers are subject to planning control and must therefore obtain planning permission for any development which they propose to carry out. But the system of planning control is modified in three special types of case: development by a local planning authority within their own area; development carried out on operational land by a

(*g*) Proposals for trunk roads are subject to statutory procedures, but these procedures do not apply to such ancillary developments as service areas.

statutory undertaker; development by a local authority or statutory undertaker which requires the authorisation of a Government department.

Obtaining of Planning Permission by Local Planning Authorities

Section 270 of the Act of 1971 authorises the Minister to make regulations governing the grant of planning permission for (a) development by the local planning authority of land within their area; (b) development by other persons of land owned by the local planning authority. New procedures were introduced in 1976.

Where a local planning authority propose to carry out development on land within their area, they should (unless the development is permitted by the General Development Order (*h*)) pass a resolution "to seek permission for that development" (*i*).

Having passed the resolution they must take a number of steps (*j*):

(a) they must place a copy of the resolution and plans in the public register of planning applications;

(b) they must give notice to all persons having a "material interest" in the land (*k*);

(c) if any of the land is comprised within an agricultural holding, they must give notice to the tenant;

(d) if the development is "bad neighbour" development, as specified in article 8 of the General Development Order (*l*), they must publish notice in the local press;

(e) if the development would affect the character and appearance of a conservation area, they must publish notice in the local press and display a notice on or near the land;

(*h*) For the General Development Order, see generally Chapter 6, p. 000, *ante*.

(*i*) General Regulations, reg. 4(1).

(*j*) *Ibid*., reg. 4(2), (3), (4).

(*k*) *I.e.* either the freehold or a lease with at least seven years to run.

(*l*) See chapter 6, pp. 124, 125, *ante*.

(f) if the development is a departure from the development plan;

(g) if the authority seeking permission is the county council, they must consult the district council; similarly the district council must consult the county council;

(h) in the case of development affecting a trunk or special road, they must give notice to the Minister.

After all the necessary notices have been served or published, the local planning authority must wait until the expiry of the period allowed for the making of representations. If any representations are received, the authority must of course give them proper consideration. There is apparently no obligation upon the authority to notify the Minister, except in the case of a departure from the development plan or in the case of development affecting a trunk or special road (*m*). Provided the Minister has not called the matter in for his own consideration, the local planning authority may then pass a resolution to carry out the development. This second resolution takes effect as a planning permission deemed to have been granted by the Minister. This deemed planning permission will, however, be personal to the local planning authority and may be implemented only by that authority (*n*).

A similar procedure should be followed where the local planning authority wish to obtain planning permission in respect of land which they own but do not propose to develop themselves. Such planning permission may be either an outline or a detailed permission; and, since the development is to be carried out by other persons, the resolution authorising the development may include such conditions as the authority think fit (*o*).

The procedures outlined above do not relieve the local planning

---

(*m*) There is nothing to prevent other persons drawing the Minister's attention to the matter.

(*n*) General Regulations, reg. 4(5), (6), (7).

(*o*) *Ibid.*, reg. 5. The words "such conditions as the authority think fit" must be read subject to the requirements of the general law: see chapter 7, pp. 149 *et seq.*, *ante*.

authority of the obligation to obtain an industrial development certificate (*p*) or an office development permit (*q*). These procedures cannot be used to obtain planning permission for work involving the alteration or extension of a listed building (*r*).

An authority may wish to arrange for the function of obtaining a deemed planning permission to be exercised by an officer. In that case, a written notice given to the authority by the officer concerned will take the place of a resolution of the authority (*s*).

Development by Statutory Undertakers

For the purposes of the 1971 Act, the expression "statutory undertaker" means "persons authorised by any enactment to carry on any railway, light railway, tramway, road transport, water transport, canal, inland navigation, dock, harbour, pier or lighthouse undertaking, or any undertaking for the supply of electricity, gas, hydraulic power or water" (*t*). A local authority may be a statutory undertaking; *e.g.* a local authority may supply water for the whole or part of its area and sometimes it may be authorised to supply water to areas outside its own boundaries.

Statutory undertakers who propose to carry out development must apply to the local planning authority for planning permission, but in relation to the operational land of statutory undertakers, some minor modifications are made by Part XI of the Act of 1971.

If the application comes before the Minister (either because it is called in under section 35 or on appeal against the decision of the local planning authority) the Minister must act jointly with the Minister responsible for the type of undertaking in question, *e.g.* in the case of a gas undertaking the Secretary of

(*p*) General Regulations, reg. 8. For industrial development certificates, see chapter 6, p. 126, *ante*.

(*q*) General Regulations, reg. 9. For office development permits, see chapter 6, p. 129, *ante*.

(*r*) General Regulations, reg. 4(1), 5(1). For listed buildings, see chapter 12, *ante*, pp. 222 *et seq*.

(*s*) General Regulations, reg. 6.

(*t*) Act of 1971, s. 290.

State for Trade and Industry. At one time there was a further provision which enabled the statutory undertakers to refer the Minister's decision to special parliamentary procedure; but this was repealed by the Act of 1968 (*u*).

Development requiring Authorisation of Government Department

In many cases development by a local authority or statutory undertaker will require (apart from planning control) the authorisation of a Government department, *e.g.* the confirmation of a compulsory purchase order or consent for the borrowing of money. Section 40 of the Act of 1971 enables the Government department concerned to direct that planning permission shall be deemed to be granted. In practice, however, local authorities are expected to obtain planning permission by applying in the ordinary way (*a*).

MINERALS

As explained in an earlier chapter, the winning of minerals whether by underground or surface working constitutes development. As a physical operation, however, mineral working differs from other forms of development. In the erection of a building, for instance, the digging of foundations or the laying of bricks are only of value as part of the whole building; in mineral working, however, the removal of each separate load is of value. As LORD WIDGERY, C.J. put it (*b*): "each shovelful or each cut by the bulldozer is a separate act of development." Because of the special characteristics of mineral working, the Minister is authorised to make regulations adapting and modifying the provisions of the Act of 1971 in relation to mineral development (*c*).

(*u*) Act of 1968, s. 70(3).

(*a*) Report of the Ministry of Housing and Local Government for the period 1950/51 to 1954, p. 78. (1972) 24 P. & C. R. 309.

(*b*) *Thomas David* (*Porthcawl*), *Ltd.* v. *Penybont R.D.C.*, [1972] 1 All E.R. 733: affirmed by the Court of Appeal, [1972] 3 All E.R. 1092.

(*c*) Act of 1971, s. 264.

The current regulations were made in 1971 prior to the coming into force of the Act of 1971. The regulations refer therefore to various provisions of the Acts of 1962 and 1968, but they are kept in force by the new Act and references in the regulations to specific provisions of the Acts of 1962 and 1968 should now be read as references to the corresponding provisions of the new Act.

The Act of 1971 (*d*) also facilitates the obtaining of working rights by order of the High Court under the Mines (Working Facilities and Support) Act 1966 as amended (*e*).

Modifications of the Act in relation to the Control of Development (*f*)

The winning and working of minerals constitute development for the purposes of the Act of 1971 in that they are a "mining operation". As such mineral development is not a "use" of land (*g*) but the Minerals Regulations provide that it shall be treated as a use for certain purposes in connection with the administration of planning control. The effect of the Act and Regulations is as follows.

Grant of temporary permission.—Section 30 of the Act of 1971 provides that, on a grant of planning permission, a condition may be imposed requiring the removal of a building or works or the discontinuance of any use of land at the expiration of a specified period. By treating mineral development as a use of land for the purposes of section 30 the Mineral Regulations make it possible to impose a condition requiring the discontinuance of mining operations after a certain period (*h*).

Duration of planning permission.—The normal rule is that a grant of planning permission will lapse if development is not commenced within five years. In the case of mineral development

(*d*) *Ibid.*, s. 265.
(*e*) Mines (Working Facilities and Support) Act 1974.
(*f*) The modifications of the Act of 1971 in relation to compensation are dealt with at p. 300, *post*.
(*g*) Act of 1971, s. 290. And see chapter 5, p. 80, *ante*.
(*h*) Minerals Regulations, reg. 3.

this period is extended to ten years; for this purpose development is to be taken as having commenced on the earliest date on which any of the mining operations to which the planning permission relates began to be carried out (*i*).

Enforcement notices.—An enforcement notice may require the demolition or alteration of any buildings or works or the discontinuance of any use of land. The Minerals Regulations treat mineral development as a use for this purpose, and also for the purposes of section 89 of the Act so that the mineral operator can be prosecuted if he fails to comply with the enforcement notice (*k*). Where mining operations are carried out without planing permission, the enforcement notice must be served within four years of the development being carried out (*l*). But in the event of non-compliance with a condition, the Regulations provide that an enforcement notice may be served at any time within four years *after the non-compliance has come to the knowledge of the local planning authority* (*m*). As Parliament has expressly enacted that an enforcement notice in respect of conditions imposed on planning permission for mineral working should be served within four years of the actual breach of condition (*n*) it is questionable whether this particular "modification" of the Act is valid.

The Minerals Regulations do not apply to mineral working by the National Coal Board nor to the winning and working of minerals in connection with agriculture (*o*). There may therefore be difficulty in imposing time limits upon these forms of mineral working and in serving enforcement notices.

(*i*) Minerals Regulations, regs. 6, 7.

(*k*) *Ibid.*, reg. 3.

(*l*) Act of 1971, s. 87(3) (a). Since "each shovelful or each cut by the bulldozer is a separate act of development", the four-year rule does little more than protect the mineral operator from any liability to restore the land; it certainly does not prevent the service of an enforcement notice to restrain further unauthorised working: *Thomas David (Porthcawl), Ltd.* v. *Penybont R.D.C., supra.*

(*m*) Minerals Regulations, reg. 4.

(*n*) Act of 1971, s. 87(3) (b).

(*o*) Act of 1971, 271, s. 264 (4).

Working Rights by Order of the High Court

The power to obtain working rights to facilitate mineral development has existed, quite independently of planning legislation, since 1923. In the first place it has been found that minerals might be left unworked because the land was or had been copyhold land or was subject to a lease or some restriction, or because the minerals were owned in such small parcels that they could not be conveniently worked. Secondly, even where these difficulties did not apply, a mineral operator might require some ancillary working right such as the right to let down the surface, to construct airways and shafts, or to obtain a water supply.

The Mines (Working Facilities and Support) Act 1966 (replacing earlier legislation) provides machinery by which such working rights can be obtained. The applicant, wishing to search for or work minerals, must first approach the Department of Industry (*p*) who will if satisfied that there is a *prima facie* case refer it to the High Court (*q*).

Right to work minerals.—The Act of 1966 enables the High Court to make an order granting to the applicant the right to work minerals provided:

(a) that the applicant has an interest in the minerals or, if the minerals are owned in small parcels, in minerals adjacent to them;

(b) that there is a danger for certain reasons of the minerals being left permanently unworked;

(c) that it is not reasonably practicable to obtain the necessary rights by private negotiation;

(d) that it is expedient in the national interest that the rights should be granted.

The working of minerals may also be impeded by restrictions in a mining lease or other documents of title. Under the Act of 1966, as originally enacted, the court might grant the right to work

(*p*) The powers of the Ministry of Power were transferred to the Department of Industry in 1970.

(*q*) Originally the Railway and Canal Commission.

certain specified minerals free from these restrictions if this result could not be achieved by private negotiation and would be in the national interest. The Mines (Working Facilities and Support) Act 1974 extends this provision to all minerals other than coal.

Ancillary rights.—The Act of 1966 also enables the High Court to make an order for the grant of ancillary rights provided conditions (c) and (d) are satisfied.

Section 265 of the Act of 1971 (re-enacting provisions in the Acts of 1947 and 1962) authorised the Minister and the Secretary of State for Industry to make regulations to facilitate the making of orders conferring the right to work minerals where the land was allocated for mineral working in the development plan. The regulations provided that where the development plan allocated any land for mineral working and there was danger for any reason that the minerals would be left unworked, the court might grant the necessary working rights; and for this purpose it was to be assumed that the working of the minerals would be in the national interest.

Section 265 of the Act of 1971 has now been repealed by the Mines (Working Facilities and Support) Act 1974. It follows that the development plan can no longer be relied on as conclusive evidence that the working of the minerals would be in the national interest.

Chapter 15

HIGHWAYS AND PLANNING

The general law of highways is a subject of some complexity and, in any event, is outside the scope of this book. But some aspects of planning law are concerned with highways and in order to understand these it will be helpful to begin with a brief general account of the law of highways.

What is a Highway?

A highway is usually defined as land whether made or unmade, over which all Her Majesty's subjects have the right to pass and to re-pass. The fact that all members of the public have this right of passage distinguishes a highway from various private rights of way (such as easements) and rights of way for the benefit of a limited section of the public (such as a churchway to enable the inhabitants of a village to go to and from church).

A highway is not necessarily open to vehicles. At common law highways may be either:

(a) footpaths;
(b) bridleways over which there is also the right to ride or lead a horse;
(c) drift-ways over which there is in addition the right to drive animals; and
(d) carriageways over which in addition to all the above there is the right to drive vehicles.

The right of the public to use a carriageway for foot passage and for horses and other animals may be restricted on motorways and trunk roads by order of the Minister under legislation now embodied in the Highways Act, 1959. This Act also recognises a further category of highway—namely a cycle track (*a*).

Creation of Highways

At common law the normal method of creating a highway is by "dedication and acceptance"; that is, the owner of the land dedicates it as a highway and the public accept it. Dedication and acceptance may be formal but are often implied as where a landowner permits the public to use a road for a long period without counter-measures (*b*) to rebut the presumption that he intends dedication; or where an estate developer lays out a road communicating at both ends with existing highways.

Nowadays many highways are created by public authorities under statutory authority; for example, where the Minister of Transport builds a trunk road or a local authority lays out roads as part of a housing estate.

Highways created before 1835 were automatically "repairable by the inhabitants at large"; that is, at the public expense. With the rapid growth of population and towns in the nineteenth century, this could have imposed a serious burden on the public authorities who had no control over the creation of highways. The Highway Act, 1835, made no change in the law relating to the creation of highways but provided that no new highway should become repairable by the inhabitants at large unless it was made up to the satisfaction of the public surveyor of highways. Then, in 1875 came the first of the "private street works codes".

Section 150 of the Public Health Act, 1875, enabled any urban authority to require the owners of properties adjoining any unadopted highway or private street to carry out specified works for making up, sewering and lighting the street; if any frontager failed to do so, the authority might carry out the work at his expense. This was followed by the Private Street Works Act, 1892, under which the authority gave each owner notice of their

(*a*) Highways Act 1959, s. 295(1).
(*b*) For example, by displaying a notice or by periodically closing gates.

intention to do the work and to charge him for it in proportion to the length of his frontage (*c*).

The 1892 Act applied to all rural districts and to any borough urban district which adopted it in place of the 1875 Act. Both systems are preserved by the Highways Act, 1959, which refers to "the code of 1875" and "the code of 1892". In some areas there are local Act provisions which either replace or supplement these codes. Where a street is made up under any such private street works legislation the local authority may then declare the street to be maintainable at public expense or they may be compelled to adopt it if a sufficient majority of the frontagers so require.

The National Highway System

Prior to 1936, all roads in Great Britain were the responsibility of the local authorities. The Minister of Transport was empowered to make grants to local authorities for the construction and maintenance of highways, but he had no power to undertake construction and maintenance. In 1936 the first Trunk Roads Act was passed. It specified a number of major roads which were henceforth to be trunk roads and vested them in the Minister of Transport as highway authority; more roads were declared to be trunk roads under an Act of 1946. In addition, the Minister of Transport was empowered to direct that any existing road should be a trunk road and he was given power to construct new trunk roads. He might also direct that any existing trunk road should cease to be a trunk road.

The next step in the creation of a national highway system was the passing of the Special Roads Act, 1949. This enabled highway authorities in pursuance of schemes, either made by the Minister of Transport as a highway authority or made by the local highway authority with the approval of the Minister of Transport, to provide roads restricted to use by particular classes

(*c*) The authority may modify this to take account of the "degree of benefit" derived by any particular owner.

of traffic only. It is in pursuance of these powers that the high-speed motorways designated by the letter "M" have been constructed.

The greater part of the Trunk Road Acts and of the Special Roads Act has been replaced by the Highways Act, 1959, but there is no material change in the earlier provisions.

The siting of trunk roads and special roads is of fundamental importance to the planning of town and countryside, and it is not surprising that the Minister is required to give consideration to "the requirements of local and national planning including agriculture" (*d*). The functions of the Minister of Transport under the Highways Act, 1959, have now been vested in the Secretary of State for the Environment, referred to throughout this book as "the Minister". This should result in a greater degree of co-ordination between transportation and planning policies.

Where the Minister proposes to make a trunk road order or a scheme for a special road, he must publish notice in the *London Gazette* and in local newspapers and he must allow time for objections to be lodged. If there are any objections, the Minister must (except in certain specified circumstances) cause a public local inquiry to be held. Thereafter, he will decide whether to make the order or scheme, either in its original form or with modifications (*e*).

The fact remains, however, that in preparing development plan schemes, whether under the old (*f*) or the new system (*g*), the local planning authority will have little or no control over the siting of trunk and special roads. As regards the older type of development plan, it is expressly provided that orders and schemes relating to trunk roads and special roads are to have effect as if they were included in the development plan (*h*)—a formula which in effect enables the Minister to superimpose trunk

(*d*) Highways Act, 1959, ss. 7(2), 11(6).
(*e*) *Ibid.*, 1st Schedule.
(*f*) See chapter 4, p. 53, *ante*.
(*g*) See chapter 4, p. 59, *ante*.
(*h*) Act of 1971. Sch. 5, para. 5.

roads and special roads on the development plan. As regards the new structure and local plans, the Act of 1971 provides that neither the Minister nor the local planning authority shall be obliged to consider representations or objections which are in substance representations and objections with respect to orders and schemes for trunk and special roads (*i*).

Local Highways

Highways, other than trunk roads and special roads vested in the Minister of Transport, are the responsibility of the local highway authorites. Since 1st April, 1974, the local highway authority is the county council. District councils, however, may exercise certain functions in respect of footpaths, bridleways and urban roads which are neither trunk roads nor classified roads; certain powers are also given to parish councils.

Most applications for planning permission will, however, be determined by the district council; since many applications for planning permission involve highway considerations, the district council may need to consult the county council as highway authority, and in some cases the county council may issue directions to the district council (*k*).

Where land is defined in a development plan as the site of a new road, or as being for a road-widening, the highway authority must purchase the land they actually require for the construction or widening of the road. At the same time, the new or widened road may confer considerable benefits on adjoining landowners. Section 206 of the Highways Act 1959 (*l*) replacing section 48 of the Act of 1947, enables the authority, in certain circumstances to charge the expense of construction (as distinct from the cost of the land) to the owners of adjoining property. The circumstances are:

(a) that the land has been defined in the development plan as

(*i*) Act of 1971, s. 16.
(*k*) G.D.O. Art. 11A, 13 (1) (c).
(*l*) As amended by the Local Government Act 1972, Sch. 30.

the site of a new road, or as being required for the widening of a road of less than byelaw width; and

(b) it must have been designated in the development plan as land to which section 206 of the Highways Act, 1959, is to apply.

When the development plan has been confirmed the appropriate council may make an order declaring the land (including in the case of a street widening, the existing street) to be a "private street". This has the effect of bringing into operation the private street works code for that district (that is, either the code of 1875, the code of 1892 or any local enactments) together with certain modifications made by the Construction and Improvement of Private Streets Regulations. When the street has been made up or widened to the satisfaction of the authority, it becomes a highway maintainable at the public expense (*m*).

Stopping up and Diversion of Highways

The common law rule is "once a highway, always a highway". The effect is that in common law there is no power whatever to stop up or divert an existing highway. There are, however, various statutory powers, some of which specifically relate to the requirements of good planning.

Stopping up by the Minister

Under section 209 of the Act of 1971, the Minister may make an order to stop up or divert a highway if it is necessary to do so in order to enable development to be carried out in accordance with a grant of planning permission or by a government department.

The order may require the provision of an alternative highway or the improvement of an existing highway, and for this purpose the Minister or a local highway authority may compulsorily acquire the necessary land. The order may also require any other

(*m*) Town and Country Planning (Construction and Improvement of Private Streets) Regulations, 1951; S.I. 1951 No. 2224, reg. 10.

authority or person to pay or contribute towards (a) the cost of any works required by the order (b) the repayment of any compensation paid by the highway authority under the Restriction of Ribbon Development Act, 1935, in respect of the highway to be stopped up or diverted. The persons likely to be charged in this way are, of course, the persons responsible for the development to be assisted by the stopping up or diversion. Thereafter, however, the new or improved highway may become maintainable at the public expense.

Under section 214, the Minister may make an order to stop up any public right of way over land held by a local authority (not necessarily the local planning authority); he must be satisfied that an alternative right of way has been or will be provided, or that an alternative right of way is unnecessary.

The procedure for orders by the Minister under section 209 or section 214 is prescribed by section 215.

The Minister must publish notice of the proposed order in the *London Gazette* and the local press, and a copy of the notice must be prominently displayed at each end of the stretch of highway which is to be stopped up or diverted. Time must be allowed for objections; if objections are received from any local authority, statutory undertaker or from any person apparently affected by the order, the Minister must hold a public local inquiry unless in the special circumstances an inquiry is unnecessary. Thereafter the Minister will decide whether or not to make the order either in its original form or subject to modifications. If the order requires any person to pay or contribute towards the cost of a new or improved highway or to repay compensation paid on an earlier occasion, that person may require the order to be subject to special parliamentary procedure.

In the case of mineral development, the order may provide for the stopping up or diversion for a limited period, after which the original highway is to be restored (*n*).

(*n*) Mineral Workings Act, 1951, s. 32.

At one time no steps could be taken until planning permission had actually been granted. Now, however, the Minister may in certain cases (*e.g.* where there is an appeal in connection with the application for planning permission) make the draft order before the actual grant of planning permission. This enables the two matters to be dealt with concurrently and thus save possibly many months of delay; but the Minister cannot make the final order until planning permission has been granted (*o*).

Stopping-up and Other Action by Local Authorities

Under section 210 of the Act of 1971 a footpath or bridleway may be stopped up or diverted by order of the local planning authority for the purpose of enabling development to be carried out in accordance with a grant of planning permission or by a government department; if the planning permission was granted by an authority exercising delegated powers, the order should be made by that authority.

Section 214 enables a local authority (not necessarily the planning authority) to make an order stopping up any footpath or bridle-way over land held by them for planning purposes; the authority must be satisfied that an alternative right of way has been or will be provided, or that an alternative right of way is unnecessary.

Before making an order under either of these sections, the authority concerned must publish a notice stating the effect of the order and indicating the time and manner in which representations and objections may be made. If there are no representations or objections, the authority may themselves confirm the order. Otherwise, the order must be submitted to the Minister who will hold a public local inquiry or other hearing before deciding whether or not to confirm the order (*p*).

Local planning authorities also have powers to convert highways used by vehicles into footpaths. These powers may be used

(*o*) Act of 1971, s. 216.
(*p*) Act of 1971, s. 217; Sch. 20.

where the local planning authority have adopted a proposal for improving the amenity of part of their area (*q*), *e.g.* convert a highway into a pedestrian precinct; having taken this preliminary step, the authority apply to the Minister for an order (*r*). Thereafter the procedure is the same as for orders by the Minister for the stopping up or diversion of a highway (*s*). The local planning authority are liable in compensation for injurious affection to any person having lawful access to the highway (*t*).

(*q*) *Ibid.*, s. 212(1). This power cannot be used over a trunk road or a road classified as a principal road.

(*r*) *Ibid.*, s. 212(2).

(*s*) See p. 264, *ante*.

(*t*) Act of 1971, s. 212(5). Injurious affection can be mitigated by exercise of the Minister's power to authorise the use of the footpath or bridleway by specified vehicles: *ibid.*, s. 212(3).

CHAPTER 16

THE CONDUCT OF A PLANNING INQUIRY

The powers and duties of planning authorities cover a very wide field, but they can conveniently be classified under three main heads: (i) the making of schemes of various kinds (including the development plan); (ii) giving a decision on applications put forward by landowners or developers; (iii) enforcement notices.

Where a planning authority (whether the local planning authority or the Minister) make a scheme, the persons likely to be affected by it have the right to make objections or representations; any person putting forward an objection or representation will usually have the right to be heard at a public local inquiry or at least a private hearing by a person appointed for the purpose, that is, an Inspector. There is an exception to this rule in the case of structure plans where the Minister will hold an "examination in public" at which no one will have any statutory right to be heard.

Where the local planning authority give a decision on an application, the applicant has the right to appeal to the Minister, who must consider the appeal unless it is clear that the local planning authority could not in law have given any other decision: the applicant always has the right to make representations to the Minister and usually has the right to be heard by a person appointed by the Minister. If the application has been referred to the Minister for decision—for instance under section 35 of the Act of 1971—the applicant and the local planning authority always have the right to make representations before the Minister gives his decision and usually the right to ask for a hearing.

Any person served with an enforcement notice has the right to appeal to the Minister; if there is an appeal both the appellant and the local planning authority have the right to ask for a hearing.

What form a hearing shall take is decided by the Minister, but usually it is a public local inquiry. At a public local inquiry, the Inspector has power to require evidence on oath, to subpoena witnesses and to require the production of documents (*a*); these powers are not available at a hearing.

The great majority of public local inquiries and hearings relate to appeals against planning decisions, and appeals against enforcement notices. Considerable importance also attaches to inquiries into development plans and major highway schemes. We will consider each of these in turn.

APPEALS AGAINST PLANNING DECISIONS

Preliminary

The procedure for appeals to be determined by the Minister is now governed by the Inquiries Procedure Rules 1974: where the appeal is to be determined by the Inspector himself (*b*) the Determination by Inspectors Rules 1974 apply. The procedure is similar in either case up to the close of the inquiry or hearing.

Not later than twenty-eight days before the inquiry the local planning authority must send to the appellant and to every "section 27 party" a written statement of their case (*c*). A "section 27 party" is anyone who has made representations to the Minister under section 27 of the Act of 1971 re-enacting section 17 of the Act of 1962 (*d*).

The local authority's statement of their case is to deal with four matters (*e*):

(1) It must contain a statement of the submissions which they propose to put forward at the inquiry.

(2) It must include a list of all the documents (including

(*a*) Local Government Act 1972, s. 250.

(*b*) See pp. 140 *et seq.*, *ante.*

(*c*) Inquiries Procedure Rules, rule 6(2); Determination by Inspectors Rules, rule 7(1).

(*d*) See p. 139, *ante.*

(*e*) Inquiries Procedure Rules, rule 6(2), (3), (4); Determination by Inspectors Rules, rule 7(1), (2), (3).

maps and plans) to which they intend to refer at the inquiry; and it must be indicated where and when these documents can be inspected and copied.

(3) It must mention any relevant direction given by the Minister or the Minister of Transport and must include a copy of the direction and the reason given for its making.

(4) It must include any expressions of view given by any Government department on which the authority propose to rely.

In addition, any member of the public has the right to inspect the statement of case (*f*).

The local planning authority must not depart from their statement of case without the leave of the Inspector (*g*).

The Minister may require the appellant also to submit a written statement of the submissions which he proposes to put forward at the inquiry and a list of all documents to which he intends to refer (*h*); the appellant will not be allowed to depart from this statement without the leave of the Inspector (*i*). The Minister has said however that the power is used "only sparingly and in exceptional circumstances" (*j*). This may seem to favour the appellant at the expense of the local planning authority.

Procedure at the Inquiry

The procedure at a public local inquiry into an appeal against a planning decision is as follows:

1. The Inspector opens the proceedings by stating the purpose of the inquiry. The appellant and the local planning authority then "enter their appearance": that is the advocate for each party

(*f*) Inquiries Procedure Rules, rule 6(5); Determination by Inspectors Rules, rule 7(4).

(*g*) Inquiries Procedure Rules, rule 10(5); Determination by Inspectors Rules, rule 12(5).

(*h*) Inquiries Procedure Rules, rule 6(6); Determination by Inspectors Rules, rule 7(5).

(*i*) See note (*g*) *supra*.

(*j*) Letter dated September, 1966 to the Town Clerk of the London Borough of Haringey, quoted in 1966 J.P.L. 618.

states his name and indicates what witnesses he proposes to call. The Inspector then asks if any other interested parties wish to be heard.

2. Unless the Inspector directs otherwise (*k*), the appellant "opens". The appellant's advocate makes an opening speech in which he will summarise the history of the case to date, the more important facts on which he intends to rely and the arguments in favour of the appeal being allowed.

3. The appellant's advocate then calls his witnesses. The Inspector has the power to require evidence to be given on oath, but this is rarely done at an inquiry of this sort. The rules of evidence are less formal than in a court of law; although admissible as a matter of law in planning inquiries (*l*), hearsay evidence is unsatisfactory and may well be disregarded by the Inspector. The evidence may be given as in a court of law by question or answer; but, what would not be allowed in a court of law, it may be given instead by the witness reading his proof of evidence. The matters on which evidence may be required are discussed later in this chapter. Each witness may expect to be cross-examined by the advocate for the local planning authority and by any section 17 party; the Inspector has a discretion to allow other interested persons to ask questions of the witness. The advocate for the appellant will then re-examine his witness. Questions may also be asked by the Inspector; sometimes the Inspector reserves his questions until after re-examination, but it is more appropriate for such questions to be put prior to re-examination.

4. It is also permissible to put in letters and other documents supporting the appellant's case, but it should be remembered that such documents (unless agreed by the local planning authority) are not so impressive as oral evidence by a witness which is open to cross-examination.

(*k*) Inquiries Procedure Rules, rule 10(2); Determination by Inspectors Rules, rule 12(2).

(*l*) *T. A. Miller* v. *Minister of Housing and Local Government*, [1968] 2 All E.R. 633.

5. The advocate for the local planning authority then calls his witnesses who will, of course, be subject to cross-examination and to questions from the Inspector. After calling his witnesses he makes his speech on behalf of the authority.

6. The section 17 parties then have the right to state their case and the Inspector may allow other interested persons to make statements. This may be done by a lawyer or professional representative or by the interested persons themselves.

7. The advocate for the appellant then makes his final speech.

8. The Inspector closes the inquiry and inspects the site in the company of representatives of the appellant and the local planning authority.

Hearings

The procedure at a hearing is the same as at a public local inquiry except that members of the public will not normally be present, or if present, will not be permitted to take part in the proceedings.

The Minister's Decision

The form of the Inspector's report and the Minister's powers thereon are also to some extent governed by the Inquiries Procedure Rules.

The Inspector must in his report set out specific findings of fact and his recommendations; he is free not to make a recommendation, but in that case he must give his reason for not doing so (*m*). In addition, the Inspector invariably includes in his report a paragraph headed "Conclusions"; these are the opinions which the Inspector has drawn from his findings of fact, and it is upon these conclusions that his recommendation will be based.

The Inspector's duty to record findings of fact was considered in *Continental Sprays, Ltd.* v. *Minister of Housing and Local Government* (*n*). The appellants contended that the Inspector

---

(*m*) Inquiries Procedure Rules, rule 14(1).
(*n*) (1968), 19 P. & C.R. 774.

should make findings on all the principal material issues of fact arising from the evidence given at the inquiry. Without deciding whether the Inspector should have done so, MEGAW, J. held that the Court was not entitled to review the evidence and decide what were the principal material issues of fact arising therefrom.

This decision was followed by WILLIS, J. in *William Boyer & Sons, Ltd.* v. *Minister of Housing and Local Government* (*o*) and again in *W. J. Simms, Sons and Cooke, Ltd.* v. *Minister of Housing and Local Government* (*p*).

The Minister may disagree with the Inspector on a finding of fact; he may receive some new evidence (including expert opinion on a matter of fact); or he may take into consideration issues of fact not raised at the inquiry. If, in any of these circumstances, he is minded to disagree with the Inspector's recommendation he must inform the appellant, the local planning authority and the section 17 parties. Any of these persons then has twenty-one days in which to make either written representations or to require the inquiry to be re-opened (*q*). The Minister is not obliged to notify the parties and give them the opportunity of making further representations where he disagrees with the Inspector's conclusions; but the Minister should consider whether what the Inspector has described as a conclusion is really a finding of fact (*r*).

The Minister is to notify his decision with his reasons to the appellant, the local planning authority, the section 27 parties and any other person who attended the inquiry and asked to be notified. The Minister usually sends a copy of the Inspector's report with his decision letter; if he does not do so, any of these

---

(*o*) (1969), 20 P. & C.R. 176.

(*p*) (1969), 210 Estates Gazette 705. This was a case arising out of the Minister's decision on a development plan amendment and related compulsory purchase orders.

(*q*) Inquiries Procedure Rules, rule 14(2).

(*r*) *Lord Luke of Pavenham* v. *Minister of Housing and Local Government*, [1967] 2 All E.R. 1066, overruling the decision of LAWTON, J. at first instance.

persons may ask for a copy (*a*). Instead of formally setting out his reasons, the Minister will often adopt the Inspector's conclusions. This is an acceptable procedure; but, where the Inspector's conclusions were so worded as to be meaningless, the court held that the Minister had failed to give any reasons and quashed his decision (*b*).

The Inspector's Decision

Where the Inspector himself gives the decision, there will be no report to the Minister and the Inspector is under no statutory obligation to record findings of fact. However, if he proposes to take into account new evidence (including expert opinion on a matter of fact) or any new issue of fact, he must not come to a decision without first notifying the appellant, the local planning authority and the section 27 parties (*c*). Any of these persons then has twenty-one days in which to make further representations or to ask for the inquiry to be re-opened.

The Inspector will notify his decision in the same manner as the Minister (*d*). The decision letter must enable the appellant to understand upon what grounds the appeal had been decided and be in sufficient detail to enable him to know what conclusions the Inspector had reached on the principal issues in controversy (*e*).

Enforcement Notice Inquiries

The procedure at an inquiry into an appeal against an enforcement notice is the same as at an inquiry into an appeal against a planning decision. But the evidence is always on oath; and, because there may be some difficult questions of law of a kind which do not usually arise at an inquiry into an appeal against a

(*a*) Inquiries Procedure Rules, rule 16.

(*b*) *Givaudan & Co., Ltd.* v. *Minister of Housing and Local Government*, [1966] 3 All E.R. 696.

(*c*) Determination by Inspectors Rules, rule 14.

(*d*) *Ibid.*, rule 16.

(*e*) *Ellis* v. *Secretary of State for the Environment* (1974), unreported; *Hope* v. *Secretary of State for the Environment*, [1975] J.P.L. 731.

planning decision, the Inspector may sit with a legal assessor. There are as yet no inquiries procedures rules but the Dobry report recommends that such rules should be made.

Structure and Local Plan Inquiries

It was explained in an earlier chapter that, when a structure plan is submitted to the Minister, he will hold an "examination in public" into selected issues, and he will decide whom to invite to appear at the inquiry. Although the Minister has power to make regulations regarding the procedure to be followed at this form of inquiry, he has decided not to do so for the time being; he has issued a code of practice instead (*f*).

As regards local plans, the local planning authority will be under a duty to hold a public local inquiry for the purpose of considering objections which have been duly submitted (*g*). The objectors will have the right to appear at this inquiry.

Although the inquiry is for the purpose of considering objections, it would be appropriate for the local planning authority to "open". That is to say, the advocate for the local planning authority would make an opening speech and call evidence in support of the plan generally. There may be some cross-examination on general issues of the authority's witnesses at this stage. The objectors would then present their respective cases. If there are many objections, a programme might be arranged so that each objector may know when his case will be heard. At the public inquiries into the older type of development plan, the manner in which an objection was heard was often arranged between the planning authority and the objector; in some cases the objector opened, but in others the local planning authority opened. Whatever arrangements are made, the objector needs to support his case by proper evidence and the local planning authority will probably call evidence with regard to the particular objection.

(*f*) See p. 66, *ante*.
(*g*) Act of 1971, s. 13(1). And see chapter 4, pp. 73, 74, *ante*.

Otherwise, it may be expected that the inquiry will follow much the same lines as an inquiry into a planning appeal.

In exceptional cases, the Minister may call in a local plan for consideration by himself. It follows that the Minister may hold a public inquiry instead of the local planning authority doing so. A public inquiry held on behalf of the Minister is likely to follow the pattern described above.

Highways Inquiries

A public inquiry must be held where there are objections to highway schemes put forward by the Minister or by the local highway authority under the Highways Act 1959. These highway schemes will, of course, include proposals for new motorways and trunk roads. Recent public inquiries have engendered a good deal of controversy and some have been disrupted by angry objectors.

There are now Highways Inquiries Procedure Rules (*h*). These rules came into operation on 10th June, 1976, but did not apply to inquiries the arrangements for which had already been announced. The rules apply to inquiries into highway schemes whether proposed by the Minister or by the local highway authority.

The rules give procedural rights to certain categories of objector described in the rules as "statutory objectors". They include objectors who own or occupy land which may be required for the carrying out of the scheme and objectors who are likely to be entitled to claim compensation under Part I of the Land Compensation Act 1973 in respect of the use of the new highway (*i*).

Where the scheme is put forward by the Minister himself, he must not later than 28 days before the inquiry is held send a statement of his case to each statutory objector together with a list of the documents, maps and plans which are to be referred to at the inquiry (*k*). If the Minister intends to rely on the views

(*h*) S.I. 1976 No. 721.
(*i*) Highways Procedure Rules, rule 3 (1).
(*k*) *Ibid.*, rule 5(1), (3).

of any other government department, a statement of those views must be included in the rule 5 statement (*l*).

The Minister must make available a representative to give evidence at the inquiry in elucidation of the rule 5 statement; and, if any other government department is supporting the scheme, they must also provide a representative to give evidence. These departmental representatives are to be subject to cross-examination except that the Inspector is to disallow any question which he considers is "directed to the merits of government policy" (*m*). It is not clear whether the need for a particular motorway or trunk road is a matter of government policy.

There are somewhat similar rules for inquiries into schemes put forward by local highway authorities.

Preparing the Evidence

The outcome of a planning inquiry may well depend on the care with which the evidence is prepared; for this reason, the preparation of the evidence should not be left to the last moment. Evidence should be given on the following matters:

(i) any fact which may possibly be disputed by the other side;

(ii) any questions of technical or expert opinion which may assist the Inspector and, after him, the Minister in coming to a conclusion;

(iii) any intentions which the landowner or developer may have as to the future use or development of the land.

We will consider each of these in turn.

Evidence of Facts

Any facts which may be disputed by the other side should be proved by proper evidence. On the other hand, there is no need for witnesses to give evidence of facts which have already been agreed by the other side, and it is quite unnecessary for the appellant's surveyor and for the planning officer to include in

(*l*) *Ibid.*, rule 5(2).
(*m*) *Ibid.*, rules 6 and 7.

their evidence details of the application and of the planning authority's grounds of refusal; the Inspector has been supplied with copies of these documents before the inquiry and in a properly conducted case they will have been sufficiently referred to by the appellant's advocate in his opening speech.

Where evidence of facts is given, care should be taken to see that they are both reliable and pertinent. For instance, the local planning authority may allege that the extension of the appellant's factory would attract a great number of vehicles and in support of this may give evidence of the number of vehicles parked on a certain day in the road outside the existing premises; the figure given by the planning officer may be perfectly correct, but it is of little value unless there is some evidence to connect these vehicles with the appellant.

Technical and Expert Evidence

The foundation of a sound case is the evidence of fact, but evidence of a different kind—that is, technical or expert evidence—may be required as well. The need for technical or expert evidence may be considered under the following headings:

(1) *Interpretation of facts.*—The facts given in evidence or admitted by the other party may require interpretation. Thus, the report of the survey may contain data about the future of industry in the area (*e.g.* figures relating to trade, employment, factory space, industrial trends) and the local authority may claim that these data indicate the need for certain specific planning proposals. A suitably qualified person—*e.g.* an economist—might show, however, that the data support other conclusions.

(2) *Special problems.*—Planning inquiries sometimes involve consideration of a question of a highly technical nature; for example, the Essex chalkpit inquiry involved consideration of the amount of dust likely to result from certain quarrying operations and the effect of such dust on agriculture. Such evidence is likely, of course, to be both factual and interpretative, but it can only be given by specialist witnesses.

(3) *Questions of design and amenity.*—A planning inquiry may involve questions as to the design of buildings and other forms of visual amenity. These are more matters of opinion rather than of fact, but it may be appropriate to call architects and similar experts whose opinions may be of assistance to the Inspector.

(4) *Planning policy.*—The ultimate arbiter of planning policy is, of course, the Minister, but here again there are acknowledged experts whose opinions will carry weight.

Evidence of Intentions

In many cases there is no need for the landowner or prospective developer to give evidence; the evidence necessary to support the case may be given more appropriately by other witnesses. There are, however, cases in which it is necessary to refer to the intentions of the landowner or developer as to the future use or development of the site; in such cases that person ought to be available to give evidence. A mere statement by counsel of his client's intentions unsupported by evidence, is unsatisfactory because counsel cannot be cross-examined. This is illustrated by *Re, London (Hammersmith) Housing Order, Land Development Ltd.'s Application* (*n*):

> At a public local inquiry by the Minister to consider the confirmation of a compulsory purchase order in respect of part of the White City, counsel for the owners of the land sought to state the intentions of his clients as to the future use of the property. He had already stated that he did not intend to call any evidence. The Inspector refused to allow the statement as to intentions to be made. HELD: the Inspector was right.

Although the case referred to an inquiry into objections to a compulsory purchase order, it is submitted that the rule in this case would apply equally to development plan inquiries. On an appeal against a refusal of planning permission it is not necessary for the landowner or prospective developer to give evidence that he intends to use the land for the purposes for which

(*n*) [1936] 2 All E.R. 1063.

he has applied for permission, but he may need to give evidence of his intentions in other respects. Thus, on the hearing of an appeal against a refusal of permission for the retention of an unauthorised caravan site, a director of the appellant company stated that they proposed to provide access roads and other improvements; cross-examination revealed, however, that the cost of these improvements would be likely to be beyond the company's financial resources.

Cross-Examination

Each witness must expect to be cross-examined. The purpose of cross-examination is to test the accuracy of facts given by the witness, the inferences which he has drawn from the facts and the soundness of any opinions he has put forward. It is both the right and the duty of the cross-examiner to be as searching as possible, and the witness should not resent this. On the other hand, the witness has the right to be treated with courtesy: as a judge once reminded an over-zealous young advocate, to cross-examine does not mean to examine crossly. Some witnesses, however, forfeit respect and may annoy the cross-examiner by evasiveness or by unwillingness to admit even simple points.

There is a further aspect of cross-examination which is not always fully understood at planning inquiries. In cross-examination, an advocate who has not yet presented his own case ought to put to the witness any points of substance on which he proposes to lead evidence in due course; this enables the witness to comment on the points in question. This does not mean, of course, that the advocate must put the whole of his case to every witness whom he cross-examines; what he should do is to put his points to the most suitable witness.

The Role of the Planning Officer

At many inquiries, the only witnesses for the local planning authority are the planning officer (or one of his deputies) and other servants of the council. There is some confusion as to their role and the kind of evidence which they ought to give. And their position is sometimes delicate because their professional opinions do not always coincide with the views of the council. The fundamental issue seems to be whether the planning officer is there simply to give evidence as to the facts and considerations which led the council to their decision, or whether he is also there to give expert evidence on the issues involved.

The Minister appears to take the view that the planning officer's role is limited to explaining the council's position. In one appeal, counsel for the appellant in his cross-examination asked the council's witness for his personal opinion; the witness was reluctant to give his own opinion, and the Inspector refused to press him to do so. The Minister in his decision letter said that the Inspector had acted quite properly "since the views of individual officers of the council are not considered to be relevant to the issue before the Minister" (*o*).

This is hardly satisfactory; indeed, one learned journal has described the Minister's statement as "one of the most extraordinary ever to appear in a planning appeal decision" (*p*). If expert evidence has any relevance at a planning inquiry, the planning authority should be able to call such evidence and it seems illogical to suggest that they cannot call their own professional officers for that purpose. Moreover, what is the position if the other side call expert evidence, but the views of the council's professional officers are considered to be irrelevant? How in these circumstances is the Inspector to evaluate the evidence? (*q*).

(*o*) [1968] J.P.L. 708.
(*p*) [1968] J.P.L. 708.
(*q*) For the views of the Town Planning Institute on the position of the planning officer see a statement issued in 1961 and re-printed in [1961] J.P.L. 94.

Addendum to Part I

PLANNING IN GREATER LONDON

The whole structure of local government in Greater London has been changed by the passing of the London Government Act 1963. The Act provided for the establishment of: (1) a Greater London Council covering the whole of the former administrative counties of London and Middlesex, some parts of the counties of Essex, Kent and Surrey and the former county boroughs of East Ham, West Ham and Croydon; and (2) thirty-two London boroughs, plus the City of London. The new councils were elected in 1964 and took office on April 1, 1965. The Act provides that in the Greater London Area planning control under the Act of 1962 and similar statutes is to be administered on a two-tier basis; that is some functions are exercised by the Greater London Council and some by the London borough councils (*a*).

The Greater London Council is the local planning authority for Greater London "as a whole" (*b*). One of the duties of the Council is the preparation of a general development plan for Greater London to "lay down considerations of general policy with respect to the use of land in the various parts of Greater London, including guidance as to the future road system" (*c*). This plan has now been prepared and was submitted to the Minister in September 1969. A lengthy inquiry into the plan was conducted by a panel of experts under the chairmanship of Mr. F. H. B. Layfield Q.C. The report of the panel was published early in 1973. The plan was ultimately confirmed by the Minister in 1976. It is now the duty of each of the London borough councils as well as the City of

(*a*) For the purposes of this Addendum, the expression "London borough" is to be taken as including the City of London.
(*b*) Act of 1963, s. 24 (1).
(*c*) *Ibid.*, s. 25 (3).

London to prepare a local plan (*d*). The detailed contents are prescribed by the Development Plans for Greater London Regulations (*e*).

The two-tier system of development plans for Greater London is very similar to the system of structure and local plans to be introduced in other parts of the country under Part II of the Act of 1971: indeed the Greater London Plan has been described as really the first of the new type of structure plan (*f*). For the purposes of the Planning Acts and similar statutes the development plan for any district of Greater London is to be taken as the plan prepared under the London Government Act (*g*).

Applications for planning permission and/or for a determination under section 53 are made to the London borough council concerned (*h*). In some specified cases the application is forwarded to the Greater London Council for decision as to whether permission should be granted or refused (*i*); in certain other cases the London borough council must not grant permission without first referring the application to the Greater London Council (*k*). If the London borough council wish to grant permission for development which is inconsistent with the Greater London plan they must refer the application to the Greater London Council; if the proposed development is inconsistent with the local development plan, they must refer the application to the Minister (*l*).

Where a London borough council propose to grant listed building consent, they must consult the Greater London Council, and this Council may not authorise the borough council to grant consent without first notifying the Minister (*m*).

(*d*) *Ibid.*, s. 25 (4).

(*e*) S.I. 1966 No. 48, as amended by the Development Plans for Greater London (Amendment) Regulations 1975, S.I. 1975 No. 1680.

(*f*) [1969] J.P.L. 234.

(*g*) Act of 1971, s. 20(2): Act of 1972, s. 4(2).

(*h*) G.D.O. art. 7(1).

(*i*) Local Planning Authorities in Greater London Regulations 1965, S.I. 1965, No. 679, reg. 3.

(*k*) *Ibid.*, reg. 4.

(*l*) *Ibid.*, reg. 5.

(*m*) Act of 1971, Sch. 11, para. 6.

PART II

FINANCIAL PROVISIONS

SUMMARY

CHAPTER 17

THE NATURE OF THE FINANCIAL PROBLEM

So far in this book we have dealt with the purposes and machinery of planning control. But planning control involves certain financial problems which are called the "Compensation—Betterment Problem". Put quite simply, this is the problem of what is to be done about (a) owners whose property is reduced in value by action taken under planning legislation; and (b) owners whose property is increased in value by such action. It is scarcely too much to say that the twin problem has bedevilled planning control ever since 1909.

THE HISTORICAL BACKGROUND

Compensation for Planning Restrictions

English law has adopted two contrasting principles with compensation for the deprivation of rights over land. On the one hand, the courts have insisted that property shall not be compulsorily acquired without full compensation—unless Parliament provides to the contrary. As was said in *A.-G.* v. *De Keyser's Royal Hotel, Ltd.* (*a*):

> "It is a well-established principle that, unless no other interpretation is possible, justice requires that statutes should not be construed to enable the land of a particular individual to be confiscated without payment."

Or, as it was put more recently in *Belfast Corpn.* v. *O.D. Cars, Ltd.* (*b*):

> " . . . the intention to take away property without compensation is not to be imputed to the legislature unless it is expressed in unequivocal terms."

(*a*) [1920] A.C. 508.
(*b*) [1960] A.C. 490; [1960] 1 All E.R. 65.

On the other hand, compensation is not payable for restrictions on the user of property unless Parliament expressly so provides. Through the Public Health Acts and similar legislation, Parliament has either directly restricted the user of land or authorised local authorities to do so. In only a few cases, however, has it been thought necessary to provide for the payment of compensation (*c*).

Strictly speaking, the restrictions imposed by planning legislation fall within the second category: in other words, planning legislation restricts an owner's use of his property but it does not take away the property from him. On the other hand, some of the restrictions imposed or authorised by the Planning Acts go far beyond anything in, say, the Public Health Acts. They can be fairly said to take away rights in property. The byelaws relating to new buildings and streets may restrict the way in which a man develops his land, but under planning legislation the appropriate authorities may forbid him to develop at all (*d*).

Until 1947 at least, Parliament recognised that many planning restrictions were in effect confiscatory of property rights. For the purposes of compensation planning restrictions were divided into those which were confiscatory and those which were merely regulatory and thus akin to public health restrictions.

The Acts of 1909 to 1925 provided for compensation to any person "injuriously affected" by any provisions in any planning scheme subject, *inter alia*, to the following exceptions:

(a) No compensation was payable for any provision in a scheme which could have been imposed as a byelaw without payment of compensation;

(b) provision might be made in the scheme itself for excluding compensation in respect of restrictions on the density, height or character of buildings, if the Minister was satisfied that it was reasonable to exclude compensation having respect to the situation and nature of the land.

(*c*) See *Belfast Corpn.* v. *O.D. Cars, Ltd.*, *ante*.

(*d*) Byelaws may prevent development where the site is too small to satisfy the requirements as to space about buildings, but this is exceptional.

The same approach was adopted in the Act of 1932. Compensation was payable to persons whose property was injuriously affected by any provisions in the scheme or by the carrying out by the responsible authority of any work under the scheme. As under earlier legislation, the scheme might exclude compensation for certain restrictions; the list of matters in respect of which compensation could be excluded was extended to restrictions on the use of land or buildings if these were needed for the protection of health or the amenities of the neighbourhood.

Betterment

"Betterment" has been defined as "any increase in the value of land (including the buildings thereon) arising from central or local government action, whether positive, *e.g.* by the execution of public works or improvements, or negative, *e.g.* by the imposition of restrictions on other land (*e*). The word "betterment" is sometimes used to describe not only the increase in value of the property but also the amount of such increase in value recovered from the owner.

Betterment resulting from positive action by a public authority can be recovered in a number of different ways—

(1) *A direct charge* on the owner of any property bettered by the public works. Thus an Act of 1662 provided for the widening of certain streets in London and for the recovery of a contribution for "melioration" (*i.e.* betterment) from owners and occupiers of property the value of which was enhanced by the widening.

Between 1890 and 1894, the London County Council, when promoting local Bills authorising various public works, unsuccessfully attempted to obtain powers for the recovery of betterment. In 1894, however, the House of Lords appointed a Select Committee on Betterment. The Committee reported that the principle "is not in itself unjust" but that it would be difficult to assess the

(*e*) Final Report of the Expert Committee on Compensation and Betterment (Uthwatt Committee), para. 260.

effect of public works in raising the value of neighbouring lands. Thereafter, the London County Council obtained a betterment clause in a number of local Acts passed between 1895 and 1902. The experiment was not a success; the trouble and expense involved were found to be out of all proportion to the amounts received (*f*).

(2) *Set-off.*—In assessing compensation for lands compulsorily acquired, regard must be had to any increase in value of other lands belonging to the same owner which will result from the carrying out of the work for which the land is being acquired.

Under this method it is possible to recover betterment only from persons directly affected by a compulsory purchase. The principle of set-off was introduced into the early Housing Acts in connection with slum clearance schemes (*g*), and it has been adopted in a few other cases. By virtue of the Land Compensation Act, 1961, it now applies to all compulsorily purchased land (*h*).

(3) *Recoupment.*—The purchase and re-sale by the authority of land adjoining a public improvement and likely to be increased in value by it: if the property does in fact increase in value, the authority secures the whole of the increase. Recoupment clauses have been included in local Acts authorising road improvements by the London County Council.

The advent of planning legislation in 1909 raised the problem of betterment in a new form. Earlier statutes had been concerned only with betterment resulting from positive action in the form of public works. Planning control, however, produces betterment in a different way. If building is prohibited or restricted on certain land—for instance, land to be kept in a green belt or open space—two results may follow. First, adjoining land on which building is to be permitted may be increased in value because of the amenity created by the green belt or open space. Secondly, the restriction on the amount available for development may

(*f*) *Op. cit.*, paras. 267–269.
(*g*) See now the Housing Act, 1957.
(*h*) Section 9.

intensify the demand for land on which building will be permitted.

Without the compulsory purchase of large areas of building land, betterment resulting from planning control can only be recovered by a direct charge on the land concerned; that is, the first of the methods described above. The Acts of 1909 to 1925 adopted the method and authorised the recovery of one-half of any increase in the value of property due to the coming into operation of a scheme. This was no more successful than the London County Council's experiment; it is believed that no betterment was ever recovered under these Acts.

The Act of 1932 went further and provided for the recovery of seventy-five per cent of any increase in value due either to the coming into operation of a scheme or the execution of works by the responsible authority under the scheme.

The Uthwatt Report

The Act of 1932 had not been in force seven years when the Second World War broke out, and by 1942 only 5 per cent of England and 1 per cent of Wales were subject to operative schemes. It is difficult to judge whether the Act of 1932 would have been a success over a longer period, and whether enough could have been raised by way of betterment to meet the liability for compensation. The historical precedents in relation to betterment were certainly not encouraging, and the liability to compensation deterred authorities from full use of their powers of planning control.

In short, now that the law empowered local authorities to limit an owner's right to make whatever use of his land he wished the authorities were finding that to use such powers, though they wished to do so, was too expensive a process. It was said to be prohibitively expensive on two grounds. In the first place, the compensation often arose in the interests either of the nation as a whole, or of the people in a very wide area, while it had to be borne by a local authority. Restrictions were often most needed round the fringe of towns, and the authorities concerned were usually those of small rural areas whose resources were very limited. Even with the large authority the size of the prospective compensation bill alarmed them. Secondly, compensation was said to include inflationary elements which made the amount to be paid excessively large. On the other hand, while in theory such authorities could recoup all or part of such expenses by means of betterment, it was said that in practice they could rarely secure it.

It was this state of affairs that led the Barlow Commission to say that "the difficulties that are encountered by planning authorities under these provisions are so great as seriously to hamper the progress of planning throughout the country" (*i*). The Commission accordingly recommended that "the Government should appoint a body of experts to examine the questions of compensation, betterment, and development generally . . ." (*k*).

Acting on this advice, the Government in January, 1941, appointed what came to be known as the Uthwatt Committee to consider a number of matters including compensation and betterment. The Committee considered that the burden of compensation was greatly increased by two particular factors which they described as "floating value" and "shifting value". These concepts are important because right or wrong they have profoundly influenced the policies of successive Governments, and they may fairly be described as the basis of the present system of compensation for planning restrictions.

"Floating Value."—This concept was noted by an earlier Government Committee (*l*), and their explanation is as simple as any:

> "If all building except agricultural is permanently prohibited over wide areas, compensation must be paid for the loss of

(*i*) Barlow Report, para. 248.
(*k*) *Ibid.*, para. 250.
(*l*) Report on the Preservation of the Countryside (1936) from the Minister of Health's Town and Country Planning Advisory Committee.

potential building value over these areas. It may be that on any reasonable estimate that can be formed not more than 100 houses are likely to be built in a 100,000-acre rural zone in the lifetime of the scheme, so that over the whole zone the loss of 'potential building value' on prohibition of any building would be only 100 houses. But potential building value is necessarily a 'floating value' and it is practically impossible to predict where it will settle. Hence, if the 100,000 acres are held in many ownerships, and claims by individual owners for loss of potential building value come to be separately adjudicated (as under the present system they must be), the total resulting bill for compensation is likely to be enormous, and greatly to exceed in the aggregate the amount of the real loss."

Or, as it was put by the Uthwatt Committee (*m*):

"Potential development value is by nature speculative. The hoped-for building may take place on the particular piece of land in question, or it may take place elsewhere; it may come within five years, or it may be twenty-five years or more before the turn of the particular piece of land to be built upon arrives. The present value at any time of the potential value of a piece of land is obtained by estimating whether and when development is likely to take place, including an estimate of the risk that other competing land may secure prior turn. If we assume a town gradually spreading outwards, where the fringe land on the north, south, east and west is all equally available for development, each of the owners of such fringe land to the north, south, east and west will claim equally that the next development will 'settle' on his land. Yet the average annual rate of development demand of past years may show that the quantum of demand is only enough to absorb the area of one side within such a period of the future as commands a present value.

Potential value is necessarily a 'floating value', and it is impossible to predict with certainty where the 'float' will settle as sites are actually required for purposes of development. When a piece of undeveloped land is compulsorily acquired, or development upon it is prohibited, the owner receives compensation for the loss of the value of a probability of the floating demand

---

(*m*) Uthwatt Report, paras. 23, 24.

settling upon his piece of land. The probability is not capable of arithmetical quantification. In practice where this process is repeated indefinitely over a large area the sum of the probabilities as estimated greatly exceeds the actual possibilities, because the 'float', limited as it is to actually occurring demands, can only settle on a proportion of the whole area. There is therefore over-valuation.' "

"Shifting Value."—This concept was explained by the Uthwatt Committee as follows (*n*)—

"The public control of the use of land, whether it is operated by means of the existing planning legislation or by other means, necessarily has the effect of shifting land values; in other words, it increases the value of some land and decreases the value of other land, but it does not destroy the land values. Neither the total demand for development nor its average annual rate is materially affected, if at all, by planning ordinances. If, for instance, part of the land on the fringe of a town is taken out of the market for building purposes by the prohibition of development upon it, the potential building value is merely shifted to other land and aggregate values are not substantially affected, if at all. Nevertheless, the loss to the owner of the land prohibited from development is obvious, and he will claim compensation for the full potential development value of his land on the footing that but for the action of the public authority in deciding that development should not be permitted upon it, it would in fact have been used for development. The value which formerly attached to his land is transferred and becomes attached to other land whose owners enjoy a corresponding gain by reason of the increased chance that their land will be required for development at an earlier date.

A similar shift of value takes place if part of the land is taken out of the market for building purposes by being purchased for a public open space or other public purpose."

In an attempt to solve these problems, the Uthwatt Committee recommended what was in effect the nationalisation of the development rights in land outside built up areas. The land would remain in private ownership, but development would require the

(*n*) Uthwatt Report, para. 26.

consent of the State which would thereupon acquire the land, if necessary by compulsory purchase, either for development by a public authority, or for re-sale or lease to a private developer (*o*).

The 1947 Act Solution

The Act of 1947 in some respects went even further than the Uthwatt Committee had recommended. In effect, it nationalised the development rights in all land, including land in built up areas. On the other hand, it did not provide for the acquisition by the State of all land required for development purposes. Although extensive powers of compulsory purchase were conferred upon public authorities, land required for private development would not normally be acquired by the State; instead, the existing owner would, so to speak, re-acquire the development rights by paying a "development charge".

The word "nationalisation" was not used in the Act of 1947; nor indeed was it expressly provided that the development rights in land should be transferred to the State. But the transfer of development rights to the State was clearly enough the underlying theory. In practice this was achieved in the following ways:

(a) development must not be carried out without planning permission;
(b) if permission was refused or granted subject to conditions, the owner of the land was not entitled to compensation because he no longer possessed the development rights;
(c) if permission was granted for development, the owner would pay a development charge representing the difference in the value of the land with the benefit of that permission and its existing use value;
(d) if the land were compulsorily acquired, the compensation would be limited to existing use value;
(e) as a measure of compensation for the loss of development

(*o*) Uthwatt Report, para. 56.

rights landowners were entitled under Part VI of the Act of 1947 to make a claim for a once-for-all payment from the Government.

Although the financial provisions set out in paragraphs (b) to (e) have been drastically changed, it is necessary to consider the claims under Part VI of the Act of 1947 in rather more detail.

Part VI Claims

Two types of claim were possible under Part VI of the Act of 1947. Section 58 provided for a global sum of £300 millions as compensation for landowners generally for loss of development value. Section 59 provided for additional payments in respect of certain war damaged land.

Under Section 58, the owner of a freehold or leasehold interest could submit a claim for compensation for loss of development value representing the difference between the "unrestricted" and "restricted" values of his interests on 1st July, 1948. The unrestricted value was that which the interest would have had if the Act of 1947 had not passed; the restricted value was its value on the assumption that permission would not be granted for any development other than Third Schedule development (which is described below).

The claims as agreed or determined by the Lands Tribunal were to be paid by the Treasury in stock not later than the 1st July, 1953. If the amount of the claims were to exceed £300 million, then it would not be possible to pay them all in full. Certain claims relating to land considered "near ripe" for development were to be given priority and paid in full; the non-priority claims were to be paid *pro rata* to the residue of the £300 million. In fact, the total approved claims amounted to £340 millions of which approximately £100 millions represented priority claims; the non-priority claims would then have been met at 16s. in the £.

The claims were not, in fact, paid out in this way because the new Government which came into office in 1951 decided to replace the financial provision of the Act of 1947 by a different scheme; this was effected by the Acts of 1953 and 1954.

The Section 59 Scheme

The War Damage Act, 1943, provided Government compensation for war damaged land and buildings. If the damage was capable of repair, the owner of the property received a cost of works payment when the repairs were done. If, however, the building were a total loss the owner received a "value payment" representing the difference between the before and after damage value of the property. This value payment was assessed on the assumption that the owner would be able to realise any development value which the site might possess. Thus where an old dilapidated building was totally demolished by a bomb and there was the prospect of a profitable future development, the development value might be considerable. In such a case the then development value would increase the after-damage value of the site and thus reduce the war damage payment. The Act of 1947, however, took away this development value, and to avoid double loss on the part of the owner, section 59 of the Act of 1947 provided supplementary compensation for loss of development value in such cases. This compensation was paid in full in cash. The fact that such a payment was made may still be of significance as will be explained in later chapters.

Third Schedule Development

Lastly, in this review of the financial provisions of the 1947 Act, it must be noticed that certain forms of development, considered to be within the existing use of land, were exempted from the "nationalisation" scheme. These developments were set out in detail in the Third Schedule to the Act of 1947 and for this reason were, until recently, referred to as "Third Schedule development". The Third Schedule to the Act of 1947 became the Third Schedule to the Act of 1962, but is now Schedule 8 of the Act of 1971 and so will henceforth be referred to in this book as "Schedule 8 development". Schedule 8 development may be described as development consistent with, or required for the existing use of the land or building in question. For instance, the conversion of a large house into flats is development and requires planning permission (*p*), but the house remains in residential use. Or again, a farmer wishes to erect barns or cowsheds; this involves development and requires planning permission, but they are developments required for the existing use of his farm in contrast to a general building development.

It must be emphasised that Schedule 8 development requires planning permission. But under the Act of 1947 it did not attract development charges and in assessing loss of development value any potential development of this kind was included in the existing use or restricted value of the land. Moreover, even under the Act of 1947, compensation was payable if planning permission was refused or granted subject to conditions for certain forms of what is now Schedule 8 development (*q*).

The 1954 Act Solution

The financial provisions of the Act of 1947 were unpopular and widely criticised. Among the more informed sources of criticism were the Law Society, the Royal Institution of Chartered Surveyors and the Chartered Auctioneers and Estate Agents Institute.

All these bodies criticised the financial provisions as discouraging to development. It is difficult to judge how far the liability to development charge did in fact discourage development. At that time, development was restricted by the post-war shortage of labour and materials and a strict system of building licensing was in force. It seems likely that development was proceeding as far as the country's resources would permit.

There seems little doubt, however, that the development charge increased the cost of development. The framers of the Act of 1947 supposed that the liability to development charge would

(*p*) Act of 1971, s. 22(3) (a).
(*q*) See chapter 18.

result in land changing hands at existing use value, and the Central Land Board were given powers of compulsory purchase to deal with cases where landowners were not willing to sell at existing use value. In fact, land was generally bought and sold at prices substantially in excess of existing use value, and to that extent the development charge operated as a kind of tax; the Central Land Board made little use of their powers of compulsory purchase.

In November 1952, the Government published a White Paper announcing a drastic revision of the financial provisions of the Act of 1947. The Government proposed in effect to hand back to private ownership the development rights in land as they existed immediately before the Act of 1947, but not as altered for better or worse by the operation of planning control since that date. The Government appear in this to have been influenced by the doctrine of shifting value explained earlier in this chapter.

These proposals were put into effect by the Act of 1953—an emergency measure to deal with the more urgent problems—and by the Act of 1954. These two Acts did not affect the powers of control over development provided by the Act of 1947, but the financial consequences of granting or refusing permission were altered. If permission were granted, the owner no longer had to pay development charge (*r*). If permission were refused or granted subject to conditions, then (with some exceptions) owners of legal interests in the land were entitled to compensation, provided a claim for loss of development value had been established under section 58 of the Act of 1947. Similarly, if land were compulsorily acquired, the compensation was to include the amount of the section 58 claim as well as the existing use value. In consequence of all this, the obligation to pay the £300 millions in one lump sum was abolished, the full amount of the established claim being available to provide compensation as and when a loss of development value was actually incurred—namely, when

(*r*) This liability was abolished by the Act of 1953 with effect from November 1952.

planning permission was refused or granted subject to conditions or when land was compulsorily acquired.

Provision was also made for compensating landowners or developers who had suffered loss in consequence of the operation of the Act of 1947 prior to 1st January, 1955—the date on which the Act of 1954 came into force. Part I of the Act of 1954 provided a complicated scheme of payments for dealing with some of these cases—notably, where land had changed hands at less than its full value because of the developer's prospective liability to development charge or where land had been compulsorily acquired at existing use value. These payments could be made only if a claim had been established under section 58 of the Act of 1947, and the making of the payment reduced the amount of the established claim.

Loss might also have been suffered under the Act of 1947 by the refusal of planning permission or the imposition of conditions, or by the revocation or modification of permission already granted. In these cases, a claim for retrospective compensation might be made under Part V of the Act of 1954, provided a section 58 claim had been established and was still subsisting; that is, had not been extinguished under Part I. (As an alternative to paying compensation under Part V, the Minister was authorised to give permission for the development in question or for some other profitable development). Any compensation paid under Part V reduced the amount of the established claim.

The established claim, or what was left of it after payments under Parts I and V, was then converted into an "unexpended balance of established development value". This provides the basis of compensation for restrictions on development (other than Schedule 8 development) imposed on or after 1st January, 1955. Compensation for restrictions on Schedule 8 development continues to be payable under the rules originally established by the Act of 1947. There are now, therefore, two sets of rules for compensation for planning restrictions—namely, one scheme for restrictions on Schedule 8 development, and another more complex scheme for restrictions on what is now known as "new development", that is, development outside Schedule 8.

Compensation for restrictions on new development is payable only if there is an unexpended balance and this will exist only if a claim was established under section 58 of the Act of 1947, and the amount of the compensation will not exceed the unexpended balance. No new claims may be made under section 58, and there is no provision for increasing the amount of the established claims to take account of the decline in the value of money. And, of course, the landowner is denied any increase of development value resulting from the development plan zoning—often a very substantial item indeed.

For these reasons the Act of 1954 was in its turn subjected to a good deal of criticism, and in 1959 Parliament decided to revert to full market value (including the benefit of any enhancement due to the development plan) as the basis of compensation for compulsory purchase. The Act of 1954, however, is left untouched in relation to compensation for planning restrictions.

The Land Commission

Following the General Election of 1964, a fresh attempt was made to deal with the compensation—betterment problem. The Labour Party's election programme contained a proposal to set up a Land Commission which would acquire all land about to be developed—a proposal similar to the recommendation of the Uthwatt Committee (*s*). The Commission would pay existing use value plus an increment to the owner, but not the full market value.

The new Labour Government subsequently came to the conclusion that it would be administratively impracticable for the proposed Land Commission to take over all land required for development. In a White Paper published in September 1965 (*t*) the Government announced that they would introduce legisla-

(*s*) See pp. 291, 294, *ante*.
(*t*) "The Land Commission", Cmnd. 2771.

tion to set up a Land Commission with power to acquire land for development at current use value plus a part of the development value. But if land not acquired by the Commission were to change hands on an unrestricted basis there would be a two-tier price system; one price for land acquired by the Commission and another for land bought by other persons whether public authorities or private developers. To avoid this situation the White Paper explained that a betterment levy would be imposed on development value when realised by sales or leases of land, and to the extent that development value has not been realised in previous sales or leases when it is realised by actual development of the land. The levy would be fixed in the first instance at the rate of forty per cent of the net development value and would be collected by the Commission and paid into the Exchequer. A landowner would thus realise the same net amount from the sale of his land whether he was selling to the Land Commission, another public authority or to a private purchaser.

These proposals were given effect in the Land Commission Act which received the Royal Assent on 1st February, 1967. Most of the provisions came into effect on 6th April, 1967. No betterment levy was payable on development commenced before 6th April, 1967, and for this development was deemed to have commenced if a start had been made on road works or sewers for a project or if a trench for foundations had been dug. As a result the amount of betterment levy collected in the three years following the passing of the Act was comparatively small: and, following the change of Government in 1970, the Land Commission Act was repealed.

CHAPTER 18

COMPENSATION FOR RESTRICTIONS ON SCHEDULE 8 DEVELOPMENT (FORMERLY THIRD SCHEDULE DEVELOPMENT)

The concept of Schedule 8 development, that is development which for certain purposes is deemed to be within the existing use of land—has been explained in the previous chapter. It is now necessary to consider Schedule 8 in more detail.

As originally enacted, it dealt only with development deemed to be within the existing use of land or buildings on 1st July, 1948; it did not apply to buildings erected (*a*) or uses commenced after that date. The Act of 1954 extended Schedule 8 to refer also to buildings erected and uses begun after 1st July, 1948. In this form the Schedule was re-enacted in the 1962 Act. Early in 1963, however, the Government came to the conclusion that the fear of liability to compensation for restrictions on rebuilding or extension of existing premises—notably offices—was deterring planning authorities from exercising proper control. The Act of 1963 was passed to deal with this problem by amending the Schedule.

Some paragraphs of Schedule 8 refer to "a material date"; this is either the 1st July, 1948, or the date on which the Schedule has to be applied in any particular case (*b*). For instance, where the Schedule has to be applied for the purposes of section 169 of the Act of 1971, the material date would presumably be the date of the planning decision which gives rise to the claim for compensation.

The extension of the Schedule to buildings erected or uses begun after 1st July, 1948, may apply even where the develop-

(*a*) Except for buildings substituted for previously existing buildings in accordance with paragraph 1 of Schedule 8.
(*b*) Act of 1971, Sch. 8, para. 12.

ment has been carried out in contravention of planning control. If at the material date the planning authority have not served an effective enforcement notice in respect of the offending development, the landowner is entitled in most cases to claim the benefit of the Schedule.

Where the development was the subject of a temporary permission, the extension of the Schedule is limited to the period of the permission (*c*).

Classes of Development

Schedule 8 specifies the following classes of development:

Part I.—Development not ranking for Compensation under Section 169

1. The rebuilding, as often as occasion may require, so long as the cubic content (*d*) of the original building is not exceeded by more than the prescribed amount of—
   (a) any building in existence on 1st July, 1948;
   (b) any building destroyed or demolished between 7th January, 1937, and 1st July, 1948;
   (c) any building in existence at a material date.

Where the original building was erected after 1st July, 1948, no increase in cubic content is permitted. In every other case the prescribed amount is one-tenth or 1750 cubic feet whichever is the greater, in the case of a dwelling house: one-tenth in the case of any other building.

It is also to be assumed that the right of rebuilding would be subject to the restrictions on floor space introduced by the Act of 1963 and now to be found in the Act of 1971 (*e*).

(*c*) Act of 1971, Sch. 8, para. 10.

(*d*) As ascertained by external measurement: where two or more buildings in the same curtilage are used as one unit for the purposes of any institution or undertaking, the cubic content of the original building is to be taken as the total cubic content of these buildings; ***ibid.***, paras. 9 and 11.

(*e*) Act of 1971, Sch. 18.

2. The use as two or more separate dwellings of any building used at a material date as a single dwelling.

Part II.—Development ranking for Compensation under Section 169

3. The enlargement, improvement or other alteration, as often as occasion may require, of any such building as mentioned in paragraph 1—or of any building substituted for it—subject to the same restriction as to increase in cubic content and floor space.

This paragraph, it is thought, applies only to physical alterations and not to a change of use. Moreover, improvements or other alterations which do not materially affect the external appearance of the building are not development at all except for war damage repairs and the provision of underground rooms (*f*).

4. The carrying out on land used at a material date for agriculture or forestry of any building or other operations required for that use; the erection, enlargement or improvement of the following is excluded, however:

(a) dwelling houses;

(b) buildings used for the purposes of market gardens;

(c) buildings used for other purposes not connected with general farming operations or with the cultivation or felling of trees.

5. The winning and working, on land held or occupied with land used for agricultural purposes, of any minerals reasonably required for that use.

6. Any change of use from one purpose to another within any use-class specified in the Use-Classes for Third Schedule Purposes Order.

This Order and the original Use-Classes Order made in 1948 for the purposes of section 12(2) of the Act of 1947 were in identical terms. However, the original order made under what is

---

(*f*) Act of 1971, s. 22(2) (a).

now section 22(2) has been amended on a number of occasions (*g*) with the result that the two Orders are no longer identical; some of the use-classes and some of the definitions (*h*) are now different. Where, however, the two orders are in identical terms, the Third Schedule Order need not be considered because the change of use in question will not be development at all.

7. Where part only of a building erected before 1st July, 1948, or other land is used for a particular purpose, the use for that purpose of an additional part not exceeding one-tenth (*i*) of the part used for that purpose on 1st July, 1948, or on the day thereafter, when the building or land first began to be so used.

8. The deposit of waste materials or refuse in connection with mineral working on a site used for that purpose at a material date.

Compensation in Respect of Schedule 8 Development

Compensation is payable in respect of restrictions on Schedule 8 development under section 169 of the Act of 1971. The conditions are as follows:

(a) the development must fall within Part II of the Schedule;

(b) planning permission must have been refused, or granted subject to conditions, by the Minister—either on appeal or under section 35 of the Act of 1971;

(c) it must be shown that the value of the interest in respect of which the claim is made is less than it would have been but for the Minister's decision;

(d) the claim must be submitted to the local planning authority within six months of the Minister's decision unless the Minister agrees to an extension of time (*k*).

(*g*) See now the Use-Classes Order, 1972.

(*h*) Compare, for instance, the respective definitions of "shop".

(*i*) Measured in the case of buildings by cubic content, and in the case of other land by area; Act of 1971, Sch. 8, para. 9.

(*k*) General Regulations, reg. 14.

Refusal of Planning Permission

Where the proposed development consists of the extension of an industrial building, it may be necessary to obtain an industrial development certificate from the Department of Trade. In the absence of such a certificate, an application for planning permission will be of no effect—except that the planning authority must consider whether they would have refused permission if a certificate or permit had been obtained; if so, they must notify the applicant accordingly and a claim for compensation under Part II of the Schedule can then be made as if permission had been refused by the Minister (*l*). No claim for compensation can be made if the authority decide that they would have granted permission because in that case it is the action of the Department of Trade and not of the planning authority which prevents the development being carried out.

There is no corresponding procedure where an office development permit is refused; presumably, because the powers of the Department of the Environment over office development were originally due to expire in 1972.

Value of Interest

There is no definition of the words "interest in land" in this Part of the Act of 1971 but it would appear from the rules for assessing compensation in section 178 that the interest must be either the freehold or a tenancy, or at least an option to purchase (*m*); a claim may be made by a mortgagee but not in respect of his interest as such, and he must account to the mortgagor for any compensation he receives.

The amount of the compensation will be the difference between (*n*):

(a) the value of the interest as affected by the Minister's decision; and

---

(*l*) Act of 1971, ss. 72(1), 169(5).
(*m*) *Oppenheimer* v. *Minister of Transport*, [1941] 3 All E.R. 485.
(*n*) Act of 1971, s. 169 (2).

(b) the value it would have had if the Minister had granted the permission or had granted it unconditionally, as the case may be. If, in refusing permission the Minister undertakes to give permission for any other development, regard must be had to that undertaking in assessing compensation (*o*).

Disputes as to the payment of compensation are dealt with by the Lands Tribunal (*p*) subject to right of appeal by way of case stated to the Court of Appeal on points of law. The liability for compensation falls on the local planning authority not the Minister (*q*).

These rules may be illustrated by *A. L. Salisbury, Ltd.* v. *York Corpn.* (*r*).

In 1953 the planning officer wrote to the owners of shops in a certain street asking them to consider, in the event of their rebuilding, or altering the front elevations, setting the ground-floor back by 5 feet to create an arcade. All the shopkeepers agreed except the claimants who in 1958 applied for permission to rebuild the front without setting back the ground floor. Permission was refused by the Minister on appeal.

A claim for compensation was then made under paragraph 3 of the Third Schedule, was disputed by the Corporation and was accordingly referred to the Lands Tribunal.

HELD: the loss of display space entailed in setting back the ground floor would not reduce the rental value of the shop since an arcaded front would in the narrow streets of York greatly improve the flow of pedestrians and lead to more custom. Accordingly no compensation was payable.

(*o*) Act of 1971, s. 169(3).
(*p*) *Ibid.*, s. 179.
(*q*) *Ibid.*, s. 169(2).
(*r*) (1960), 11 P. & C.R. 421.

CHAPTER 19

COMPENSATION FOR RESTRICTIONS ON NEW DEVELOPMENT

Compensation is payable under Part VII of the Act of 1971 for restrictions on new development—that is development other than Schedule 8 development—provided the following conditions are satisfied:

(1) A planning decision must have been made on or after 1st January, 1955, whereby permission for new development was refused or granted subject to conditions.

(2) The land in question must have an unexpended balance of established development value at the time of the decision.

(3) The claimant's interest in the land must have been depreciated in value as a result of the decision.

(4) Compensation must not be excluded under section 147, 148 or 149.

These conditions must now be considered in detail.

THE PLANNING DECISION

The words "planning decision" mean a "decision made on an application under Part III of this Act" (*a*). Applications under Part III of the Act include applications for planning permission and for any detailed consents required as a result of a grant of permission on an outline application. A decision on either type of application may therefore give rise to a claim for compensation.

Although the expression "application under Part III" is also wide enough to include applications for consents required by a tree preservation order, a building preservation order or under the Advertisements Regulations, it is not likely that any of these would give rise to a claim for compensation under this scheme.

(*a*) Act of 1971, s. 290.

Many of the matters for which consent is required under a tree or building preservation order are not development at all; moreover, where development is involved a separate application would have to be made for planning permission. In the case of advertisements compensation is expressly excluded (*b*).

The refusal of the appropriate Department to grant a certificate for office or industrial development is not, it is thought, a decision on an application under Part III of the Act of 1947; such a refusal does not therefore give rise to a claim for compensation. But, where an industrial development certificate has been refused, the owner of the land can ask the local authority to state whether they would have granted permission if such a certificate had been issued; if they would have refused permission, a claim for compensation can be made (*c*).

Nature of the Decision

The decision may be that of the local planning authority (or a local authority exercising delegated powers) or of the Minister on appeal or under section 35 of the Act of 1971. It is not necessary that the decision should have been the subject of an appeal to the Minister (*d*).

If the local planning authority fail to give a decision within the proper time, the applicant may appeal to the Minister as if permission had been refused (*e*). It is submitted that this does not operate as a deemed refusal for the purpose of claiming compensation.

The Unexpended Balance

The origin of the unexpended balance has been explained in chapter 17 but certain points require further explanation.

Although a claim under section 58 of the Act of 1947 could be

(*b*) Act of 1971, s. 147.

(*c*) *Ibid.*, ss. 72(1), 151. As to the position where an office development permit is refused see p. 307, *ante*.

(*d*) *Ibid.*, s. 134(1).

(*e*) See p. 137, *ante*.

made in respect of each separate interest in the land, there can be only one unexpended balance for any piece of land. Where more than one claim was established the unexpended balance is the aggregate of the established claims as subsisting on 1st January, 1955 (*f*).

In converting one or more established claims into an unexpended balance, an addition of one-seventh is made (*g*). This is intended to be in lieu of interest from 1st July, 1948 to 1st January, 1955, but no further additions can be made.

The unexpended balance attaches to the land: that is, upon a sale or gift of the land, the benefit of the unexpended balance passes automatically to the new owner.

The conversion of the established claims as subsisting on 1st January, 1955, give the amount of the *original* unexpended balance. This amount can be ascertained by applying to the Minister for a certificate under section 145 of the Act of 1971. The original balance may be reduced or extinguished in certain cases and may be increased in others.

The Minister cannot be asked for a certificate as to the amount of such variations in the unexpended balance, except by a public authority who have served notice to treat for the land.

Reduction or Extinguishment of Original Unexpended Balance

Where compensation is paid under Part VII of the Act of 1971 in respect of the depreciation of one or more interests in land, the amount of the compensation is to be deducted from the unexpended balance which will be reduced or extinguished accordingly (*h*). If the planning decision extended to part only of the land, the unexpended balance will be apportioned, and it will be the balance attaching to the part affected by the planning permission which will be reduced or extinguished.

(*f*) *I.e.* after deducting any payment made under Part I or V of the Act of 1954.

(*g*) Act of 1971, s. 136(3).

(*h*) *Ibid.*, s. 141.

Where land is compulsorily acquired by or sold to an authority possessing compulsory powers, the unexpended balance will be extinguished. If the compulsory acquisition or sale extends to part only of the land, the unexpended balance will be apportioned. The situation is further complicated where there are separate interests in the land. Thus, where there is a leasehold as well as the freehold interest, the authority may acquire both or they may acquire the freehold and wait for the lease to expire in the ordinary way. In the latter event (provided the lease has more than a year to run) the unexpended balance will be reduced by the amount attributable in the freehold. Similar principles apply where (as may occasionally happen) the authority acquire the leasehold but not the freehold.

Where land has been compulsorily purchased, compensation will be payable for damage sustained in consequence of the severance of the land from other land held therewith. Compensation will also be payable in respect of injurious affection to any land whether or not it was held with the acquired land. It would be outside the scope of this book to go into details of a subject which is in effect part of the law of compensation for compulsory purchase. It should be noted, however, that any unexpended balance attaching to the severed or injuriously affected land may be reduced or extinguished in consequence of the compensation paid for the severance or injurious affection (*i*).

Where compensation is paid by the local planning authority for the revocation or modification of planning permission, the Minister may make a contribution to the expense incurred by the authority and that will reduce any unexpended balance attaching to the land (*k*).

In the four cases described above the unexpended balance has

(*i*) Where notice to treat in respect of the acquired land was served between 1st January, 1955, and 29th October, 1958, compensation for severance and injurious affection was governed by the Act of 1954, s. 36. As to the effect on the unexpended balance where notice to treat was served on or after the latter date, see Act of 1971, s. 143.

(*k*) See chapter 20.

been reduced or extinguished because a payment has been made out of it the basis of such payment being that the owner of the land has been prevented from realising the development value of the land. The Government considered it equally logical that the unexpended balance should be reduced or extinguished where the owner is allowed to realise the development value. Speaking on the Second Reading of the Bill in the House of Lords, the Lord Chancellor said (*l*)—

> "That balance, *of course*, is progressively reduced to take account of payments and of the realisation of development value by building or other development."

The unexpended balance is reduced by the value of any new development (that is, development other than Schedule 8 development) initiated at any time on or after 1st July, 1948 (*m*). The value of the development will broadly speaking be the amount by which the value of the land with planning permission for the development in question exceeds the value which the land would have if permission for that or any other new development were refused. The valuation is to be made by reference to the prices prevailing at the time the valuation is made (*n*); this will not be the time when the new development was carried out but the next occasion on which the unexpended balance has to be ascertained (*o*).

These provisions do not apply to (i) land in respect of which compensation has become payable under section 59 of the Act of 1947; (ii) any development initiated before 1st July, 1955, in respect of which a development charge has been incurred or would have been incurred but for one of the statutory exemptions (*p*).

Increase in Unexpended Balance

The unexpended balance will be increased where any compensa-

(*l*) House of Lords Debates, vol. 189, col. 444. Author's italics.
(*m*) Act of 1971, s. 141.
(*n*) *Ibid.*, Schedule 16, para. 2.
(*o*) *Ibid.*, s. 140(1).
(*p*) *Ibid.*, s. 141(2), (3).

tion is repaid as explained in chapter 21. It may also be increased in a few exceptional cases where compensation has been paid for severance or injurious affection under section 36 of the Act of 1954 (*q*).

Depreciation of the Claimant's Interest

The claimant must be able to show that the value of his interest in the land has been depreciated in consequence of the planning decision in question (*r*). The only interests which qualify for this purpose are a fee simple and a tenancy (*s*). No claim can be made in respect of other interests in the land such as a mortgage or a rent charge. In certain circumstances a mortgagee can require the Minister to pay any compensation money direct to him, and should the mortgagor fail to make a claim the mortgagee may do so instead. Similar provisions are made in respect of rent charge owners (*t*).

It may happen that the claimant's interest extends to land which has not been affected by the planning decision, if so, the claimant is entitled to compensation only in respect of the land actually affected. Similarly his interest may extend to land, which, although affected by the planning decision, has no unexpended balance; in that case, he can claim only in respect of so much of the land as has an unexpended balance.

Exclusion of Compensation

Even if all other necessary conditions have been fulfilled, no compensation can be claimed in the following cases:

(1) *Change of use.*—No compensation is payable for a refusal of permission for any development which consists of or includes the making of a material change in the use of any building or

---

(*q*) This would only happen in a few cases between 1st January, 1955 and October, 1958.

(*r*) Act of 1971, s. 146(1).

(*s*) *Ibid.*, s. 134(4).

(*t*) See the Compensation Regulations, regs. 9, 10, 12.

other land (*u*). The drafting of this particular provision has been the subject of much criticism. It clearly excludes compensation in such cases as the change of use of existing premises from, say, a house to offices; and it is equally clear that no compensation is payable for refusal of permission to change the use of land where no building or other operations are involved. The difficulty arises over such cases as refusal of permission to build, say, houses on agricultural land. This is not development *consisting* of a change of use because building operations are excluded from the word "use" (*v*), but it might be argued that it *includes* a change of use in that where planning permission is given for the erection of a building, the permission is to be construed as including permission to use the building for the purpose for which it is designed (*a*). The Government emphasised that it was not intended to exclude compensation in such cases, but it must always be remembered that statements in Parliament are not authority for the construction of a statute.

(2) *Advertisements.*—No compensation is payable for a refusal of consent for the display of advertisements (*b*).

(3) *Conditions.*—No compensation is payable in respect of the following conditions (*c*):

(i) a condition as to the number or disposition of buildings on land—but for this purpose a condition prohibiting development of a specified part of the land is to be treated as a refusal of permission as respects that part of the land and so may attract compensation (*d*);

(ii) as to the dimensions design, structure or external appearance of any building or the materials to be used in its construction;

(iii) as to the manner in which the land is to be laid out,

(*u*) Act of 1971, s. 147(1).
(*v*) Act of 1971, s. 290.
(*a*) *Ibid.*, s. 33(2).
(*b*) *Ibid.*, s. 147(1).
(*c*) *Ibid.*, s. 147(2).
(*d*) *Ibid.*, s. 147(6).

including the provision of facilities for parking, loading or fuelling vehicles;

(iv) as to use of buildings or other land;

(v) as to the location, design or construction of any means of access to a highway, other than a service road;

(vi) any condition imposed on permission for mineral working.

(4) *Statutory Conditions.*—No compensation will be paid in respect of conditions as to the duration of planning permission or in respect of any condition imposed by the Department of the Environment or Industry when granting either an industrial development certificate or an office development permit (*e*).

(5) *Premature development.*—No compensation is payable for a refusal of permission if the reason (or one of the reasons) given for the refusal is that the development would be premature having regard to either:

(a) the order or priority, if any, indicated, in the development plan (for example, in the programme map) for the development of that area; or

(b) any existing deficiency in the provision of water supplies and sewerage services, and the period within which any such deficiency may be expected to be made good.

If, however, fresh application is made after a lapse of seven years, and permission is again refused on either of these grounds, compensation will be payable (*f*).

(6) *Unsuitability of land.*—No compensation will be paid for a refusal of permission if the reason (or one of the reasons) given is that the land is unsuitable for development on account of liability to flooding or subsidence (*g*).

(7) *Land acquired by public authorities.*—Land may have been compulsorily acquired by or sold to an authority possessing compulsory purchase powers, and a planning decision made after the date of notice to treat or the contract of sale. In that case, the

(*e*) Act of 1971, s. 147(3).
(*f*) *Ibid.*, s. 147(4).
(*g*) *Ibid.*, s. 147(5).

authority is not entitled to compensation for that planning decision, nor is any person who derives title to the land from that authority after 1st July, 1948 (*h*).

(8) *Land belonging to statutory undertakers or the National Coal Board.*—No compensation is payable for a planning decision affecting operational land of a statutory undertaker or the National Coal Board (*i*).

(9) *Other planning permission available.*—No compensation is payable if permission is available for some other development of a residential, commercial or industrial character; that is, development consisting wholly or mainly of houses, flats, shops, industrial buildings (including warehouses) or any combination of these (*j*).

Procedure for Making and Maintaining Claims

A claim for compensation must be sent to the local planning authority for transmission to the Minister within six months of the date of the decision or such extended period as the Minister may allow (*k*). On receiving the claim the Minister must first consider whether the conditions for payment of compensation are satisfied. If they are not satisfied, the Minister will invite the claimant to withdraw his claim (*l*). If the claim is not withdrawn, the Minister must give a decision and the claimant can appeal to the Lands Tribunal (*m*).

Review of Planning Decision

At this stage, the Minister may decide to review the decision which has given rise to the claim for compensation. In this connection, he may do one of two things. First, he may decide to substitute a decision more favourable to the applicant, but he can only do this where the decision was that of the local planning

(*h*) *Ibid.*, s. 149(1), (2).
(*i*) Act of 1971, s. 149(3).
(*j*) *Ibid.*, s. 148.
(*k*) *Ibid.*, s. 154(2).
(*l*) *Ibid.*, s. 154(5).
(*m*) Compensation Regs., reg. 7.

authority (or its delegate) and there was no appeal. A decision more favourable to the applicant means:

(a) in relation to a refusal of permission, a grant of permission either unconditionally or subject to conditions, either for the whole or part of the land concerned;

(b) in relation to a grant of permission subject to conditions, either an unconditional grant or a grant subject to less stringent conditions.

Secondly, the Minister may decide to grant permission for some other form of development. This he can do, even if there has been an appeal or if he himself gave the decision on a reference under section 35 of the Act of 1971.

Before giving a formal direction for either of these purposes, the Minister must give notice of the proposed direction to the local planning authority and to any person who has claimed compensation and has not withdrawn his claim. The authority or the claimant may then make objections and ask to be heard by a person appointed by the Minister for the purpose.

If the Minister decides to go ahead with the proposal, he will embody them in a formal direction notice of which is given to the local planning authority and the persons claiming compensation. The latter may wish at this stage to modify the claim for compensation because the effect of the direction will almost certainly be to reduce the amount of the claim if not to extinguish it altogether (*n*).

Determination of Compensation: Amount

In order to determine the amount of compensation, it is necessary first to consider whether the whole of the land in question is "qualified land", that is, any part of the land affected by the planning decision which at the time of the decision has an unexpended balance (*o*).

(*n*) Act of 1971, ss. 38, 39.
(*o*) *Ibid.*, s. 106.

The following situations may then arise (*p*):

1. Where there is only one claim, and the whole of the land affected by the planning decision is qualified land, then the amount of compensation will be the lesser of the following amounts.

(a) the amount by which the value of the claimant's interest, or so much of it as subsists in the qualified land, is depreciated in value by the planning decision;

(b) the amount of the unexpended balance attaching to the qualified land.

2. Where the whole of the land is qualified land, but there is more than one claim in respect of the same area of qualified land, then it is necessary to consider whether the aggregate amount of compensation payable in respect of all the claims would exceed the amount of the unexpended balance. If the aggregate would exceed the amount of the unexpended balance—but not otherwise—the unexpended balance must be allocated between the interests concerned. The amount so allocated to each interest will then be the maximum amount payable in respect of that interest.

It may happen that no claim has been made in respect of one or more of the interests in the qualified land. It is clear that any such interest is to be ignored; it is not to be brought into the allocation so as to reduce the amount of the unexpended balance available for those who have made claims.

3. In the preceding two paragraphs, it has been assumed that the whole of the land is qualified land and that (if there is more than one claim) the separate claims relate to the same area. Where these conditions are not satisfied, the amount of compensation payable in respect of any interest is to be determined as follows:

(i) first, there must be ascertained the amount by which any interest in the whole or part of the land affected by the decision has been depreciated in value;

(*p*) *Ibid.*

(ii) secondly, the land concerned must be divided into as many separate parts as are necessary to ensure that each part either (a) consists of qualified land with one or more interests relating to the whole of it; or (b) is not qualified land;

(iii) the depreciation in the value of the interest (as ascertained in paragraph (i)) is then to be apportioned between the separate parts mentioned in paragraph (ii); this apportionment is to be made according to the nature of the separate parts and the effect of the planning decision in relation to each of them.

The amount of the compensation payable in respect of each interest will be the aggregate of the amounts payable in respect of each part, subject, of course, to the amount of the unexpended balance available in respect of those parts; this will involve apportionment of the unexpended balance.

Determination of Compensation: Procedure

In determining the amount of compensation, the Minister is to "cause such investigations to be made and such steps to be taken as he may deem requisite . . . ." These may include a hearing before a Ministry Inspector, but there is no obligation upon the Minister to give the opportunity of an oral hearing. Having taken such steps as he deems requisite, the Minister must prepare a statement of his findings, notice of which is given to the claimant, and (if the findings involve an apportionment of the unexpended balance) to any other person interested in the land (*q*).

Any person who has received notice of the Minister's findings may then appeal to the Lands Tribunal (*r*).

Registration of Compensation

Where the amount of compensation exceeds £20, the Minister may notify the county council or county district council of the

(*q*) Compensation Regs., reg. 6.
(*r*) *Ibid.*, reg. 7.

details and the authority are to register the notice in the register of local land charges (*s*).

Minerals

Claims for compensation in respect of minerals will be affected by the Minerals Regulations made under the Act of 1962 and kept in force under the Act of 1971. The Regulations modify the financial provisions of the Act in its application to minerals.

Some of these modifications result from the fact that minerals may be held separately from the land in which they lie. Where ownership of surface and minerals was severed before July 1st, 1948, a claim for loss of development value is treated as a separate unexpended balance (*t*). Where the freehold is severed after that date, the unexpended balance (if any) is also to be apportioned between the minerals and the remainder of the land (*u*).

(*s*) Act of 1971, s. 158.
(*t*) Mineral Regulations, reg. 9 (2).
(*u*) *Ibid.*, reg. 9 (1).

Chapter 20

COMPENSATION FOR REVOCATION OR MODIFICATION OF PERMISSION

The circumstances in which planning permission may be revoked or modified have been described in an earlier chapter. There are two sets of cases. First, where permission has been granted on an application, that permission may be revoked or modified by an order under section 45 of the Act of 1971. Where such an order is made, compensation will be payable under section 164 of the Act. Secondly, where permission has been granted by the General Development Order, 1963, that permission may be withdrawn by a direction under article 4 of the Order requiring an application to be made for express permission. If such permission is refused or is granted subject to any conditions other than those prescribed by the Order, compensation can be claimed under section 164.

The Act of 1947 had provided that compensation should be paid for—

(a) any expenditure rendered abortive by the revocation or modification;

(b) loss or damage directly attributable to the revocation or modification, but only exceptionally would this include compensation for the depreciation in the value of the land.

These provisions gave effect to the principle of the Act of 1947 that, in the absence of special circumstances, compensation should not be paid for loss of development value. With the partial restoration of development values to private ownership under the Act of 1954 that basis was obviously no longer applicable. The Act of 1954 accordingly provided that in cases arising on or after 1st January, 1955, the compensation payable for revocation or modification should include loss of development value, whether or not the land has an unexpended balance of established development value.

CLAIM FOR COMPENSATION

Particulars of Claim

Compensation for revocation or modification may therefore include compensation in respect of the following:

(a) expenditure in carrying out work rendered abortive by the revocation or modification of permission, and—whether or not any work has actually been done—this may include expenditure on plans and other preparatory matters (*a*).

(b) loss or damage directly attributable to the revocation or modification, *e.g.* expenses incurred in securing release from a building contract entered into *after* the grant of the permission which has been revoked or modified;

(c) depreciation in the value of any interest in land resulting from the revocation or modification.

Depreciation in the Value of any Interest

It would appear from the rules for assessing compensation contained in section 178 of the Act of 1971 that the interest must be either the freehold or a tenancy, or at least an option to purchase (*b*); a claim may be made by a mortgagee but not in respect of that interest as such, and he must account to the mortgagor.

The amount of the compensation for depreciation will be the difference between (a) the value of the interest with the benefit of the permission prior to its revocation or modification; and (b) the value of the land subject to the revocation or modification, assuming that permission would be given for appropriate Schedule 8 development (*c*).

(*a*) Act of 1971, s. 164(1). *Holmes* v. *Bradfield R.D.C.*, [1949] 1 All E.R. 381.
(*b*) *Oppenheimer* v. *Minister of Transport*, [1941] 3 All E.R. 485.
(*c*) Act of 1971, s. 164.

The assumption that permission would be available for Schedule 8 development is reasonable where the permission which has been revoked or modified related to "new development". But it creates a problem where the permission which has been revoked or modified was for Schedule 8 development. As originally enacted section 22 of the Act of 1947 dealt with this problem by incorporating section 20 with the result that compensation was payable for the revocation or modification of permission for development falling within Part II of the Schedule but not where the development was within Part I. With the repeal of subsection (5) by the Act of 1954 this no longer applied. The practical solution, however, is to apply for compensation as if permission had been refused or granted subject to conditions under section 164 of the Act of 1971 but, if the liability for compensation is disputed, it may be necessary to apply again for the permission which has been revoked or modified with a view to obtaining a decision which will form the basis of a claim under section 164.

Procedure

A claim for compensation under section 164 of the Act of 1971 must be made within six months of the order or decision, unless the Minister agrees to an extension of time (*d*). The compensation is payable by the local planning authority (*e*). Any dispute as to the payment of compensation may be referred to the Lands Tribunal (*f*).

CONTRIBUTION BY THE MINISTER

Compensation under section 164 of the Act of 1971 is payable by the local planning authority and is not dependent upon an unexpended balance. But instead of first granting permission and later revoking or modifying it, the authority might well have refused permission or granted it subject to conditions at

---

(*d*) General Regulations, reg. 14.
(*e*) Act of 1972, s. 164.
(*f*) *Ibid.*, s. 179(1).

the outset. Had that been done, compensation would not have been payable under section 164 but it might have been payable under Part VII by the Minister.

The Act of 1971 contains provisions under which the Minister may, if he thinks fit, contribute towards the compensation actually paid by the local planning authority. Where compensation for depreciation exceeds £20, the local planning authority are to give notice thereof to the Minister together with particulars of any apportionment (*g*). The Minister may come to the conclusion that, had permission been refused or granted as modified, in the first place, compensation would have been payable by him under Part VII of the Act; in that case he may (*h*) pay to the local planning authority an amount not exceeding the *lesser* of the following (*i*):

(a) the amount of the compensation for depreciation paid by the authority;

(b) the unexpended balance at the date of the making of the order in respect of which the compensation was paid.

Where such a contribution has been paid it is logical that the amount of the unexpended balance should be reduced accordingly and provision for this purpose is made by the Compensation Regulations. On the other hand, it would be unreasonable that the unexpended balance should be reduced as a result of a transaction between the Minister and the local planning authority without the owner of the land having the opportunity of presenting objections.

The Compensation Regulations require the Minister to give notice of his intentions to any person having an interest in the land or who is likely to be affected by the reduction of the

---

(*g*) Act of 1971, s. 166.

(*h*) The use of the word "may" suggests that the Minister has a discretion, but when the Bill for the 1954 Act was in Standing Committee of the House of Commons, the Minister said that the intention was that the contribution should be paid. H. of C. Official Report, Standing Committee C, 16th June, 1954, cols. 618–621.

(*i*) Act of 1971, s. 167.

unexpended balance (*k*); these persons then have the right to object on certain specified grounds (*l*) and, if these objections are not accepted by the Minister to appeal to the Lands Tribunal (*m*).

(*k*) *E.g.* a mortgagee.
(*l*) Reg. 14.
(*m*) Reg. 15.

Chapter 21

REPAYMENT OF COMPENSATION

Where compensation has been paid for loss of development value, and permission is subsequently granted for some profitable form of development, it is only reasonable that the compensation should be repaid. The Act of 1971 contains provisions for the repayment of the following classes of compensation:

(1) compensation under either Part II of the Act of 1954, Part VI of the Act of 1962 or Part VII of the Act of 1971 in respect of planning restrictions on new development imposed after 1st January, 1955 (*a*);

(2) compensation under either Part IV of the Act of 1954, Part VII of the Act of 1962 or Part VIII of the Act of 1971 in respect of orders revoking or modifying planning permission after 1st January, 1955 (*b*);

(3) compensation under Part V of the Act of 1954 in respect of planning restrictions or the revocation or modification of planning permission between 1st July, 1948, and 1st January, 1955 (*c*);

(4) Payments under section 59 of the Act of 1947 for loss of development value in connection with certain classes of war damaged land (*d*).

Types of Repayment

No provision is made for the repayment of compensation under section 169 of the Act of 1971 for restrictions on Schedule 8 development (*e*) or of payments under Part I of the Act of 1954(*f*).

(*a*) See chapter 19, *ante*.
(*b*) See chapter 20, *ante*.
(*c*) See p. 300, *ante*.
(*d*) See p. 297, *ante*.
(*e*) See chapter 18, *ante*.
(*f*) See p. 300, *ante*.

Where compensation for revocation or modification of planning permission is concerned, it is only the compensation for depreciation in the value of the land (as distinct from compensation for abortive expenditure, etc.) that is to be repaid.

The provisions as to the repayment of compensation should be clearly understood by solicitors and surveyors; failure to advise the client properly may render the solicitor or surveyor liable for professional negligence.

The compensation will not necessarily be repaid by the person who received it. The compensation will have been paid to the owners of the freehold or leasehold interests in the land at the time. Repayment must be made by the person who subsequently carries out certain types of development, who may be a successor in title to the person receiving the compensation. This liability to repay must therefore be taken into account in considering terms of sale or lease.

It is no doubt for this reason that successive Acts make careful provision for entering compensation payments in the register of local land charges. In the case of compensation under paragraph (1) and (2) above, the Minister is to serve a "compensation notice", notifying the local authority of any payment exceeding £20, who are then to enter the details in the register of local land charges. The compensation notice may apportion the payment as between different parts of the land; and if it does so, the details of the apportionment will also be entered in the register of local land charges. If there is no apportionment, it is to be assumed that the compensation is distributed rateably over the land (*g*). Similar provisions as to apportionment and registration applied to compensation under Part IV of the Act of 1954 and payments under section 59 of the Act of 1947 (*h*).

If, for any reason, the details of a compensation payment are not entered in the register of local land charges, the provisions

---

(*g*) Act of 1971, ss. 158, 166.
(*h*) Act of 1954, ss. 39, 57.

as to repayment do not apply as against a purchaser of the land (*i*).

Where a compensation notice has been registered, certain types of new development must not be carried out until a specified sum has been paid or received (*k*). Where the compensation arises under paragraphs (1), (2) or (3) above, the repayment provisions apply to:

(a) development of a residential commercial or industrial character, being development which consists wholly or mainly of houses, flats, shops, offices or industrial buildings (including warehouses);
(b) mineral development;
(c) any development which having regard to its probable value, the Minister considers should be subject to the provisions for repayment of compensation.

Paragraph (c), however, does not apply if the owner of the land has obtained from the Minister a certificate that it is not reasonable that the compensation shall be repaid.

In the case of payments under section 59 of the Act of 1947 the repayment provisions apply to all classes of development without exception (*l*).

The amount of the compensation to be repaid is determined by reference to a "development area", that is, the land on which the proposed development is to be carried out. If the development area is identical with or includes the whole of the land mentioned in the compensation notice, the amount to be repaid will be the amount specified in the compensation notice; in other cases it will be an appropriate proportion to the amount shown in the compensation notice. The Minister may remit the whole or any part of the repayment if he thinks it necessary to encourage the development to take place, but this is entirely within his discretion (*m*).

(*i*) *Stock* v. *Wanstead and Woodford B.C.*, [1961] 2 All E.R. 433; *Ministry of Housing and Local Government* v. *Sharp*, [1970] 1 All E.R. 1009.
(*k*) Act of 1971, ss. 159, 168.
(*l*) *Ibid.*, s. 258.
(*m*) *Ibid.*, s. 160.

PART III

COMMUNITY LAND AND DEVELOPMENT LAND TAX

SUMMARY

CHAPTER 22

COMMUNITY LAND: GENERAL PROVISIONS

As we have seen in an earlier chapter, there have been various attempts to deal with the compensation-betterment problem (*a*). The latest attempt is embodied in the Community Land Act 1975, and the Development Land Tax Act 1976. This new legislation is concerned not only with the recoupment of betterment. It is also designed to enable local authorities to plan more positively and to decide where development takes place. The new legislation thus has two main objectives. As set forth in a White Paper (*b*), these are:

"(a) to enable the community to control the development of land in accordance with its needs and priorities; and

(b) to restore to the community the increase in value of land arising from its efforts".

The first objective implies two things: that there is a need for more positive planning and that the powers available under other legislation—such as the Planning Acts and the New Towns Act—are insufficient. The White Paper asserted that the existing system of planning control was largely negative.

> "The community, via its elected local authority and, in the final analysis central government, can veto proposals for development, but the initiative is left largely in private hands. The community does not at present have sufficient powers always to plan positively, to decide where and when particular development should take place" (*c*).

(*a*) See chapter 17, *ante*.
(*b*) Cmnd. 5730, para. 16.
(*c*) *Ibid.*, para. 3.

The White Paper proposed, therefore, that major development of land should take place only after the land has passed through public ownership. To this end, local authorities will for a period of some years following "the first appointed day" (*d*) be *enabled* to acquire land needed for "relevant development", that is all development other than comparatively small developments (*e*). At any time, however, the Minister may make an order—usually known as a "duty order"—imposing upon the appropriate authorities a *duty* to acquire all land required for specified classes of development. And after "the second appointed day" it will be the duty of all local authorities to acquire all land needed for relevant development (*f*). Planning permissions granted after the first appointed day may be suspended pending a decision on whether or not the land is to be brought into public ownership (*g*).

The second objective—restoring to the community the increase in value due to its efforts—is to be achieved in the first instance by means of the development land tax. This is payable wherever development value is realised—typically on the sale of land for development. Where land is compulsorily purchased—whether under the Community Land Act or under other powers—development land tax will be deducted from the compensation so that the acquiring authority will pay the net amount. But where an authority subsequently dispose of land held under the Community Land Act, they will normally charge full market value.

The development land tax is intended to be an interim measure only. After the second appointed day (*h*) compensation for compulsory purchase will be restricted to "current use value" thus excluding development value altogether.

(*d*) This was 6th April, 1976.
(*e*) See p. 335, *post*.
(*f*) The Rt. Hon. John Silkin, the Minister concerned, has said that the second appointed day is not likely to be fixed for at least ten years.
(*g*) See chapter 23, *post*.
(*h*) See note (*f*), *supra*.

Definitions

The Act of 1975 introduces certain new concepts, the most important of which are "development land" and "relevant development". These must now be considered.

Development land is defined as "land which in the opinion of the authority concerned is needed for relevant development within ten years of the time at which they are acting" (*i*). This means that it is for the local authority concerned to decide whether or not land is development land. They must, however, be satisfied that the land is needed for "relevant development" and in deciding whether it is so needed, they must have regard to the development plan and to certain other matters (*k*). "The time at which they are acting" means, it is submitted, the time when they are discharging a particular function, *e.g.* drawing up or reviewing their land acquisition management scheme, or when deciding whether to acquire a particular piece of land.

Relevant Development

"Relevant development" is defined, by exclusion, as all development (as defined in the Act of 1971 (*l*)) except that comprised in three categories (*m*):

(1) exempt development;
(2) building of a single dwellinghouse;
(3) excepted development.

Development in category (1) is entirely outside the scheme of the Act of 1975. Thus, the powers of compulsory purchase conferred by the Act cannot be used for the acquisition of land which is suitable only for such development. Development within categories (2) and (3) is within the powers of compulsory purchase conferred by the Act of 1975. However:

(*i*) Act of 1975, s. 3(1).
(*k*) See p. 341, *post*.
(*l*) See chapter 5, *ante*.
(*m*) Act of 1975, s. 3(2).

(a) it can never be the subject of a "duty order" (*n*) and thus can never fall within the category of land which authorities will in due course be obliged to acquire;

(b) it is outside the procedures for the suspension of planning permissions (*o*);

(c) if an authority wish to acquire land by compulsory purchase for such development, the modified procedures, described in a later chapter (*p*), will not apply.

The definitions of these three categories of what may be called "non-relevant development" must now be considered.

Exempt Development

This is any development specified in Sch. 1 of the Act of 1975, namely:

(1) development permitted by the General Development Order or which would be so permitted but for an article 4 direction (*q*);

(2) the carrying out on land used for the purposes of agriculture or forestry, of building or other operations required for the purposes of that use other than the erection of dwellinghouses;

(3) the winning and working, on land held or occupied with land used for the purposes of agriculture, of minerals reasonably required for the purposes of this use.

Development of the land set out in paragraphs (2) and (3) is for the most part development permitted by the current General Development Order. However, development of this land will be exempt development even though it does not comply with the conditions and limitations implied by the General Development Order; furthermore, whereas development might cease to be exempt development under paragraph 1 because of changes in the

(*n*) See p. 343, *post*.
(*o*) See chapter 23, *post*.
(*p*) See chapter 24, *post*.
(*q*) See chapter 6, p. 120, *ante*.

General Development Order, such changes cannot affect paragraphs (2) and (3) above.

Building of a single dwellinghouse.—To fall within this category of exempt development, the development must consist exclusively of the erection of a single dwelling, but it may include such ancillary things as garages and outhouses (*r*).

Excepted Development.—This is development prescribed by regulations made by the Minister. The Community Land (Excepted Development) Regulations (*s*) prescribe thirteen classes of excepted development. Their scope may be seen by considering some of the more important classes. The first three classes relate to land which was, so to speak, in the pipe line for development on 12th September, 1974, the date on which the White Paper was issued. Class 1 refers to "any development the carrying out of which is authorised by planning permission granted on or before 12 September 1974". This will presumably cover development authorised by an outline permission. A planning permission granted on appeal after 12th September, 1974, will fall within Class 1 if the decision appealed against was made before that date or, where the appeal arises from the failure of the local planning authority to give a decision, if that decision should have been given before that date (*t*). There may, however, be cases in which a planning authority resolved to grant planning permission before 12th September, 1974, but sent to the applicant the notice of their decision after that date. In *R.* v. *Yeovil B.C. Ex parte Trustees of Elim Pentecostal Church* (*u*) the Divisional Court held that there was no grant of planning permission until notice was sent to the applicant: if that is the correct view, then development does not fall within Class 1 of the Excepted Development Regulations unless notice was sent to the applicant

---

(*r*) Act of 1975, s. 3(3).

(*s*) S.I. 1976 No. 331.

(*t*) Act of 1975, s. 6(3). As to the time within which the local planning authority should give a decision, see chapter 6, p. 137, *ante*.

(*u*) (1971), 23 P. & C.R. 39.

on or before 12th September, 1974 (*a*). Finally, it should be noted the effect of Class 1 will be of limited duration because of the time limits on the validity of permissions (*b*).

Class 2 covers development consisting wholly or mainly of the building of dwellinghouses or industrial buildings on any land, the freehold of which has been owned (*c*) by a builder or developer of residential or industrial property (*d*) (not necessarily the same builder or developer) since 12th September, 1974. To obtain the benefit of this exception, notice must have been given not later than the prescribed date (*e*) to one of the authorities concerned in whose area the land is situate. There are no limits to the size of developments excepted under Class 2 or as to the time within which such development must be carried out.

Class 3 covers the erection of industrial buildings on any land, a material interest (*f*) in which has been owned (*g*) since 12th September, 1974, by an industrial undertaker (*h*) (not necessarily the same industrial undertaker). Here again there is no limit to the size of the development. It should be noted that the exception will cover extensions to and the re-erection of existing industrial buildings (*i*).

Classes 4 and 5 cover respectively the erection of industrial buildings of a total gross floor space of up to 1,500 square metres and of other buildings of a total gross floor space of up to 1,000

(*a*) See also chapter 6, p. 139, *ante*.

(*b*) See chapter 7, p. 166, *ante*.

(*c*) This need not be the legal estate; a *binding* contract for the acquisition of the freehold will suffice: Excepted Development Regulations, reg. 2(4).

(*d*) For definition of "builder or developer of residential property" see Excepted Development Regulations, reg. 2(1).

(*e*) The prescribed date was 6th October, 1976 unless application for planning permission was made between 6th April, 1976 and 5th October, 1976.

(*f*) "Material interest" means the freehold or a lease with at least seven years to run: Act of 1975, s. 6(1).

(*g*) See note (*c*), *supra*.

(*h*) An industrial undertaker is any person carrying on any such process or research as is mentioned in the definition of industrial buildings contained in the Act of 1971, s. 6, as to which see chapter 6, p. 127, *ante*.

(*i*) Act of 1975, s. 6(1).

square metres (*j*). The effect of these two classes is to remove quite substantial developments from the categories of "relevant development". The limit of 1,000 square metres of gross floor space for non-industrial buildings will cover such developments as housing developments of up to ten to twelve houses or twenty flats; small commercial buildings; most recreational buildings; churches, meeting halls. Class 5 also covers cases of mixed use such as shops with offices or flats above them. Both classes cover the rebuilding or extension of buildings (*k*).

Class 6 refers to the erection on any land of one or more buildings to be used for agriculture. As we have seen, the carrying out on land which is used for the purposes of agriculture of any building or other operations required for the purposes of that use (other than the erection of dwellinghouses) is exempt development (*l*). The practical effect of Class 6 would seem to be to treat the erection of agricultural buildings on land not used for agriculture as excepted development.

Class 7 covers the rebuilding, enlargement, improvement or other alteration of existing buildings, or of buildings demolished within the previous ten years provided the gross floor space does not exceed the original floor space by more than ten per cent (*m*).

Finally in this review, it should be noted that most changes of use are excepted development by virtue of Class 11.

The Minister may enlarge or restrict the categories of excepted development by making new or amended regulations (*n*).

The Authorities

In England, the powers and duties conferred by the Act of 1975 are to be exercised for the most part by the county councils and the

(*j*) Gross floor space is to be ascertained by external measurement of that space whether or not the building is to be bounded (wholly or partly) by external walls.

(*k*) Act of 1975, s. 6(1).

(*l*) See p. 336, *ante*.

(*m*) For "gross floor space" see note (*i*), *supra*.

(*n*) Act of 1975, s. 53(4).

district councils. The new town development corporations and the planning boards for the Lakes District and the Peak District national parks are also authorities for the purposes of this Act (*o*). The Minister may create a joint board for the areas, or parts of areas, of two or more authorities (*p*). Thus, in England, the authorities concerned are the planning authorities together with the new town development corporations. It follows that all land in England will be in the area of at least two authorities.

In Wales, however, there is a quite different system: in the first instance the responsibility for discharging the appropriate functions is given to the Land Authority for Wales—a new body established by the Act (*q*)—and, where appropriate, the new town development corporations. The elected local authorities may be given powers by the Land Authority either by delegation (*r*) or under agency agreements (*s*). However, when a duty order (*t*) is made in respect of any area in Wales, the local authorities for that area will have powers of compulsory purchase and also functions in regard to the suspension of planning permissions.

Land Acquisition and Management Schemes

It will be seen that throughout England, functions under the Act of 1975 are exerciseable from the outset by at least two authorities, usually the county council and the district council. In an attempt to resolve the problems which this duplication might cause, the Act provides for a Land Acquisition and Management Scheme for each county defining the responsibilities for each authority in the area. The duty of preparing the scheme for each county and of keeping it up to date is imposed upon the county council and the other authorities in the area acting jointly: the schemes do not require the approval of the Minister but he has

---

(*o*) Act of 1975, s. 1 (1) (a).
(*p*) *Ibid.*, s. 2.
(*q*) *Ibid.*, s. 8.
(*r*) *Ibid.*, s. 14(4).
(*s*) *Ibid.*, s. 14(7).
(*t*) See p. 343, *post*.

powers of supervision which will enable him *inter alia* to resolve disputes between authorities (*u*).

The purpose of the Land Acquisition and Management Scheme is essentially to decide "who does what". It should not be confused with the programmes for acquisition which the authorities are expected to draw up each year (*a*). There will be no Land Acquisition and Management Scheme in Wales.

General Powers and Duties of Authorities

On 6th April, 1976, it became the duty of each authority in exercising certain functions to have regard to (a) the desirability of bringing development land into public ownership, and of developing that land themselves or of making it available for development by others; and (b) the desirability of securing the proper planning of their area (*b*). The "functions" referred to are the functions of these authorities under the Act of 1975 itself and also their functions concerning the acquisition, management and disposal of land under the Act of 1971 and, in the case of a new town development corporation, under the New Towns Act 1965 (*c*).

"Development Land", as we have seen (*d*), is land needed for relevant development within ten years of the time when the authority are exercising any particular functions. In deciding whether any particular piece of land is development land in this sense, the authority are required to have regard to a number of matters. First, and naturally enough, they are required to have regard to the provisions of the development plan; that is, the structure plan, any local plans affecting the area in which the land is situate, and the 1947-type development plan so far as it is

---

(*u*) Act of 1975, s. 16, Sch. 5.
(*a*) See p. 343, *post*.
(*b*) Act of 1975, s. 17(1).
(*c*) *Ibid.*, s. 17(5).
(*d*) See p. 335, *ante*.

still in force (*e*). Second, the authority are to have regard to whether planning permission for any relevant development has been granted or has been refused (*f*). If permission has been refused, it does not necessarily follow that the land will not be treated as development land; this would seem to depend on the reasons why a particular application was refused. Third, the authority are to have regard to any other considerations which would be material for determining an application for planning permission for any relevant development; in other words, the authority should consider whether they would grant planning permission if an application were made (*g*).

It is expected that the authorities concerned will take the initiative in identifying development land, and the result of the initiatives will be seen in the preparation of land policy statements and programmes of acquisition. But land may also be identified as needed for relevant development by persons seeking to bring land into development. Accordingly, where application is made for planning permission for relevant development, the authorities concerned are required to consider whether they wish to acquire the land; and the planning permission may be suspended in the meantime. Where planning permission is suspended in this way, certain owners or occupiers are enabled to serve a blight notice compelling the authority concerned to acquire the land forthwith. The suspension of planning permission will be considered further in the next chapter.

The authorities concerned are also enabled to identify land for relevant development by designating "disposal notification areas". Any person proposing to dispose of a material interest in land situate in a disposal notification area will be under a duty to give notice to the authority concerned. That authority must then serve a counter-notice indicating whether or not they propose to acquire

---

(*e*) Act of 1975, s. 17(2) (a). For development plans generally, see chapter 4, *ante*.
(*f*) Act of 1975, s. 17(2) (b).
(*g*) *Ibid.*, s. 17(2) (c).

the land. This may in turn trigger off the service of a blight notice. The provisions as to disposal notification areas will be considered later in this chapter.

It is the clear intention of the Act of 1975 that decisions as to whether any particular land is brought into public ownership, or as to when that should be done, should be made within the existing planning framework. In practice these decisions are likely, for the next few years at least, to be affected by financial considerations. The Minister requires each authority to prepare "rolling programmes" for the acquisition of land under the Act of 1975: that means that each year the authority will prepare a programme for the ensuing five years. The rolling programmes for each authority are to be based on a "land policy statement" which will set out the authority's policy on such matters as the anticipated needs for land for housing and industry, policy for acquiring sites in terms of general location and size of parcels, release of land already in public ownership for private development. There is no statutory authority either for the rolling programmes or for the land policy statements, but the Minister has indicated that he expects authorities to draw up these documents (*h*).

Extended Powers and Duties

Although at first the authorities will be enabled to acquire land needed for relevant development, the intention is that ultimately they should be under a duty to acquire such land. It seems that this duty will be imposed on a piecemeal basis. At any time the Minister may make a "duty order" requiring the authorities within the area, or part of the area, of a county council to acquire all land needed for "designated relevant development", that is, such types of relevant development as are specified in the

---

(*h*) See in particular circulars 121/75 and 26/76 (Community Land Circulars 1 and 6).

order (*i*). The date on which a duty order comes into force is to be known as "a relevant date" (*k*).

When a duty order comes into force, it will be the duty of the authorities in the area concerned to acquire all outstanding material interests in land (*l*) which is needed for the purposes of designated relevant development (*m*). This duty will not extend to land which is not needed for designated relevant development within the ensuing ten years and to certain other cases (*n*).

Before making a duty order, the Minister must consult the authorities concerned (*o*), and the order is likely to designate those classes of relevant development which appear at that time to give rise to the more pressing needs for land. But it is intended that ultimately all relevant development shall become designated relevant development throughout Great Britain through the making of duty orders. It is probable therefore that for many areas there will be more than one duty order.

When all relevant development has become designated relevant development throughout Great Britain, the Minister may make an order fixing "the second appointed day" (*p*). Thereafter, compensation for compulsory purchase (whether under the Act of 1975 or any statutory powers) will be on the basis of "current use value", except in the case of certain lands owned by charities or where a financial hardship tribunal has awarded additional compensation.

Disposal Notification Areas

Any authority under the Act of 1975 may—for the purpose of obtaining information about disposals of development land—

(*i*) Act of 1975, s. 18(1).
(*k*) *Ibid.*, s. 18(6).
(*l*) "Material interest" means the freehold or a lease with at least seven years to run: *Ibid.*, s. 6(1).
(*m*) Act of 1975, s. 18(3).
(*n*) *Ibid.*, s. 18(4).
(*o*) *Ibid.*, s. 18(2).
(*p*) *Ibid.*, s. 7.

declare any land in their area to be a disposal notification area (*q*). Thereafter, any person who proposes to dispose of a material interest in the land must (with certain exceptions) give notice to the authority concerned. The authority then have four weeks in which to serve a counter-notice stating whether or not they propose to purchase the land (*r*).

The service of a counter-notice that the authority intend to purchase the land does not impose on that authority any duty to take steps to acquire the land within any specified period, but certain categories of owner-occupier may be able to serve a blight notice (*s*). Service of a counter-notice that the authority does not intend to purchase the land does not, however, deprive the authority concerned of the power to do so. Any area of land may lawfully be declared to be a disposal notification area. However, the Minister has advised authorities to adopt a cautious approach; a disposal notification area should be declared only where an authority propose to acquire a significant area of land for development where early acquisition of the land is intended, and where there is adequate planning backing (*t*).

Procedure for Declaring DNA

Any of the authorities under the Act of 1975 may declare land within their area to be a disposal notification area. All that is required is for the authority to pass a resolution (*u*). The area should be indicated on a map which is to be kept available for public inspection, and notice of the resolution should be entered in the local land charges register (*a*). The public have no rights of objection, and the Minister's approval is not required. But the authority should inform the Minister, and he may at any time terminate or modify the declaration (*b*).

(*q*) Act of 1975, s. 23(1), (2).
(*r*) *Ibid.*, s. 23 (5), (6), (7).
(*s*) See chapter 11, p. 210, *ante*.
(*t*) Circular 26/76 (Community Land Circular 6), para. 101.
(*u*) Act of 1975, s. 23(2).
(*a*) *Ibid.*, Sch. 8, para. 1.
(*b*) *Ibid.*, Sch. 8, para. 1.

In England, all land is in the area of at least two authorities for the purposes of the Act of 1975. It is therefore possible for the same land to be within more than one disposal notification area. That would mean that any person proposing to dispose of that land would have to give two or more notices.

As mentioned above, the Minister may terminate or modify a disposal notification area. The authority concerned may also do so at any time by passing a resolution to that effect (*c*).

The Duty to Notify

A detailed consideration of the duty to notify proposed transactions in land in a disposal notification area would be outside the scope of this work but a general outline will be appropriate (*d*). Anyone who proposes to dispose of a material interest in land in a disposal notification area, or who proposes to enter into a binding contract to dispose of such an interest must (subject to some exceptions) give notice of his proposal to the authority concerned. This will cover sale of the freehold interest, grant of a lease for seven years or more, assignment of a lease with at least seven years to run (*e*).

The exceptions fall into two classes. First, there are cases to which the provisions as to notification do not apply. These include disposals by way of gift. The implication is that, even if notice were given, it would be invalid and the authority concerned would not be entitled to serve counter-notice: consequently, there would be no right on the part of the landowner to serve a blight notice. Second, there is one case in which notice may but need not be given. This relates to the disposal by an individual of his private residence (*f*), that is, the whole or part of a dwellinghouse which

---

(*c*) Act of 1975, Sch. 8, para. 5.

(*d*) For a fuller treatment of the subject, references may be made to Community Land Encyclopaedia, paras. I (463) *et seq.*

(*e*) Act of 1975, ss. 6(1), 23(5).

(*f*) The reference to an "individual" clearly excludes any body corporate: possibly, it also excludes the personal representatives of a deceased individual: *Webb* v. *Warwickshire C.C.* (1971), 23 P. & C.R. 63. But where two is at the time his only or main residence along with gardens or grounds which the individual has for his own occupation and enjoyment up to an area of one acre (including the site of the house) (*g*). The voluntary service of notice in the case of a private residence could lead ultimately to the service of a blight notice (*h*).

---

or more individuals jointly own a private residence it is submitted that they would be within the statutory provision (Interpretation Act 1889). Trustees are included: Act of 1975. Sch. 8, para. 4(2).

(*g*) Act of 1975, Sch. 8, para. 4.

(*h*) For the general conditions applicable to the service of blight notices, see chapter 11, *ante*, pp. 210 *et seq*.

CHAPTER 23

COMMUNITY LAND: SUSPENSION OF PLANNING PERMISSION

The new legislation is not intended to prevent private owners of land from making their own applications for planning permission for relevant development. Indeed, it is envisaged that private applications will be one of the means by which the authorities will be enabled to identify land needed for relevant development. And, although it is the intention that ultimately relevant development should take place only on land which has passed through public ownership, it is clear that for some years much relevant development will take place on land which has not first been acquired by one of the statutory authorities.

It is important, however, for the smooth working of the Act that, where an application has been made for planning permission, the authorities concerned should have an opportunity of deciding whether the land should be acquired or not and, if so, that it should be acquired before any development takes place. It is equally important that the owners of such land should know where they stand. Accordingly, the Act of 1975 requires that where an application for planning permission is made, the authorities concerned should make an early decision whether or not to acquire the land and if that they decide to acquire, the planning permission should be suspended for a limited time to enable them to do so. Planning permission may be granted by the Minister as the result of an appeal against an enforcement notice (*a*); if the permission is for relevant development, the permission may also be suspended. Where a planning permission is suspended, it remains in force, but cannot be implemented for the time being.

(*a*) See chapter 9, p. 181, *ante*.

If relevant development is carried out whilst the planning permission is suspended, the local planning authority may serve an enforcement notice under the Act of 1971 (*b*); and, if the land is compulsorily acquired, the value of such development is to be ignored in assessing compensation (*c*).

The provisions as to the suspension of planning permission vary according to the date on which the application was made and the time when the permission was granted. There are three situations:

(1) Planning permission for relevant development granted after 12th September, 1974, and before the relevant date (*d*) on an application made before 6th April, 1976.

(2) Planning permission for relevant development granted before the relevant date on an application made on or after 6th April, 1976.

(3) Planning permission granted on or after the relevant date irrespective of when the application was made.

We will now consider each of these situations in detail. Two points, however, should be noted first. There can be no suspension of planning permissions *granted* before 6th April, 1976, because they are permission for "excepted development" (*e*). There are special rules regarding the date of planning permissions given by the Minister on appeal. Where the Minister gives permission on an appeal against a decision of the local planning authority, that permission is deemed to have been granted on the date of the decision of the local planning authority: where the appeal arises from the failure of the local planning authority to give a decision within the proper time the permission is deemed to have been granted on the date by which the decision should have been given (*f*).

(*b*) Act of 1975, s. 22(1).

(*c*) *Ibid.*, s. 22(2).

(*d*) The relevant date on which the development for which planning permission has been granted becomes "*designated* relevant development" by virtue of a duty order. See chapter 22, p. 343, *ante*.

(*e*) See p. 337, *ante*.

(*f*) Act of 1975, s. 6(3). As to the date by which the decision of the local planning authority should be given, see chapter 6, p. 137, *ante*.

PLANNING PERMISSION FOR RELEVANT DEVELOPMENT GRANTED AFTER 12TH SEPTEMBER, 1974, AND BEFORE THE RELEVANT DATE ON AN APPLICATION MADE BEFORE 6TH APRIL, 1976

In this case, a person who owns a material interest (*g*) in the whole of the land, and who is entitled to possession as against every other owner of a material interest, may serve a notice (called a "notice of election") requiring the authorities concerned to decide whether or not they intend to acquire the land (*h*). The effect of such a notice is automatically to suspend the planning permission for the time being (*i*).

Upon receiving the notice of election, each of the authorities concerned must then serve within three months a counter-notice indicating either an intention to acquire the land to which the planning permission relates or an intention not to acquire that land. Failure by any of the authorities to serve a counter-notice within three months will mean that that particular authority will be deemed to have abandoned their power of compulsory purchase (*k*). All this seems to imply that more than one authority may serve a notice of intention to acquire, but in practice no doubt only one of the authorities would do so (*l*).

Notice of Intention to Acquire

The service of such notice does not bind the authority contractually, but it gives the authority a period of twleve months in which to complete "the first step towards acquisition of the land". This occurs when the authority have either entered into a binding contract to purchase the land by agreement (*m*) or have

(*g*) *I.e.* the freehold or a lease with at least seven years to run. Act of 1975, s. 6(1).

(*h*) Act of 1975, s. 19(2), Sch. 7, para. 4.

(*i*) *Ibid.*, s. 19(6).

(*k*) *Ibid.*, Sch. 7, para. 4.

(*l*) The Land Acquisition and Management Scheme—as to which see p. 340, *ante*—may afford guidance to the authorities on this point.

(*m*) This, it is submitted, would include a contract which left the price to be fixed by arbitration (*e.g.* by the Lands Tribunal) if not otherwise agreed.

published notice of the making of a compulsory purchase order. If the authority fail to complete the first step towards acquisition of the land within this period of twelve months, they are deemed to have abandoned their power of compulsory purchase for five years (*n*). The question whether the planning permission then ceases to be suspended depends on the position of the other authorities concerned, and is discussed later in this chapter (*o*).

Even if the authority complete the first step towards acquisition of the land by publishing notice of the making of a compulsory purchase order within the time allowed, it does not follow that the Minister will confirm the compulsory purchase order; or, the order may be quashed by the court. In either of these events the planning permission ceases to be suspended, but the authority can make a further compulsory purchase order and submit it for confirmation (*p*). If the compulsory purchase order is confirmed, the authority must then serve notice to treat in respect of all outstanding material interests within twelve months (*q*); if they fail to do so, they are deemed to have abandoned their power of compulsory purchase for five years (*r*). In that event the planning permission would probably cease to be suspended but this is discussed later (*s*). If the authority successfully complete the acquisition, the planning permission ceases to be suspended so that the authority concerned can carry out the development or alternatively dispose of the land with the benefit of the planning permission (*t*).

Notice of Intention not to Acquire

A notice of intention not to acquire the land comprised in the

(*n*) Act of 1975, Sch. 7, para. 1(1), (3), (5).
(*o*) See p. 352, *post*.
(*p*) Act of 1975, Sch. 7, para. 2(2).
(*q*) This contrasts with the normal rule that notice to treat must be served within three years of the confirmation of the compulsory purchase order: Compulsory Purchase Act 1965, s. 4.
(*r*) Act of 1975, Sch. 7, para. 1(1), (3).
(*s*) See p. 352, *post*.
(*t*) Act of 1975, Sch. 7, para. 2(1).

planning permission may be unconditional or conditional. Where the notice is unconditional, the authority concerned abandon their power of compulsory purchase for five years (*u*). The authority concerned may, however, indicate that their intention not to acquire the land is subject to one or more conditions (*a*). The conditions which may be imposed are specified in the Act of 1975; they include for example a condition that no relevant development is carried out on the land except in accordance with the originating planning permission (*b*). There is no right of appeal against such a condition, but the validity of any such condition may be challenged in the High Court (*c*).

Where an authority serve a notice of intention not to acquire the land, they abandon their power of compulsory purchase for five years but with the qualification that the power revives upon a failure to comply with the conditions (*d*).

End of Suspension

The suspension comes to an end when either:

(a) all the authorities concerned have abandoned, or are deemed to have abandoned, their power of purchase; or

(b) one of those authorities purchase the land (*e*).

Where an authority have given notice of intention to purchase, but subsequently are deemed to have abandoned their power of purchase, the planning permission will remain suspended, unless and until the authorities concerned have abandoned their powers of purchase. In practice, as suggested earlier, probably only one authority would seek to acquire the land; in that event, the other authorities concerned would have abandoned their powers of purchase at a fairly early stage.

(*u*) Act of 1975, Sch. 7, para. 1(1), (2), (3).
(*a*) *Ibid.*, Sch. 7, para. 7(1), 8(4).
(*b*) *Ibid.*, Sch. 7, para. 8. The "originating planning permission" is the permission which gave rise to the authority's counter-notice of intention not to acquire the land.
(*c*) Act of 1975, Sch. 7, para. 7(3), (4).
(*d*) *Ibid.*, Sch. 7, para. 1(1), (2), (3).
(*e*) *Ibid.*, Sch. 7, para. 2(1).

When a planning permission ceases to be suspended, any time limits to which that permission was subject (*f*) are extended for a period equal to that for which it was suspended (*g*).

Planning Permission for Relevant Development Granted before the Relevant Date on an Application Made after 5th April, 1976

The procedures described above, in relation to planning permission granted as a result of an application made before 6th April, 1976, operate only if the landowner chooses to serve a notice of election. But where the application is made after 5th April, 1976, the landowner has no such choice: the procedures under section 20 operate automatically. Each of the authorities concerned must serve on the applicant and on all other parties named in a certificate under section 27 of the Act of 1971 (*h*) a notice stating whether or not it is intended to acquire the land if planning permission is granted (*i*).

The authorities concerned are not entitled to wait and see if planning permission is granted; they must come to a decision whether or not to acquire the land within the time allowed to the local planning authority for giving notice of their decision whether or not to grant planning permission—normally two months (*k*). If an authority fail to give notice of intention either to acquire or not to acquire within the time allowed, that authority will be deemed to have abandoned their power of compulsory purchase for five years (*l*).

These rules are modified where the application for planning permission is deemed to arise from an appeal against an enforcement notice under section 88 of the Act of 1971 (*m*). In such

(*f*) See chapter 7, p. 166, *ante*.
(*g*) Act of 1975, s. 22.
(*h*) See chapter 6, p. 126, *ante*.
(*i*) Act of 1975, Sch. 7, para. 5(1).
(*k*) See chapter 6, p. 137, *ante*.
(*l*) Act of 1975, Sch. 7, para. 5(4).
(*m*) See chapter 9, p. 181, *ante*.

cases, the authority should wait and see whether the Minister does grant planning permission: if he does, the authorities concerned then have three months in which to serve notice of intention whether they intend to acquire the land or not (*n*).

Notice of Intention to Acquire

This form of notice indicates that, if planning permission is granted, the authority concerned intend to acquire the land. In this connection, it should be remembered that, if the local planning authority refuse permission, the Minister may subsequently grant it on appeal. If planning permission is granted, it will be suspended from that moment pending acquisition by the authority concerned (*o*). Having served notice of intention to acquire, the authority must act expeditiously. They must complete the first step towards acquisition (*p*) within twelve months of serving the notice; however, if the local planning authority refuse permission, the authority must complete the first step within twelve months of the date on which the applicant gave notice of appeal (*q*). In all other respects, the procedure and the consequences of not complying with the time scales are the same as in a section 19 case (*r*).

Notice of Intention not to Acquire

The notice may be unconditional or conditional, and the consequences of each are the same as under section 19 (*s*). Two points should be noted. First, service of an intention not to purchase does not of itself deprive the authority of their power of compulsory purchase for five years; it is the service of such a notice combined with the grant of planning permission which has this effect. Where such a notice is served and permission is subsequently

---

(*n*) Act of 1975, Sch. 7, para. 5(3).
(*o*) Act of 1975, s. 20(3)
(*p*) See p. 350, *ante*.
(*q*) Act of 1975, Sch. 7, para. 1(1), (3).
(*r*) See p. 351, *ante*.
(*s*) See p. 351, *ante*.

refused the authority retain their power of compulsory purchase. Second, if planning permission is granted after all, and the authorities concerned have served notice of intention not to acquire, then the planning permission is never suspended at all and comes into full effect at once.

End of Period of Suspension

The rules are the same as in the case of section 19 permissions (*t*).

PLANNING PERMISSION GRANTED ON OR AFTER THE RELEVANT DATE

As we have seen (*u*) "the relevant date" is the date on which a duty order designating certain classes of relevant development comes into force in a particular area. From that date, the authorities concerned will be under a duty to acquire all outstanding material interests in land which is needed for the purposes of designated relevant development within the ensuing ten years.

It is therefore expected that, where planning permission is given for designated relevant development, the land comprised in the permission will be acquired by one of the authorities concerned. It follows that the authorities are not required to serve notice of intention either to acquire or not to acquire the land. It also follows that all planning permissions for relevant development granted on or after the relevant date are automatically suspended with only very limited exceptions (*a*).

The planning permission will not be suspended in the following cases:

(1) where one of the authorities concerned owns the land and itself carries out the development (*b*);

(2) where an authority has acquired the land and disposes of it to enable the development to be carried out (*c*);

(3) where an authority seeks to acquire the land compulsorily but the Minister refuses to confirm the compulsory

(*t*) See p. 352, *ante*.

(*u*) See pp. 343, 344, *ante*.

(*a*) Act of 1975, s. 21(2).

(*b*) *Ibid.*, s. 21(2) (a).

(*c*) *Ibid.*, s. 21(2) (b), (4).

purchase order (*d*). If a planning permission has been suspended, the suspension will cease as soon as these conditions are satisfied.

We will consider each of these cases in turn.

(1) Development by an Authority

Two conditions must be satisfied here. First that there are no outstanding material interests in the land; in other words, the freehold and any leasehold interest with at least seven years to run must be owned by one of the authorities concerned, or by a charity and have been owned by that or another charity since 12th September, 1974 (*e*). It does not matter how the land came into the ownership concerned: it may have been acquired under the the Act of 1975 or it may have been acquired under other statutory powers, *e.g.* the Housing Acts. The second condition is that the development covered by the planning permission is carried out by or on behalf of an authority.

(2) Land Disposed of by an Authority

In this case three conditions must be satisfied. First that there are no material interests outstanding and that the authority then dispose of a material interest in the land by selling the freehold or granting a lease for more than seven years. Second, the authority disposing of the land must approve the carrying out of the development in accordance with the planning permission. Third, the authority concerned must give a certificate that the first two conditions have been satisfied.

(3) Compulsory Purchase Order not Confirmed

Since it is the intention of the Act that land required for relevant development should be brought into public ownership, it will presumably be quite exceptional for the Minister to refuse to confirm a compulsory purchase order.

(*d*) Act of 1975, s. 21(2) (b), (3).
(*e*) *Ibid.*, s. 4.

CHAPTER 24

COMMUNITY LAND: ACQUISITION AND DISPOSAL

ACQUISITION AND DISPOSAL OF LAND

As we have seen, one of the main purposes of the Act of 1975 is to bring land needed for relevant development into public ownership with a view either to its being developed by one of the authorities concerned or to its being made available for development by others.

For this purpose, section 15 of the Act of 1975 gives the authorities extensive new powers for bringing land into public ownership. They may acquire by agreement or by compulsory purchase any land which they consider suitable for development. They cannot however use these powers to acquire land for "exempt development" (*a*). Normally, of course, these powers of acquisition will be used to acquire land for "relevant development", but they may also be used to acquire land for "excepted development" (*b*): in practice, the Minister is likely to require special reasons for using these powers of acquiring land for "excepted development".

Where an authority acquire land for relevant development, they may also acquire (1) any adjoining land which is required for executing works for facilitating the development and use of that land (*c*); (2) land needed to replace common land, open space or a fuel or field garden allotment which has been acquired for relevant development (*d*).

(*a*) Act of 1975, s. 15(1), (2). For the definition of "exempt development", see p. 336, *ante*.

(*b*) For the definition of "excepted development", see p. 337, *ante*.

(*c*) The acquisition of adjoining land for these purposes will, it is submitted, have to be supported by evidence: the *ipse dixit* of the authority is unlikely to be sufficient: *Coleen Properties, Ltd.* v. *Minister of Housing and Local Government*, [1971] 1 All E.R. 1049.

(*d*) Act of 1975, s. 15(3).

These new powers of acquisition are additional to other powers of compulsory purchase, *e.g.* under the Housing Acts and the Planning Acts. The authorities concerned may well prefer to use these new powers wherever possible because of certain procedural advantages.

Procedure for Compulsory Purchase

The compulsory purchase of land requires the authorisation of the Minister. The authority concerned must make a compulsory purchase order and submit it for confirmation in accordance with the procedure laid down in the Acquisition of Land (Authorisation Procedure) Act 1946. There are, however, some modifications of that procedure.

Notice of the making of the compulsory purchase order must be given in the normal manner under the Act of 1946 and opportunity given for objections, but under the Act of 1975 the Minister may disregard (that is, he need not even consider) an objection made on the ground that the acquisition is "unnecessary or inexpedient" (*e*). As has been said: "It is difficult to conceive of any ground of objection which cannot be said to fall foul of this provision" (*f*). The reference to the acquisition being "unnecessary" is probably intended to enable the Minister to disregard objections made on the ground that the proposed development would as well be achieved without bringing the land into public ownership; but the use of the word "inexpedient" seems to go well beyond that.

If the Minister agrees to consider an objection, the question arises as to whether the objectors have the right to a hearing or must rely simply on written representations. Under the normal procedure, the Minister must give the objectors and the authority the opportunity to present their case at a public local inquiry or other hearing. But under the Act of 1975 the Minister has a

(*e*) Act of 1975, Sch. 4, para. 2(6). There is a similar provision in the New Towns Act 1965. It is understood that this has rarely, if ever, been used: V. Moore "Community Land, the New Act".

(*f*) Land Development Encyclopaedia, I, 311.

discretion to dispose with an inquiry or hearing in the following circumstances (*g*):

(a) where planning permission for relevant development is in force in respect of land comprised in the order and was granted by the Minister after a public local inquiry; or

(b) where a local plan has been adopted or approved under the Act of 1971 and the grant of planning permission for relevant development would be in accordance with that plan (*h*); or

(c) where a local plan is not in force, but the grant of planning permission for relevant development would be in accordance with the development plan.

The development plan mentioned in (c) above may be either a structure plan or a development plan made under the Acts of 1947 and 1962 and still in force. A structure plan, however, is essentially a statement of policies and general proposals; it will not allocate land for development in such detail that a landowner should be deprived of the opportunity of arguing his objections to a compulsory purchase order at a public local inquiry or other hearing.

In addition, the Minister has power to direct by order that for a specified period (not exceeding five years) references to a local plan in paragraph (b) above shall include (i) a draft local plan which has been through the statutory procedures for public participation and (ii) other plans in respect of which there have been adequate opportunities for public participation. This is, however, subject to one important exception: the Minister will not be able to dispense with a public inquiry or hearing if there is an objection from the occupier of a dwellinghouse (*j*).

Management and Disposal of Land

Having acquired land under the Act of 1975, the authority concerned will have to decide whether to develop it themselves

(*g*) Act of 1975, Sch. 4, para. 2(3).
(*h*) For local plans, see chapter 4, *ante*.
(*j*) Act of 1975, Sch. 4, para. 3.

or whether to release it for development by others; and, of course, they will have to decide when to develop the land or to release it. Decisions may also have to be made as to what use should be made of the land in the meantime. In reaching decisions on these various matters the authority are required to have regard to a number of matters (*k*):

(i) the needs of persons living or carrying on business or other activities in the area, or wishing to do so;
(ii) the needs of builders and developers engaged in, or wishing to engage in, the carrying out of development in the area;
(iii) the needs of agriculture and forestry;
(iv) the needs and obligations of local authorities, new town authorities and parish and community councils;
(v) the needs and obligations of charities;
(vi) the needs and obligations of statutory undertakers;
(vii) such other matters as the Minister may direct.

Prior Negotiating Rights

Where the authority concerned decide to dispose of land for private development, certain persons may have "prior negotiating rights". These persons are (a) anyone who owned a material interest in the land immediately before it was acquired; (b) a person who applied for planning permission for development of the same type as that for which the land is being made available. In either case the application for prior negotiating rights must have been made before the land was acquired.

In such cases, the authority must, before committing themselves to disposing of the land, give the applicant the opportunity to negotiate for the purchase of a material interest in the land or to negotiate for the right to carry out development on some other terms acceptable to the authority (*l*). This does not amount to a

(*k*) Act of 1975, Sch. 6, para. 1 (1).
(*l*) *Ibid.*, Sch. 6, para. 2.

right of pre-emption or even of "first refusal". However as the Minister has explained:

> ". . . where there is a bona fide desire on the part of a prior negotiating right applicant to carry out development in accordance with the authority's proposals, there should be genuine negotiations with a view to making the land available to the applicant, unless there are special reasons to the contrary" (*m*).

Consent to Disposals

The disposal of land by any of the authorities concerned requires the consent of the Minister (*n*). The Minister has, however, given a general consent for a variety of specific transactions (*o*). The principles upon which the Minister has acted are:

(i) land for the building of houses for owner-occupation is to be released to builders under building agreements, the freehold generally being disposed of direct to the final purchaser: but the alternative of freehold or leasehold conveyance to the builder in the first instance is acceptable, provided that this is done in a way which enables the authority concerned to retain sufficient control over the carrying out of the development and subsequent disposal;

(ii) land for other kinds of development is normally to be disposed of leasehold, on terms which ensure that the community (*p*) shares in future increases in value: leasehold disposals in excess of 99 years will require specific consent (*q*).

(*m*) Circular 26/76 (Community Land circular No. 6), para. 65.

(*n*) Local Government Act 1972, s. 123A added by the Act of 1975, s. 42. For the disposal by new town development corporations, see New Towns Act 1965, s. 18; for disposals by the Land Authority for Wales see Act of 1975, s. 14(2).

(*o*) Circular 26/76 (Community Land circular No. 6), Annex D.

(*p*) "The community" presumably means the authority disposing of the land.

(*q*) Circular 26/76 (Community Land circular No. 6), para. 50.

It is clear that authorities will be expected to dispose of land for the best consideration that can reasonably be obtained; where for some special reason an authority propose to dispose of the land for less, specific consent must be obtained from the Minister (*r*).

Where the authority concerned dispose of the freehold to a developer, control over the future development of the land and subsequent disposals can be retained by means of agreement under section 52 of the Act of 1971 as strengthened by section 126 of the Housing Act 1974 (*s*). Where the disposal to the developer is by way of lease, control over the future development and disposal of the land can be retained by appropriate covenants in the lease.

(*r*) Local Government Act 1972, s. 123(2).
(*s*) See chapter 10, pp. 192, 194, *ante*.

Chapter 25

DEVELOPMENT LAND TAX

As we have seen in an earlier chapter, the development land tax (DLT) is the latest in a series of attempts by Parliament to deal with the compensation/betterment problem (*a*). The DLT Act 1976 is closely connected with the operation of the Community Land Act, but the incidence of the new tax is not limited to "relevant development" as defined in the Act of 1975 (*b*); it will fall on many transactions and much development outside the scope of the Act of 1975.

With certain exceptions, DLT is now charged whenever development value in land is realized. Development value is deemed to be realised whenever there is a disposal of land for a consideration which reflects the potentialities of the land for "material development" (*c*). The obvious examples of such disposals are the sale of the freehold or of a leasehold interest or the grant of a lease. But DLT is also chargeable where development value is realised by the carrying out of material development; on the commencement of a project of material development all persons owning major interests in the land are deemed to have disposed of their interests and to have subsequently re-acquired them, and will be liable to DLT accordingly.

DLT is payable at the rate of 80 per cent on the total amount of development value realized by the chargeable person in any one financial year, subject to two reliefs. The first £10,000 of realised development value in any financial year is exempt from DLT. The next £150,000 of realised development value accruing in any financial year ending before 1st April, 1979 attracts tax at the

---

(*a*) See chapter 17, *ante*.
(*b*) See chapter 22, p. 335, *ante*.
(*c*) See p. 366, *post*.

reduced rate of $66\frac{2}{3}$ per cent. These figures refer to the total amount of development value realised by the chargeable person during the financial year and not to separate transactions. Thus, if the chargeable person realises development value to the extent of £9,500 on each of two transactions (making a total of £19,000) in the same year, he will be chargeable on £9,000.

An important feature of DLT is that local authorities and other public bodies are enabled to acquire land net of tax. Before paying the consideration for an acquisition, the acquiring authority will make a deduction on account of the DLT chargeable to the vendor. If additional tax proves to be chargeable, it will be transferred by the Inland Revenue to the acquiring authority.

Disposals

Liability to DLT arises out of the actual or deemed disposal of an interest in land. The expression "interest in land" is widely defined as follows (*d*):

> "any estate or interest in land, any right in or over land or affecting the use or disposition of land, and any right to obtain such an estate, interest or right from another which is conditional on the other's ability to grant the estate right or interest".

It follows that a very wide range of transactions may be affected by DLT. These may be classified under three heads: actual disposals, part disposals and deemed disposals.

Actual Disposals

Actual disposals include the sale of the fee simple, the assignment of a lease, the grant of options and rights of pre-emption. There are however two major exclusions. First, the interest in land of a mortgagee is not an interest in land for the purposes of the DLT Act and neither the creation of a mortgage nor its redemption constitutes the disposal of an interest in land (*e*).

(*d*) DLT Act, s. 46(1).

(*e*) *Ibid.*, s. 46(2), (3).

Secondly the interest of a beneficiary in any settled property is not an interest in land for the purposes of DLT (*f*), but this must be distinguished from the interest of a beneficiary in the proceeds of sale of land held on bare trust which is treated as an interest in land (*g*).

Part Disposals

The most obvious example of a part disposal is the grant of a lease. Further examples are the grant of easements and the imposition of restrictive covenants.

The DLT Act, however, extends the concept of part disposals to cover all cases in which the owner of an interest in land receives a sum of money which is derived from that interest and that sum is not rent payable under a lease nor consideration for the acquisition by the person paying it of an interest in land. Three examples of such part disposals are specifically mentioned in the DLT Act, namely (*h*):

(a) sums received by way of compensation for any kind of damage to land or for any depreciation or risk of depreciation in the value of an interest in land;

(b) sums received in return for forfeiture of or surrender of, or refraining from exercising rights vested in the owner of an interest in land;

(*c*) sums received as consideration for the use or exploitation of land or of any assets (other than minerals) in, on or under, land.

Paragraph (a) would appear to include such matters as compensation for injurious affection resulting from compulsory purchase of neighbouring land; compensation for injurious affection resulting from the exercise of statutory powers, e.g. for the laying of sewers; compensation for planning restrictions.

(*f*) *Ibid.*, s. 46(2).
(*g*) *Ibid.*, s. 46(4).
(*h*) *Ibid.*

Paragraph (b) would include such payments as a fine charged by a landlord as a condition of consenting to a change of use of the demised premises.

Deemed Disposals

DLT is chargeable not only on actual disposals of land but also on the commencement of any project of material development. For this purpose all persons entitled to major interests in the land are deemed immediately before the commencement of the project to have disposed of their interests and to have re-acquired them at their then market value (*i*).

A major interest is any interest in land (*k*) subject to two exceptions:

(*a*) An interest in reversion on a long lease (i.e. a lease with an unexpired term of more than 35 years) under which the rents and premium payable do not, and cannot be made to, reflect any part of the development concerned (*l*). An example would be a freeholder who leased land in 1950 for 99 years at a fixed rent: since he can gain no significant benefit from development, his interest does not attract DLT. The position would be different if the lease provided for periodic rent reviews which would secure to the lessor some part of the enhanced value of the land attributable to the development.

(b) An interest worth less than £5,000 which does not confer a right to possession as defined by section 205(1) of the Law of Property Act 1925 (*m*). "Possession" here includes the right to receive rents and profits, so any freehold or leasehold interest confers a right to possession. It would seem that this category of non-major interests includes only incorporeal hereditaments such as easements and the benefit of restrictive covenants.

(*i*) DLT Act, s. 2(1).
(*k*) For definition of "interest in land", see p. 364, *ante*.
(*l*) DLT Act, s. 2(3)(a). (*m*) DLT Act, s. 2(3)(b).

We must now consider the definitions of "material development" and "project of material development".

Material Development

"Material development" is defined by section 7(7) of the DLT Act as any development (as defined in the Act of 1971 (*n*)) with the exception of:

(a) development for which planning permission is granted by the General Development Order or would be so granted but for an Article 4 Direction (*o*);

(b) development excluded from being material development by Part II of Schedule 4 of the DLT Act.

Part II of Schedule 4 excludes nine classes of development as follows:

(1) Maintenance, improvement, enlargement or other alteration of a building so long as the cubic content is not exceeded by more than one-tenth (*p*). Two or more buildings within the same curtilage will be regarded as a single building.

(2) The rebuilding of any existing building or of any building destroyed or demolished within the last ten years, provided the cubic content is not exceeded by more than one-tenth (*q*). Here again two or more buildings within the same curtilage will be treated as a single building.

(3) The carrying out on land used for purposes of agriculture or forestry of any building or other operations required for that use. The carrying out of building and other operations required for agriculture or forestry is to some extent permitted by the General Development Order but this exemption is more extensive; there are no limits upon size and the erection of dwellinghouses for agriculture or forestry would appear to be included.

(*n*) See chapter 5, *ante*.

(*o*) See chapter 6, *ante*.

(*p*) Cubic content is to be ascertained by external measurements. Any increase attributable to increase in space allocated to fire escapes, car parking, heating or air-conditioning plans or lifts or staircases is to be disregarded.

(*q*) See note (*g*), *supra*.

(4) The use of land for the display of advertisements or the carrying out of operations required for that purpose.

(5) The use of land for car parking for a period not exceeding six years or the carrying out of operations for that purpose.

(6) Change of use from one purpose to another within the same use. For this purpose the DLT Act specifies five broad use classes. It appears that all possible uses of land fall within one or other of these five use classes.

(7) The extension of the use of part of a building or land for a particular purpose by not more than one-tenth of the cubic content in the case of a building or one-tenth of the area in the case of land.

(8) The abandonment of a temporary use of land and the resumption of its normal use.

(9) Where land is unoccupied the resumption of the last normal use.

Project of Material Development

The expression "project of material development" means any project or scheme in pursuance of which any material development is, or is to be carried out (*r*).

A project of material development is deemed to begin when any specified operation comprised in the project is begun (*s*). "Specified operation" means any of the following (*t*):

(a) any work of construction in the course of the erection of a building;

(b) the digging of a trench as part of the foundations of a building;

(c) the laying of any underground pipe or main to the foundations of a building or any such trench;

(*r*) DLT Act, Sch. 1, para. 1.
(*s*) *Ibid.*, Sch. 1, para. 2(1).
(*t*) *Ibid.*, Sch. 1, para. 2(2).

(d) any operations in the course of laying out or constructing a road;

(e) any operation in the course of winning or working minerals;

(f) any change in the use of land where that change constitutes development.

It will also be important to ascertain the precise extent of the project, because this will affect the amount of DLT chargeable on commencement. The general rule is that at any given time a project of material development includes the development which is to be or has been carried out in pursuance of the project and all operations in the course of clearing the land which is to be or has been so carried out (*u*). Where both a change of use of a building and works of improvement or alteration are to be carried out, the change of use and the building works constitute a single project (*a*). The land comprised in a project consists of all land which is to be or has been so developed or cleared (*b*). There is no rule which limits the project to the area covered by existing planning permissions, but in practice this would seem to be the best guide to ascertaining the extent of the project at any time. However, where exemption from DLT is claimed on the ground that the project was commenced before 6th August 1976, the extent of the project must be ascertained by reference to planning permission and detailed approvals in force at that date. (*c*). Notice of commencement must be given to the Inland Revenue not earlier than sixty days before the project is begun and not later than thirty days after it is begun (*d*). The notice is to be in the form prescribed by the Inland Revenue and will require a description both of the land comprised in the project and of the scope of the project (*e*). Further notice must be given

(*u*) *Ibid.*, Sch. 1, para. 4(1)(a).
(*a*) *Ibid.*, Sch. 1, para. 4(7).
(*b*) *Ibid.*, Sch. 1, para. 4(1)(b).
(*c*) *Ibid.*, Sch. 1, para. 4(3), and Sch. 8, para. 36(7).
(*d*) *Ibid.*, Sch. 8, para. 36(1).
(*e*) *Ibid.*, Sch. 8, para. 36.

if at a later date the project is extended by the inclusion of additional development on the land comprised in the original notice (*f*). Notice may also be given if the scope of the project is reduced and this may entitle those concerned to a refund of DLT (*g*).

Assessment of DLT

DLT is chargeable on the realised development value accruing to any person as a result of the disposal, or the deemed disposal, of a major interest in land. The realised development value is the difference between the net proceeds of disposal and the "relevant base value" (*a*).

Net Proceeds of Disposal

The net proceeds of disposal are the consideration for the disposal less the incidental costs to the chargeable person of making it (*b*). Thus in the straightforward case of the sale of a freehold for £50,000 with allowable costs (e.g. legal and estate agent's fees of £1,000), the net proceeds of disposal will be £49,000.

Some cases, however, will not be so straightforward. "Consideration" includes any consideration for money or money's worth (*c*). The consideration on a sale might include land given in exchange. Or the purchaser may as part of the consideration enter into some covenant or agreement. So it may be necessary to value land given in exchange or to determine the value of say a restrictive covenant.

Moreover, as we have seen, DLT is chargeable on the disposals deemed to arise on the commencement of a project of material development (*d*). In these cases the consideration is taken as

(*f*) For the prescribed form see Community Land Encyclopaedia.
(*g*) See note (*f*) *supra*.
(*a*) DLT Act, s. 4(1).
(*b*) *Ibid.*, s. 4(3).
(*c*) *Ibid.*, s. 47(1).
(*d*) See p. 368, *ante*.

the open market value of the interest deemed to be disposed of (*e*). This is determined immediately before the project of material development is begun and on the assumptions (a) that it is lawful for the project to be carried out and (b) that planning permission would not be and has not been granted for any material development not comprised in the project and which has not been carried out or begun before the project is begun. Account is taken of any conditions imposed on any permission for any development comprised in the project (*f*).

Relevant Base Value

The DLT Act prescribes three formulae known respectively as Base A, Base B and Base C. The relevant base value in any particular case is the highest of the three. By taking the highest figure, the amount of realised development value (on which DLT is charged) is reduced.

Base A

This is the aggregate of (*g*):

(i) the cost of the chargeable person's acquisition of his interest in the land;
(ii) any expenditure on relevant improvements;
(iii) the amount by which the current use value of the interest at the time of disposal exceeds its current use value at the date of its acquisition or on 6th April, 1965 whichever is the later;
(iv) where applicable, the "special addition";
(v) where applicable, the "further addition".

Expenditure on Relevant Improvements.—The DLT Act contains a definition of "expenditure on improvements", but not all such expenditure is relevant for the purposes of Base A.

(*e*) DLT Act, s. 2(1).
(*f*) *Ibid.*, Sch. 1, para. 6(1).
(*g*) DLT Act, s. 5(1)(a).

"Expenditure on improvements" means any expenditure incurred by the chargeable person:

(a) in enhancing the value of his interest, being expenditure reflected in the state of the land or of the market value of his interest at the time of disposal; or

(b) in establishing or defending his title to that interest or his enjoyment of that interest.

It does not, however, include expenditure on such matters as maintenance and repairs (*h*).

In calculating expenditure on "relevant" improvements, however, there must be deducted any increase in the current use value of the interest due to expenditure on improvements (*i*). In other words, expenditure on relevant improvements is confined to expenditure which enhances the development value of the land.

Current Use Value.—This is to be ascertained on the assumption that planning permission would be granted for Schedule 8 development (*k*). Logically enough, this assumption cannot be made where compensation is payable in consequence of restrictions previously imposed on Schedule 8 development or as a result of a discontinuance order (*l*). Of course, no account can be taken of any prospective value for material development. but the DLT Act does not exclude possible value for development permitted by the General Development Order or for other development excluded from the definition of material development (*m*).

"The Special Addition".—The DLT Act recognises that many developers finance their purchases of land by borrowing and

(*h*) DLT Act, Sch. 3, para. 1.
(*i*) *Ibid.*, Sch. 3, para. 2.
(*k*) DLT Act, s. 7(2). For Schedule 8 development, see chapter 18, *ante*.
(*l*) As to discontinuance orders, see chapter 10, pp. 196 *et seq.*, *ante*.
(*m*) See pp. 365, 366, *ante*.

that in recent years interest rates have been abnormally high. Where the chargeable person bought his interest in the land before 13th September, 1974, the Base A value is increased by 15 per cent of the cost of acquisition for each year or part of a year, not exceeding four, during which he has owned his interest in the land. Where the chargeable person bought his interest in the land between 13th September, 1974 and 1st May, 1977, the special addition is ten per cent for each year or part of a year (*n*).

"The Further Addition".—Where the cost of acquisition carries the special addition, the same percentage is also added to any expenditure on relevant improvements (*o*).

Base B

This is the aggregate of 110 per cent of the current use value of the interest (*p*) and the amount of any expenditure on relevant improvements (*q*).

Base C

This is the aggregate of 110 per cent of the cost of acquisition and the amount of any expenditure on improvements (*r*). Since Base C does not include any element of current use value, all expenditure on improvements is allowable.

Exemptions and Reliefs

There are several important exemptions from liability to DLT. In addition, there are reliefs in the form of deferment of liability in some other cases.

(*n*) DLT Act, s. 6.

(*o*) *Ibid.*, s. 5(5), Sch. 3, Part II. For "expenditure on relevant improvements", see p. 371, *ante*.

(*p*) For "current use value", see p. 372, *ante*.

(*q*) DLT Act, s. 5(1)(b). For "expenditure on relevant improvements", see p. 371, *ante*.

(*r*) DLT Act s. 5 (1)(c). For expenditure on improvements, see p. 372, *ante*.

Exemptions

Exempt Bodies

All local authorities and a number of other public authorities specified in section 11 of the DLT Act are totally exempt.

Private Residences

DLT is not chargeable on realised development attributable to land which constitutes the whole or any part of an individual's only or main residence; this may include gardens or grounds which together with the site of the house, do not exceed one acre in extent or such larger area as the Commissioners of Inland Revenue may determine (*s*).

Houses Built for Owner-Occupation

There is an exemption from DLT on the deemed disposal which arises on the building of a dwellinghouse for owner occupation. Three conditions must be satisfied: (a) the owner of the relevant interest must have owned that interest, or some interest which forms part of it, on 12th September, 1974; (b) the development must consist exclusively of the building of a dwellinghouse and related development such as a garage; (c) at the time the development is commenced, the owner or a member of his family must intend to occupy the house as his sole or main residence (*t*).

The exemption can be claimed in respect of two dwellinghouses (but not more) if one of them is built on land in the curtilage of a dwellinghouse owned and occupied by the individual concerned on 12th September, 1974.

Builders Stock-in-Trade

There is an exemption for builders in respect of land owned by them on 12th September, 1974 and which formed part of their stock in trade and had at that date the benefit of planning permission (*u*).

(*s*) DLT Act, s. 14.
(*t*) *Ibid.*, s. 15.
(*u*) *Ibid.*, s. 16.

Minerals

No DLT is chargeable on realised development value accruing on the deemed disposal attributable to the winning and working of minerals. This expression includes various ancillary operations (*a*).

Where there is an actual disposal of an interest in land with planning permission for the winning and working of minerals, the consideration for the disposal is to be taken to be the market value of the interest disposed of determined on the assumption that the winning and working of minerals is not authorised and half the difference between such market value and the actual consideration (*b*). Thus if agricultural land worth £50,000 as agricultural land is sold for mineral development at £500,000, the consideration for DLT purposes will be taken as £300,000. However, the Inland Revenue will obtain some recoupment since the cost of acquisition by the mineral developer will be reduced in the same way.

Development within three years of acquisition

Where a person has acquired an interest in land and development is commenced within three years, no DLT will be chargeable on the deemed disposal provided the Inland Revenue are satisfied that no significant amount of realised development value would have accrued if the development had commenced immediately (*c*).

Land held by Charities on 12th September 1974

A charity is wholly exempt from DLT on a disposal (whether actual or deemed) of land held by them on 12th September, 1974. Moreover, if one charity owned the land on 12th September, 1974 and subsequently sold it to another charity, the second charity will not be liable to DLT on a disposal by them (*d*).

(*a*) *Ibid.*, s. 17(1), (7).
(*b*) *Ibid.*, s. 17(3), (4), (5), (6).
(*c*) *Ibid.*, s. 18.
(*d*) *Ibid.*, s. 24.

Approved Housing Co-operative Associations

Development carried out by an approved housing co-operative association or self-build society is totally exempt from DLT (*e*).

Deferments

There are four cases in which the liability for DLT which accrues on the commencement of a project of material development is deferred until there is an actual disposal of an interest in the land. These are:

(1) The carrying out of industrial development by an industrial undertaker (*f*).

(2) Development by statutory undertakers for the purposes of their undertaking (*g*).

(3) Development by a charity on land acquired by them after 12th September, 1974 where the development relates to a building or land to be used wholly or partly for the purposes of a charity (*h*).

(4) Development by the Housing Corporation or registered housing associations, not being approved co-operative housing associations or self-build societies (*i*).

(*e*) DLT Act, s. 26.
(*f*) *Ibid.*, s. 27
(*g*) *Ibid.*, s. 19.
(*h*) *Ibid.*, s. 25.
(*i*) *Ibid.*, s. 26.

INDEX

B

C

M

PRINTED IN GREAT BRITAIN BY OFFSET LITHOGRAPHY BY
BILLING & SONS LTD, GUILDFORD, LONDON AND WORCESTER